GHANA'S NEW CHRISTIANITY

P104 diff

PAUL GIFFORD

Ghana's New Christianity

Pentecostalism in a Globalizing African Economy

INDIANA UNIVERSITY PRESS
Bloomington & Indianapolis

First published in North America in 2004

Indiana University Press
601 North Morton Street
Bloomington, Indiana 47404-3797, USA

http://iupress.indiana.edu

Telephone orders 800-842-6796
Fax orders 812-855-7931
Orders by e-mail iuporder@indiana.edu

Printed in India

Cataloging information available from the Library of Congress.

1 2 3 4 5 09 08 07 06 05 04

PB ISBN: 0-253-21723-7
CB ISBN: 0-253-34474-3

CONTENTS

PREFACE AND ACKNOWLEDGEMENTS

At the outset it is necessary to outline the aims and procedures of this book in order to make clear both what I am attempting and what not, and what the book is and is not.

This is a study of Ghana's new Christianity. The churches that are its focus are obviously Pentecostal, but I have generally preferred the term 'charismatic' because they are not the traditional Pentecostal denominations that have been in Ghana for up to seventy years. The churches under discussion here are the newcomers, and I have not dealt at any length with the issue of their relationship with the older Pentecostal churches. Often, so as not to foreclose any debates, I refer to these churches simply as 'new churches'.

This study is limited to one city in one country, Greater Accra (including Tema, Madina, Adenta), although it embraces perhaps 5 million of Ghana's 18 million inhabitants. To cover all the innumerable new churches in this area is obviously impossible; a selection had to be made, and my first basis for selection was importance. To take a metaphor from English football, there is an acknowledged premier division. Most residents of Accra, if asked, would agree that Duncan-Williams, Otabil, Heward-Mills, Agyin Asare and their churches dominate the scene, along with Winners' Chapel. So these five forced themselves into consideration, or selected themselves for study. Most in Accra would equally be aware of the burgeoning crop of prophets. From all the prophets on offer, I selected the young Elisha Salifu Amoako, and I admit I might well have selected another (like Emmanuel Apraku, Owusu Bempa, Kanco Vagalas). These six churches are my primary focus. Nevertheless I have not restricted myself to them alone. In my attempt to paint an adequate picture of Ghana's new Christianity, I have ranged as widely as I could.

In attempting a book about many charismatic churches—and prepared to cast my net as widely as possible—I admit to a complicating factor of some importance. Although most would classify them into one category and readily label them 'charismatic', they are not all (even the six that are our prime concern) the same. Nor has any one of them remained static over time. In fact, one of my conclusions is that the differences between them are so marked that generalisations about 'charismatic Christianity' are rapidly becoming rather unhelpful. I have therefore walked a tightrope, attempting to allow fully for the differences between them and for their changes over time, while still claiming to describe something definable as 'the charismatic scene' in Ghana.

My aim is first to establish what this Christianity is—what is its religious vision. The task is timely. In his book *The Next Christendom: the Coming of Global Christianity* Philip Jenkins remarks that Africa will be Christianity's 'spiritual centre within a few decades'. And as he insists: 'Southern Christianity, the third Church, is not just a transplanted version of the familiar religion of the older Christian states; the New Christendom is no mirror image of the old. It is a truly new and developing entity. Just how different from its predecessor remains to be seen.'[1] So basic description is required. E. P. Thompson has remarked of British Methodism: 'Too much writing on Methodism commences with the assumption that we all know what Methodism was, and gets on with discussing its growth-rates or its organisational structures.'[2] Sometimes there is evident a similar tendency to talk about the role of Africa's new churches without establishing clearly what we are dealing with. In establishing what this Christianity is, my approach is from the supply side, rather than from the demand side. I begin from the purveyors rather than the consumers, but the supply and the demand are intimately related. I attempt to show that it is precisely because what is supplied so neatly meets public demand that these churches are outstripping others where, by contrast, the supply is not so exactly what is demanded.

Some from a more sociological background may find the lack of statistics, charts and tables a deficiency. In the following chapters I do in places refer to rates of growth, structures, class composition and social programmes, but the focus is primarily on the religious vision these churches provide. As Cox has written, 'Knowing the gods and demons of a people and listening to the prayers and curses tell us more about them than all the graphs and statistics one could assemble.'[3]

I argue that the appeal of these new churches is not that they constitute new communities providing support no longer provided by dissolving traditional structures; or that they perform social functions (like arranging marriages) that traditional procedures no longer accomplish; or that they give opportunity to the youth to exercise authority in a gerontocratic

---

[1] Philip Jenkins, *The Next Christendom: the Coming of Global Christianity*, New York: Oxford University Press, 2002, 75 (also 216) and 214.

[2] E. P. Thompson, *The Making of the English Working Class*, London: Penguin, 1980 (orig. 1963), 918.

[3] Foreword, Allan H. Anderson and Walter Hollenweger (eds), *Pentecostals after a Century: Global Perspectives on a Movement in Transition*, Sheffield Academic Press, 1999, 12.

society; or that they redress gender imbalance, or provide material assistance, employment, identity or opportunity, or bring colour (through their exuberant worship) to otherwise drab lives. They do not flourish primarily because they are a place to feel at home, or a home for the homeless, or because they meet the quest for belonging. Undoubtedly many do these things in various ways and to various degrees, but they flourish mainly because they claim to have the answers to Ghanaians' existential problems and especially to their most pressing existential problem, economic survival.

A second aim, as the book's subtitle suggests, is to engage in the debate on the socio-political role of this Christianity. This second aim is obviously distinct from the first and admits of various approaches. Yet this is a case-study of Ghana, and the years that have seen these new churches flourish are also the years of Ghana's structural adjustment, designed to bring the country into the modern world economy. I want to relate these churches to that attempted economic reform, and I am therefore concerned with the role of religion in effecting modernity—but in the particular sense in which Landes defined modernisation: 'that combination of changes—in the mode of production and government, in the social and institutional order, in the corpus of knowledge, and in attitudes and values—that makes it possible for a society to hold its own in the [twenty-first] century; that is, to compete on even terms in the generation of material and cultural wealth, to sustain its independence, and to promote and accommodate to further change.'[4] What are the ways that its new Christianity might have helped, or currently be helping, to bring Ghana into the world's modern political and economic system? The role of the international financial institutions in Ghana (and indeed in Africa as a whole) is intensely debated, and I have not been drawn into that. It will be obvious that in general lines I agree that Ghana needed the basic planks of structural adjustment (to be explained in the first chapter). My own position does not differ greatly from that embraced by African leaders themselves in the New Partnership for African Development (NEPAD), especially paragraphs 49 (expounding the 'New Political Will of African Leaders') and 79–84 (elaborating the 'Conditions for Sustainable Development') and made even more explicit in the NEPAD annexes 'Declaration on Democracy, Political, Economic and Corporate Governance' and 'African Peer Review Mechanism' adopted at the OAU/AU Durban summit in July 1992.[5]

---

[4] David S. Landes, *The Unbound Prometheus: Technological Change and Industrial Development in Western Europe from 1750 to the Present*, Cambridge University Press, 1969, 6; Landes wrote 'twentieth century'.
[5] NEPAD is a programme to redevelop Africa by promoting growth, eradicating

To identify Ghana's new Christianity, and then to analyse its role, I attended in Accra, between July 2000 and September 2001, and again in March-April and August-September 2002, as many charismatic gatherings of all kinds as I could—services, crusades, conventions, conferences, prayer meetings. Obviously not even a large team of researchers could attend them all, such is the richness of the phenomenon. However, in understanding these churches, I was considerably assisted by their media output, the broadcasts, tapes, videos and literature that they so assiduously produce. To establish the wider context, I also tried to immerse myself in events and debates and life more widely, through various means. I spoke to as many Christians as I could, from all churches. Yet in what follows I have deliberately relied far more on observation and my own reflection than on interviews. Over nineteen months I spoke with most major church leaders or their responsible lieutenants, and with as many participants in the various gatherings as possible, often arranging to meet the latter afterwards to continue discussion; also with many Ghanaians knowledgeable in politics, economics, sociology and culture. I learned a great deal from them, but this book consists primarily of personal reflection on what I observed and my personal interpretation which in many important points is at odds with what my interlocutors, including charismatic leaders and church members, told me.

Although this study focuses on Ghana, that country is not hermetically sealed. Its charismatic churches perpetually host visitors, especially North American and Nigerian, and its church leaders (not only those of the premier league) are for ever going abroad ('outside' is the Ghanaian term). Some of the broadcast media and much of the literature are from overseas. While this research was in progress, the Korean David Yonggi Cho visited Ghana for a crusade and pastors' conference, and the Nigerian David Oyedepo brought his 'Maximum Impact Summit' to Accra in mid-2002, events of great importance for Ghana's charismatic community. Even more significant for me was the 'Winning Ways' convention that Ghana hosted in early 2001. This was publicised as representing the quintessence of charismatic Christianity, featuring some of its acknowledged

---

widespread poverty and halting Africa's marginalisation. It is a merger of the Millennium Partnership for the African Recovery Programme (MAP) and the Omega plan of Senegal's President Wade, finalised on 3 July 2001. This merger gave rise to the New African Initiative approved by the OAU summit on 11 July 2001. This was further refined at the OAU Heads of State Implementation Committee (HSIC) on 23 Oct 2001, as NEPAD. I am aware that some Africans reject NEPAD as simply a framework 'developed from outside the continent and imposed on African countries' (see the declaration of Codesria-Third World Network (Africa) meeting, 23–26 April 2002 (*Graphic*, 3 May 02, 4); those who so understand NEPAD will have little sympathy with my argument here.

international stars, and seemed to be genuinely accepted as such by Ghanaian charismatics. I use the latter in particular to shed light on the transnational character of Ghana's charismatic Christianity.

I have already referred to the need to be sensitive to changes over time, especially because my perceptions in 1995 led me to claim only recently that Ghana's church leaders do not generally designate themselves 'prophets'—only to return in 2000 to discover that the usage is widespread.[6] Thus this book should be understood as a snapshot—from one particular vantage-point—in 2000–2. The charismatic scene will inevitably continue to change rapidly.

I have included as much primary material as possible in order to enable those who have not had the opportunity to immerse themselves in the phenomenon to see the data I am building on. However, marshalling such an amount of primary material does create a problem in referencing. To give full details—date, place, occasion—for every citation would have made the book over-long and unwieldy. I have therefore been persuaded to give for a spoken quotation merely a date in the text; roman type denotes a live service, and italic type a media broadcast on that day. This does not answer every question, but it obviates most and keeps the presentation manageable.

Chapter 1 presents the context in which Ghana's charismatic Christianity has flourished, and outlines the current state of the debate on Africa's economic plight, and Chapter 2 describes the shift in Ghana's Christianity over the period of the 1980s and 1990s, dwelling particularly on media output. Chapter 3 analyses the major emphases characterising Ghana's new Christianity, particularly the stress on success, its financial dynamic, and the claim to be 'biblical'. Chapter 4 focuses on the growing prophetic strain in charismatic Christianity, and Chapter 5 on another form of charismatic Christianity altogether: the politically and culturally aware Christianity of Mensa Otabil. Chapter 6 attempts to generalise about the specifically economic role of charismatic Christianity, in particular whether this Christianity should be hailed as promoting a new work ethic. Chapter 7 broaches the political role of these churches, and discusses to what extent they might be seen as changing politics through a reform of culture.[7]

---

[6] Paul Gifford, 'The Use of the Bible in African Christianity' in Niels Kastfeld (ed.), *The Bible and the Koran in African Politics*, London: Hurst, 2003.

[7] This is not my first study of Ghanaian Christianity: *African Christianity: its Public Role* (London: Hurst, 1998) attempted a briefer picture of all strains of Christianity in Ghana, compared to three other countries. Knowledge of the earlier book is not needed to understand this one, and I have tried to avoid repeating material included there, although it is sometimes referred to (abbreviated to *AC*) for background.

Many helped towards the writing of this book, too many to mention individually. Although none of them is responsible for any of the views expressed here, the following have earned my special gratitude: Dr E. Kingsley Larbi, the Rev. Kwesi Addo Sampong, Dr Charles Owiredu, Dr Abraham Akrong, Dr Emmanuel Martey, Professor Kwesi Dickson, Dr Kwabena Asamoah-Gyadu, Professor Max Assimeng, Professor John Collins, Professor Dan Smith, Mr John Temin, Ms Susan Gagliardi, Dr John Lemley, the Rev. Susan Hanson, the Rev. John Gartey, Dr Emmanuel Anim, the Rev. Abamfo Atiemo, Mrs Barbara Mends, Mrs Juliet Appiah, Mr Asumah Adams, Professor David Martin, Professor J. D. Y. Peel, the Rev. Hugh Osgood, the Rev. Patrick Claffey, Ms Jane Clifford, Professor Richard Gray and the late Professor Adrian Hastings.

I would also like to thank the members of the class on 'Christianity and African Society' which I taught at Accra's Central University College in 2000; they shaped my reflection greatly. I also thank the Leverhulme Trust, who awarded me a research fellowship for the academic year 2000–1. Lastly I thank my wife whose companionship and critical interest during this research contributed so much.

London, March 2004   PAUL GIFFORD

ABBREVIATIONS

31DWM	31st December Women's Movement
AC	*African Christianity: its Public Role* (by Paul Gifford)
ACI	Action Chapel International
AFRC	Armed Forces Revolutionary Council
AIC	African Independent (Instituted) Church
ASR	*African Studies Review*
BBC	British Broadcasting Corporation
CAC(I)	Christ Apostolic Church (International)
CAFM	Christian Action Faith Ministries
CCG	Christian Council of Ghana
CDD	Centre for Democratic Development
CEO	Chief Executive Officer
CHRAJ	Commission for Human Rights and Administrative Justice
CIA	Central Intelligence Agency
CNN	Cable Network News
CoP	Church of Pentecost
CPCS	Centre for Pentecostal and Charismatic Studies
CPP	Convention People's Party
CSIR	Centre for Scientific and Industrial Research
CUC	Central University College
DgTP	Dag's Tapes and Publications
DRC	Democratic Republic of the Congo
EC	Electoral Commission
EP	Evangelical Presbyterian (Church)
ERP	Economic Recovery Programme
EU	European Union
FM	Frequency Modulation
FORB	Forum of Religious Bodies
GDP	Gross Domestic Product
GNPC	Ghana National Petroleum Company
GRM	Global Revival Ministries
GTV	Ghana Television
HIPC	Highly Indebted Poor Country
ICGC	International Central Gospel Church
ICMC	International Christian Miracle Centre
IEA	Institute of Economic Affairs
IMF	International Monetary Fund

IVP	Inter-Varsity Press
JCPC	Jesus Connection Prayer Centre
JMAS	*Journal of Modern African Studies*
JRA	*Journal of Religion in Africa*
KJV	King James Version
LCI	Lighthouse Chapel International
LRB	*London Review of Books*
NACOE	National Consultation on Evangelisation
NDC	National Democratic Congress
NEPAD	New Partnership for African Development
NGO	non-governmental organisation
NPP	National Patriotic Party
OAU	Organisation of African Unity
OPEC	Organisation of Petroleum Producing Countries
P & P	*People and Places*
PACLA	Pan African Christian Leadership Assembly
PNDC	Provisional National Defence Council
PWCC	Pauline Walley Christian Communications
RHCI	Royal House Chapel International
SAP	Structural Adjustment Programme
SDA	Seventh Day Adventist
TJCT	*Trinity Journal of Church and Theology*
TICCS	Tamale Institute for Cross Cultural Studies
TLS	*Times Literary Supplement*
UGCC	United Gold Coast Convention
UNDP	United Nations Development Programme
USAID	United States Agency for International Development
WAATI	West African Association of Theological Institutes
WCC	World Council of Churches
WMCI	Word Miracle Church International

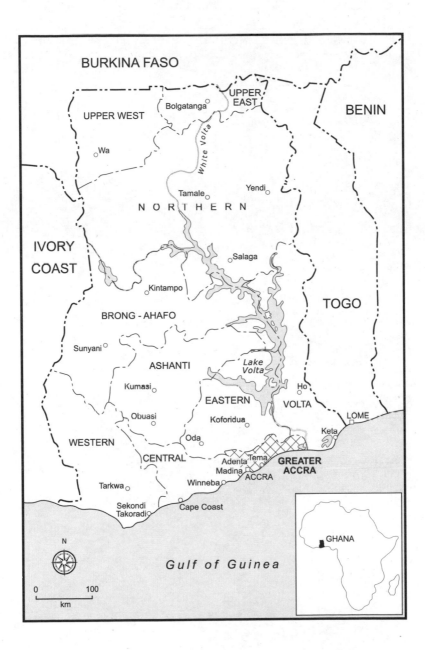

1

THE CONTEXT AND THE DEBATE

Rawlings and Ghana

Modern Ghana comprises about seventy-five ethno-linguistic groupings, of which the most numerous are the Akan, the Mossi, the Ewe and the Ga. Although the numerous slaving forts along the shore testify to hundreds of years of European presence, European contact was at first restricted to the coast. The littoral known as the Gold Coast became a British crown colony in 1874, and over the next thirty years two more protectorates were established, one over the northern territories, and one over the Ashanti Region in the centre. The Asante, members of the Twi-speaking branch of the Akan peoples, developed a powerful empire which reached its peak in the eighteenth and nineteenth centuries. The British finally occupied Asante in 1896.

The modern country became independent in 1957. The first President ('Leader of Government Business' from 1951, Prime Minister 1952–60) was Kwame Nkrumah, perhaps Africa's most famous son, who in December 1999 topped a BBC poll as the African of the millennium. He was identified with anti-colonialism, black pride and the African personality, Pan-Africanism, African unity, and industrialisation. He is still widely revered in Ghana, and political parties vie to claim his mantle, but it is also undeniable that he pioneered many of those qualities that have become the bane of African politics: 'big man' rule, the personality cult, corruption and disregard of the rule of law. Nkrumah was overthrown in 1966 in a military coup (its plotters are now acknowledged to have been assisted by the CIA). The military handed over to Kofi Busia's Second Republic (1969–72), which ended with another coup. During the ensuing years of rule by a corrupt Military Council, particularly under General Ignatius Acheampong (1972–8), Ghana bordered on collapse.

This is the context for the first coup of Flight-Lieutenant J. J. Rawlings. He had planned a coup for 15 May 1979, but it was unsuccessful and he was arrested. At his trial he was (unwisely, from the authorities' point of

1

view) given a chance to explain himself, and his passionate idealism and righteous anger against self-serving senior officers, not to mention his good looks, caught the popular imagination. Before he could be sentenced he was sprung from gaol by the lower ranks, and thrust into power as chairman of the Armed Forces Revolutionary Council (AFRC). On 16 and 26 June, with the masses chanting 'Let the blood flow', he had eight senior military officers publicly executed at Teshie firing range. Among them were three former heads of state, Generals Acheampong, Afrifa and Akuffo, and the former commanders of the navy, air force and border guards (for this reason, some prefer to call Rawlings's advent a mutiny rather than a coup). The popular mood included a good deal of envy and anger against those who were thought to have enriched themselves at the expense of the masses—'We no go sit down make them cheat us everyday.' '*Kalabule*' was the word widely used to denote this profiteering. The category of 'profiteer' was enormously broad. Market women were stripped and beaten publicly, and properties belonging to those deemed exploiters were simply 'acquired by the state'. Those were heady days, and Rawlings's charisma ensured that Ghanaians queued up to pay bills, and when he called for a national pothole-filling campaign, they willingly took part. He was persuaded (reluctantly, by some accounts) to allow general elections scheduled by the Military Council to go ahead, and after four months in power he handed over to the winner of these elections, Hilla Limann.

This was before World Bank loans could be used to give evidence of development. Limann was generally seen as ineffectual (his defenders would say that Ghana was in such straits that immediate results were out of the question, but that procedures were being put in place that in the long term would have ensured recovery). However, for Limann there was to be no long term. Although most of the AFRC had been persuaded to leave the country after power had been ceded to Limann, Rawlings had stayed in Ghana, brooding in the wings. He staged a second coup (his 'Second Coming') on 31 December 1981. This time he was associated with several left-wing ideologues, and he established in the seat of government, Christiansborg Castle, a Provisional National Defence Council (PNDC) with its initial direction vehemently socialist. Perceived wrongs were 'righted'. In addition, many personal scores were settled: for some months 'revolutionary justice' was the order of the day, and the total of those killed (or just 'missing') many have exceeded 300. This period came to a climax in June 1982 with the murder of three judges (one a pregnant woman), whose rulings were evidently felt to be opposed to some of the actions of the AFRC in Rawlings's first coming, and a retired military officer who may have fallen out with Rawlings's security supremo, Kojo Tsikata. These murders caused a strong reaction, and the PNDC had to establish a tribunal of sorts which found guilty (and had executed) the killers, including a member of the PNDC. However, doubt has always remained over who ultimately sanctioned the killings; it is known that the keys to the jeep used to carry the victims to their execution were collected from the Rawlings's kitchen table. The revulsion following these murders reined in some of the excesses.

However, bad rains, with the resulting poor harvests, and then the forced repatriation from Nigeria of up to 1 million Ghanaians without proper papers, meant that around 1982–3 Ghana reached its nadir; the country simply could not cope. Rawlings, the populist and admirer of Castro and Gaddafi, then eased out the socialists and turned to the IMF and World Bank to rebuild the country.

Western donors imposed conditionalities, and Rawlings in the early 1990s agreed to a return to civilian rule (after soundings indicated that he could win an election if it were orchestrated carefully). He engineered a new constitution (containing clauses indemnifying himself and his companions for earlier excesses), and at the last minute transformed his PNDC into a political party, the National Democratic Congress (NDC). When he won the 1992 presidential elections, the main opposition parties cried foul and boycotted the parliamentary elections a week later, which were consequently overwhelmingly won by the NDC. There were irregularities in both these elections; Rawlings at one and the same time wrote the rulebook and was referee, linesman and captain of the winning team, but he and his NDC would probably have won anyway, since by this time many rural areas were beginning to see aid-financed roads and electrification that they had not known before; for them the human rights issues that bothered the urban newspaper-reading classes were not pressing issues. In 1996 Rawlings repeated his victory over J. A. Kufuor, the candidate of the National Patriotic Party (NPP) of the more free-market, non-Nkrumahist tradition. This time the election itself was probably fairer, although the NDC's campaigning involved just as much use of incumbency and state resources.

Economic failure

Since 1983 Ghana had been undergoing structural adjustment imposed by the IMF. By the end of the 1980s, Ghana was cited by the West as an economic success story, but by the middle of the 1990s it was clear that this programme (normally called the Economic Recovery Programme— ERP) was not working. On the ground, Ghanaians (despite the roads and electricity) did not need convincing; life was incredibly hard. By the late

[margin note: 90s poverty in Ghana]

1990s there was widespread poverty with 70% of the population earning under US $1.00 a day. The basic daily minimum wage went from 2,900 to 4,200 cedis (US $0.60) in November 2000; at the same time a bottle of Coca-Cola went to 1,200 cedis, and a loaf of bread cost 2,500. A security guard (security seems to be Ghana's one growth industry) then received about 120,000 cedis a month, but his expenses were estimated at 48,000 cedis for transport, 8,400 for water, 10,000 for electricity and 50,000 for rent. How he might support any dependents was hard to imagine. In April 2001 the minimum wage again increased, from 4,200 to 5,500 cedis (about US $0.80). In health care the government had introduced user fees (a system called in Ghana 'cash and carry'), which put medical care beyond the reach of many if not most (horror stories repeatedly appeared in the media about families not being allowed to leave hospital or to retrieve a body from the morgue until the medical bills had been paid; often this was simply impossible). 50% of Ghanaian doctors leave the country within their first two years of graduation, and 80% within the first five years after graduation.[1] Education collapsed. School enrolment diminished. The UNDP estimates that one out of four children is not in school.[2] Ghana has long had elite schools, and at Legon, just outside Accra, used to have a formidable university whose graduates have risen to prominence all round the world. This tends to obscure the fact that Ghana's general education is lamentable; in 2000 illiteracy may still have been as high as 70%.[3] In 1999 the proportion of public school children regarded as mastering the level appropriate for Primary 6 in English and Maths was 8.7 and 4.0% respectively.[4]

[margin note: dependent on foreign aid]

Ghana's ERP, as the title of an important book expressed it, was both a miracle and a mirage.[5] The miracle was the growth-rate through most of the late 1980s and early '90s (about 5%, although figures are disputed). However, the growth was a mirage in that it was driven by overseas aid and public investment, not by revival of the private sector. The country was almost totally dependent on foreign aid. Ghana's average annual aid budget is about $1 billion.[6] Structural adjustment funding between 1983

---

[1] K. Y. Amoako, 'Economic Development and Reform Issues in Africa: Lessons for Ghana', lecture given at University of Ghana, Legon, August 00, unpublished paper, 12.

[2] Ibid., 13.

[3] The *Graphic*, of 12 Sept 00, 1, reported it had dropped from 69 to 49%; as also *Despatch* of 23–29 April 01, 2; this was disputed, and a figure of 34.5% adult literacy was given in the *Mail* of 21 Dec. 00, 8.

[4] See criterion-referenced test results, *Graphic*, 14 July 01, 18–21 (in 1992 the corresponding figures had been 2.9 and 1.1).

[5] Ernest Aryeetey, Jane Harrigan and Machiko Nissanke, *Economic Reforms in Ghana: the Miracle and the Mirage*, Oxford: James Currey, 2000.

[6] Amoako, 'Economic Development', 12.

and 2000 reached $6 billion.[7] Foreign Direct Investment (FDI, always a good sign of a country's economic health) was very small, and investment on the part of Ghanaians themselves was no greater. The 1.5–2 million Ghanaians overseas were remitting between $300–400 million a year, the fourth largest source of foreign exchange, but even that was mainly to support the emigrants' families or build houses for themselves, not to invest in production.[8] Indeed the country produced little. Gold, cocoa and timber maintained the same percentage of export earnings as before; alternative exports were not developed. The agricultural sector had virtually collapsed. Ghana had once been self-sufficient in rice, but by 2000 it was importing $100 million worth each year. In Accra's street markets the tomatoes were likely to come from Italy, the onions from Holland—I have even bought beans originating from Britain, which is not widely known as an agricultural exporter.

To cap it all, at the beginning of 1998 the currency started to collapse. By the end of that year the exchange rate was 2,300 cedis to one US dollar; at the beginning of 2000 it was 3,530 cedis and by the end of that year, there were 7,000 cedis—according to one means of calculation, depreciation of 100% in twelve months.[9]

The lack of success of the ERP was seldom admitted by observers because of their agendas. Rawlings was given a generally positive press in the West as supposedly one of a new breed of African leaders, like Museveni in Uganda, bringing order where chaos had reigned. Clapham thus shrewdly appraised elections in both Uganda and Ghana: 'A government that was already regarded as internationally acceptable was allowed to count as democratic.'[10] For a brief period Rawlings and Museveni together were the main evidence for the much-touted 'African Renaissance', with the leaders of Ethiopia, Eritrea, Rwanda and even, strange as it seems in retrospect, the Democratic Republic of the Congo supporting evidence. Thus President Clinton's trip to Africa in 1998 included both Ghana and Uganda, as an endorsement for their policies (and the same reason could be given for Queen Elizabeth's trip to Ghana in November 1999). The World Bank and the IMF were led to trumpet their success story in Ghana, because they had been given such a free hand that if Ghana were not a success they had little authority to direct reforms anywhere.

---

[7] *Graphic*, 8 June 01, 7.
[8] *Crusading Guide*, 10–16 Oct. 00, 5; Amoako, 'Economic Development', 11.
[9] In 1983, before ERP, the rate was 2.75 cedis to $1.00; at the introduction of ERP, the rate went from 2.75 to 30 cedis to $1.
[10] Christopher Clapham, 'Governmentality and Economic Policy in Sub-Saharan Africa', *Third World Quarterly*, 17 (1996), 818.

The irony remains that Rawlings, who had come to power to reverse an economic disaster, was, after nineteen years and seventeen years of IMF supervision, presiding over an economy in a state of collapse. Inflation was 40%, interest rates were 46%, and manufacturing was down to 4% of GDP.

Governance

During the Rawlings years the debate about Africa's plight shifted significantly. Economic reform began as just that: something economic. Structural adjustment involved floating the currency, selling off parastatals, abolishing subsidies, dismantling trade barriers and promoting exports. However, as long ago as the early 1980s the notion gained ground that development was not something purely or even primarily economic, but related to the political scene more widely. Economic performance came to be seen as a function of the political system.

One can still find proponents of the view that it is mainly external forces that are to blame for Africa's economic woes. Of course the legacy of colonialism (even of slavery), the Cold War, the debt burden and unfair terms of trade are significant. But from the 1980s a new orthodoxy emerged which attributed a substantial portion of the blame for Africa's predicament to domestic mismanagement.[11] As Kofi Annan bluntly told African leaders at an OAU summit in Togo in July 2000, 'This [our plight] is not something others have done to us. It is something we have done to ourselves. If Africa is being bypassed, it is because not enough of us are investing in policies which would promote development and preserve peace. We have mismanaged our affairs for decades, and we are suffering the accumulated effects.'[12] The Executive Secretary of the UN Economic Commission for Africa, K. Y. Amoako, also a Ghanaian, expressed it thus: 'I personally am of the view that underpinning all Africa's problems is the crisis of governance; and that the sooner we recognise this, the sooner we will be prompted to take corrective action.'[13] Governance refers to the administrative and technical aspects of the exercise of public authority. It includes ideas like transparency and accountability, pluralism, participation, predictability, openness, effectiveness of public administration, respect for human rights and property rights, a flourishing

---

[11] Amoako, 'Economic Development'; 3; George Ayittey, 'Why Africa is Poor', lecture given at IEA, 24 July 00, 4–5. For a discussion of this 'New Liberal Orthodoxy', see Nicolas van de Walle, *African Economies and the Politics of Permanent Crisis, 1979–1999*, Cambridge University Press, 2001, 137–50.

[12] *Graphic*, 12 Sept. 00, 5.

[13] Ibid., 23 Sept. 00, 1.

civil society and the rule of law.[14] This concept of governance became the key concept in analysing Africa.

Africa's characteristic mode of governance is described as 'neo-patrimonialism'. It is almost defined in contrast to 'rational-legal' administration whereby power is exercised through legally defined structures for a publicly acknowledged aim. Operating a rational-legal system are officials who, in exercising the powers of office, treat other individuals impersonally, according to criteria which the structures demand. If an official moves to a new post, she will immediately act according to the rules of this new post, and her successor in her previous position will act as she had done. This rational-legal ideal (admittedly nowhere achieved in its fullness) has proved the most efficient and legitimate way of running a complex modern state. In a neo-patrimonial state, by contrast, support is ensured by clientelism, a relationship of exchange in which a superior provides security for an inferior, who as a client than provides political support for his patron. Those lower in a hierarchy are not subordinate officials with defined powers and functions of their own, but retainers whose position depends on a leader to whom they owe allegiance. Control of the state carries with it the ability to provide (and of course to withhold) security, and to allocate benefits in the form of jobs, development projects and so on. The system is held together by loyalty or kinship ties rather than by a hierarchy of administrative grades and functions.[15]

Within this perspective we can see the contradictions involved in implementing structural adjustment in Africa. In much of Africa it was almost bound to fail, for the SAP policies 'struck directly at the basis for the economic and hence political control maintained by African governing élites over their own societies. That was indeed precisely the point.'[16] The governing élites, even if in theory forced by the debt crisis to implement SAP, have been able to thwart its implementation; indeed, 'winning', in the view of many African rulers, 'consisted in gaining as much external finance as possible, while delivering as little economic reform as possible in exchange'.[17] And although measures like floating the currencies

---

[14] See Amoako, 'Economic Development', 15, for hallmarks of a capable state; similarly, Thomas Friedman IEA/CIDA/UNDP lecture 'Understanding Globalisation', Legon, 25 April 01; according to George Ayittey: 'Democracy requires a freely negotiated constitution, an independent judiciary, an independent Electoral Commission, a transparent electoral register, and the ability of the people to exercise their democratic right to vote without fear, intimidation, violence or even vote buying', *Crusading Guide*, 3–9 Aug. 00, 1; similarly V. Antwi-Danso, *Evening News*, 28 Sept. 00, 9, and *News*, 4 Aug. 00, 9.

[15] Gifford, *AC*, 5–8; for much of this, see Christopher Clapham, *Third World Politics: An Introduction*, London: Routledge, 1985.

[16] Clapham, 'Governmentality', 812.

[17] Ibid., 813. Donor conditionality was 'largely toothless'; van de Walle, *African Economies*, 174.

to a realistic level was simple enough and could be monitored, it was a totally different case with privatising state assets. 'External pressures for privatisation presumed a distinction between "public" and "private" spheres which did not always apply even in industrialised states, and which was entirely inappropriate to most of Africa.'[18] African élites had been privatising for years; in Sierra Leone, President Siaka Stevens formed his own company with a Lebanese businessman and sold all the profitable state enterprises to himself.

In this area of governance, the Rawlings era brought Ghana only very limited advance. On the whole, Rawlings in power was not seen by Ghanaians as excessively corrupt personally (a perception conspicuously not extended to his wife), even if the lean and hungry Flight-Lieutenant had metamorphosed into a rather portly head of state. However, despite undoubted charisma, evident particularly in the early years, Rawlings's gifts did not include the ability (or, apparently, much desire) to transform governance in Ghana, build institutions or structures or systems, and establish procedures or rules or regulations. He seemed to attach little importance to such things (although his tendency to mouth words like 'transparency' while giving them no practical meaning is an intriguing psychological trait).

Far from building institutions or structures, there was not a single existing institution that Rawlings did not politicise or personalise. The judiciary came to be widely seen as serving his interests.[19] The security forces were headed by 'reliable' allies, and the '64 Battalion' (named from the date of his first coup—4 June) was thought to owe its loyalty to Rawlings himself rather than to the state. The police victimised his opponents, while leaving well-connected figures alone. The civil service served his interests, forgoing even a semblance of impartiality. The state-controlled media were transparently biased; the *Daily Graphic* and *Ghanaian Times* and GTV were at times quite unprofessional in coverage, particularly in what they omitted. 'After 18 years of the exemplary leadership of President Jerry John Rawlings…' intoned a not untypical *Graphic* editorial of 13 September 2000.[20] The *Graphic*'s columnists could be mindlessly sycophantic. A columnist criticising Rawlings in the *Mirror*

---

[18] Clapham, 'Governmentality', 813.

[19] *The World Bank Ghana Governance and Corruption Survey*, January 2001, labels Ghana's judiciary as 'highly corrupt', *Guide*, 15 June 01, 4. The Executive Director for African Human Rights Heritage extended the indictment to the Police Service, lawyers, as well as court clerks and registrars (*Times*, 21 April 01, 1).

[20] Even after the transition: 'For close to two decades he has selflessly dedicated himself to the cause of his country, Africa, the developing world, and to global peace and justice….' *Graphic*, 17 Jan 01, 7.

in June 1996 was immediately dismissed. Rawlings had a talk show taken off GTV after only five weeks in February 1998.[21]

Economic institutions were personalised, giving loans to friends and NDC mandarins (who, being well-connected, were of course under little pressure to pay anything back). The Social Security National Insurance Trust (SSNIT), the State Insurance Company (SIC)[22] and even many banks, including the Bank of Ghana, often aroused disquiet. The Divestiture Commission, selling off the State Owned Enterprises (SOE) in accordance with structural adjustment, was notoriously lacking in transparency, and many SOEs were sold to those with easy access to public funds, or to shadowy individuals fronting for important figures, and at questionably low prices (the government stake in Ghana Telecom was sold off for $100 million, when some valuations were as high as $800 million[23]). One heard stories of Rural Banks functioning as channels of cash to politically reliable rather than economically viable clients, and of course they too were under no pressure to repay. Government contracts were denied to non-NDC members and went to party faithful, or consortia of party faithful and foreign businessmen, many of them not totally above suspicion in their country of origin. Rawlings actively undermined local businessmen who he thought might pose a threat to him.

A couple of examples illustrate the manner of Ghana's governance. The presidential jet was leased to the state by no one knew whom, through a company of which the Minister of Finance was a director. The Ghana National Petroleum Company (GNPC), headed by Rawlings's friend Tsatsu Tsikata, was set up to prospect for oil. It cost the country millions of dollars, yet its board allegedly never met; it certainly produced no reports—Kwesi Botchwey, the Finance Minister of Ghana's 'miracle', admitted that he eventually resigned because Tsikata ran his own budget independent of ministerial control.[24] Ghana Airways was run with such spectacular lack of transparency that the new Kufuor administration needed months of effort to discover that the airline was $130 million in debt; in May 2002 it suffered the indignity of having one of its DC10s impounded at Heathrow for non-payment of bills. Most notorious of all was the 'Quality Grain Rice' scandal, in which a young African-American woman received $27 million to grow rice on 10,000 acres in the Volta Region. Only 575 acres were ever under cultivation, and no rice was ever produced. Much of this was made public when the woman was eventually sued by her American co-directors and found guilty by jury in Atlanta,

---

[21] *Chronicle*, 30 April–1 May 01, 5.
[22] Ibid., 7–11 Dec. 00, 1.
[23] Discussed on Radio Univers' Media Review, 9 Jan. 01.
[24] *Evening News*, 14 May 01, 1.

Georgia, on thirty-five counts of bank fraud, money laundering and making false statements, and sentenced to fifteen years' imprisonment and ordered to pay $20 million to Ghana. Why was someone with no experience of rice production ever given such a grant in the first place? The *Chronicle* described her as 'single and under 29 when she met President Rawlings around 1996… with her ample hips, powerful presence, voluptuous lips and great looks'. This is *Chronicle* code suggesting that the reason was a sexual relationship with Rawlings, as indeed a few were prepared to assert on independent radio.[25]

Local government was characterised by similar procedures. District Assemblies had one-third of their members and their District Chief Executives named directly by Rawlings. Consequently many looked after his interests rather than those of the district which they theoretically served. The District Assembly Common Fund was open to all kinds of abuse.[26] Chiefs had to support Rawlings and the NDC at the risk of being de-stooled.

Even the Electoral Commission (EC) and the Commission for Human Rights and Administrative Justice (CHRAJ) were headed by presidential appointees, and although they tended to become more autonomous over the years and indeed notched up some successes, they were not widely seen as independent bodies, operating impartially.[27] The Serious Fraud Office was generally seen as a device to harass Rawlings's perceived opponents.[28]

Consider the 31 December Women's Movement (31DWM), founded in 1982 as one of the 'revolutionary organs' of Rawlings's Second Coming, from which it took its name. In the late 1980s it transformed itself into a NGO in order better to qualify for grants from overseas donors. Nevertheless, the 31DWM, as the country's only mass women's movement, was in all but name the women's wing of the NDC. It had affiliated women's groups (like the Nurses' Association), and claimed a huge membership and staff and offices throughout the country. It undertook various projects such as craft industries, tie-dyeing, gari-processing mills and day-care centres. Its funding came through donor support, contributions from local businesses, and transfers from government ministries (like the Ministry of Health). Many of its functionaries were actually on the government payroll (e.g. as teachers). Even its critics did not deny that it accomplished some good work, but in practice it was a mass patronage machine, channelling money to party loyalists, and at election times

---

[25] *Chronicle*, 4–5 Sept. 00, 1; see also *Graphic*, 28 April 01, 14–15, and 2 May 01, 3.
[26] *Graphic*, 30 Sept. 00, 7.
[27] For Electoral Commission, see *Chronicle*, 13–14 Sept. 00, 8.
[28] *Chronicle*, 20–22 Oct. 00, 1.

serving to mobilise the countryside for the NDC. Massive grants simply disappeared into its maw.[29]

This personalised rule could go to bizarre lengths. In a much-publicised incident, Rawlings, while driving with his bodyguards in Accra one night, observed a taxi driving carelessly. Rawlings set off after the taxi, whose driver stopped the car and fled. Rawlings then got his guards to throw the taxi into a ditch. When the private media got wind of the incident, the Castle countered that, given the indiscipline on Ghana's roads, the President should be congratulated for his public-spiritedness.[30] In a more notorious incident, carried by the independent media for weeks in mid-2000, an ex-boyfriend of Rawlings's eldest daughter was detained by guards at the Castle after breaking up with her and had his head shaved with a broken bottle. When his parents heard of his detention by the military, they went to the Castle to protest, and were arrested on a charge of offensive conduct, remanded in prison without bail, and convicted.[31] The ex-boyfriend himself later sought asylum in Britain.

The personalised regime meant that although Ghana was fairly stable in West African terms, the economic gains were much smaller and more faltering than was often suggested. The statistics speak for themselves—and these are statistics which are continually rehearsed by Ghanaians. At independence in 1957 Ghana was in the same economic league as Hong Kong, Singapore, Malaysia, South Korea; all had a *per capita* income of about $400. By 2000 Hong Kong's was about $28,000, Singapore's $32,000, South Korea's $18,000 and Malaysia's $22,000, while Ghana's has decreased from $400 to between $360 and $390.[32] And if the World Bank and the IMF find it difficult openly to say why, the governance paradigm sheds some light on the reasons for Ghana's economic failure. Ghana under Rawlings tends to confirm the new consensus that political culture is a major cause of Africa's lack of development. Far from being a classic illustration of the successful implementation of structural

---

[29] Richard Sandbrook and Jay Oelbaum, *Reforming the Political Kingdom: Governance and Development in Ghana's Fourth Republic*, Accra: CDD, 1999, 21–2. For similar 'NGOs' run by African Presidents' wives, see van de Walle, *African Economies*, 165–6.

[30] *Crusading Guide*, 25–31 July 00, 1; and 1–7 Aug. 00, 1.

[31] Judge's ruling, *Chronicle*, 22–24 Sept. 00, 3. The decision was quashed by the Accra Regional Tribunal a year later (*Mail*, 3 Dec. 01, 1).

[32] The figures are not always cited consistently. The numbers given here are as cited by James Mensah, chairing IEA/CIDA/UNDP Friedman lecture, 'Understanding Globalisation', Accra, 24 April 01; Nana Akufo-Addo reported at the 'Global Forum for Combating Corruption' in The Hague, 31 May 2001: 'Ghanaian people are poorer today than they were at independence. *Per capita* income, US $420 in 1957 is now US $370. The average real wage is a quarter of what it was 30 years ago. 40% of our population live below the poverty line.' (*Graphic*, 8 June 01, 7)

adjustment, Ghana is more nearly a text-book illustration of an unaccountable neo-patrimonial regime.

It is a further irony that one who came to power burning with righteous anger against exploiters ended up nurturing a great number of them. One of the military commanders whom Rawlings had executed in 1979 was accused of using his office to obtain a bank loan of 50,000 cedis; members of his own government were plundering millions of dollars.

Political culture

In Ghana itself one sometimes hears the opinion that Africa's ills are the result of external forces,[33] but overwhelmingly the consensus seems to agree with Annan and Amoako (see above, p. 6) that the root cause is the lack of good governance. Ghana's outspoken economist George Ayittey never misses an opportunity to put forward an internalist rather than an externalist analysis.[34] Likewise Joseph Ayee, head of political science at the University of Ghana, Legon: 'In sub-Saharan Africa at least, the persistent development crisis and the recent phenomenon of failing states are due in part to poor leadership: leaders who are not committed to the development of their societies and who lack honesty and a commitment to democracy' (the context makes clear that 'in part' means 'in great part').[35] Again, Kwame Donkoh-Fordwor, Ghanaian former president of the African Development Bank: 'It is now generally agreed that one of the main reasons for the very poor political and economic record of Africa has been the failure of the countries to adopt the democratic system of government.... African countries have not succeeded in advancing their economies because their political philosophy has not been based on constitutional governance, the rule of law, sound democratic institutions, the freedom of the individual and national economic philosophy in which the private sector has a dominant role to play.'[36] V. Antwi-Danso of the Legon Centre for International Affairs, dismisses attempts to blame

---

[33] See, e.g., *Chronicle*, 22 Aug. 01, 2.

[34] See IEA lecture, 'Why ERP Failed in Ghana', 25 July 00; and see George B. N. Ayittey, *Africa in Chaos*, London: Macmillan, 1999.

[35] Joseph R. A. Ayee, *Saints, Wizards, Demons and Systems: Explaining the Success or Failure of Public Policies and Programmes*, Accra: Ghana Universities Press, 24.

[36] *Standard*, 25 March 01, 12. See also Kwame Gyasi, this time quoting Professor Sule Gambari, Under-Secretary General of the United Nations: 'Africa failed to produce a productive middle class but instead has produced a parasitic elite that lived off the fat of the land through non-productive activities dependent on political patronage.' Gyasi comments: 'What Ghana and Africa have succeeded in doing is to produce armed robbers turned into political leaders whose quest for foreign culture and stolen wealth knows no bounds, no matter the damage they wreak on the poor citizens.' (*Spectator*, 21 July 01, 3)

external factors: Ghana's economic collapse is 'due mainly to cronyism and clientelism, the result of our insipid desire to hold on to power.'[37]

In Ghana, the building of the institutions so necessary for development has not proved possible, because the ruling élites have had little incentive to introduce structures or procedures. This systematised lack of proper procedures brought considerable benefit to some, even though it lies at the root of the suffering of the majority. It is not that Ghanaians are incapable of establishing institutions; the people who matter do not want them, because it is precisely the lack of them which enables them to do so well now—witness the new houses and hotels they are erecting in Accra's new suburbs like East Legon. It was the lack of independent transparent procedures that enabled bodies like the 31DWM to operate as they did, as channels of resources and influence, and to preserve the system under which the NDC grandees thrived.

This lack of accountability characterises the political culture of Ghana. Gyekye is reluctant to see in Ghana a 'culture of corruption', finding the concept 'incoherent'.[38] One takes his point—it is not a purposely created cultural product acknowledged with pride—but it remains true that there is in Ghana a high level of acquiescence. The country's political élite can acquire considerable wealth, and there seems no shame attached to this.[39] Someone quite poor can be given a high position in politics or public administration, and within a very short time he will have a big house, cars and overseas education for his children and dependants. Everyone knows that there is no other source of income than public funds.

Yet the wealth is flaunted; indeed, if the money went into savings or investment, the point would be lost. Wealth and status go together; the former is the sign of the latter. Appearances matter—and appearances, titles and the symbols of office often matter far more than doing a job well or delivering results. Formal recognition from others is important. In a culture where the sense of time has not been greatly interiorised, hours spent by subordinates paying homage to Big Men is more important than working productively. Productivity in Ghana, though hard to assess because so much is performed in the informal sector, must be incredibly low, but when set against proper deference to Big Men, it is of little account.

---

[37] *Spectator*, 28 July 00, 9.

[38] Kwame Gyekye, *Political Corruption: a Philosophical Inquiry into a Moral Problem*, Accra: Sankofa, 1997, 13.

[39] If it be argued that this is the same the world over, compare Singapore's Lee Kwan Yew: 'The strongest deterrent is a public opinion which censures and condemns corrupt persons, in other words, in attitudes which make corruption so unacceptable that the stigma of corruption cannot be washed away by serving a prison sentence.' (*Straits Times*, 27 Jan. 1987, 11)

Some would see corruption in Ghana as discontinuous with traditional society. Thus Assimeng: 'Nothing epitomises the discontinuity in the value nexus from traditional society to contemporary social order in Ghana, as much as bribery and corruption.'[40] But most observers see traditional values as contributing to the current situation. Sandbrook and Oelbaum chart Ghana's political development precisely in terms of a well established patrimonial tradition contending with a more liberal-democratic tradition that is weaker. 'The neo-patrimonial tradition is doubtless more deeply rooted in the history and culture of Ghana, not to mention better adapted to its poverty, limited class formation, and peasant origins than the liberal-democratic tendency.'[41] They note that under Rawlings 'clientelism, personalism and corruption have returned with a vengeance';[42] one section of their book is even entitled 'Neopatrimonialism Resurgent: Rawlings as the New Nkrumah'.[43] Nugent seems to agree with this view that Ghana's tradition is important: 'In pre-colonial Asante, and no doubt in other polities as well, successful accumulation depended greatly on access to state resources and privileges.... In time-honoured fashion, those who made money were inclined to flaunt it.'[44] Gyekye admits that corruption existed in pre-colonial society, but claims that its growth was fostered by colonial and post-colonial political systems.[45]

If Sandbrook and Oelbaum described the increase of neo-patrimonialism under Rawlings, they were also cautiously optimistic. African political culture is not static or unchanging, and they showed evidence of democratic advance, noting that some institutions like the Electoral Commission and CHRAJ were finding some limited autonomy. Their study was completed in 1997. If it were updated to 2002, their conclusion might well be the same: neopatrimonialism has continued to increase, but there is also real cause for optimism, with some strengthening of elements in civil society, notably the media (especially FM radio) and the peaceful change of regime.

[40] Max Assimeng, *Social Structure of Ghana: a Study in Persistence and Change*, 2nd edn, Tema: Ghana Publishing Co., 1999, 248; see 248–52 and 186.

[41] Sandbrook and Oelbaum, *Reforming*, 44.

[42] Ibid., 28.

[43] Ibid., 11–40.

[44] Paul Nugent, *Big Men, Small Boys and Politics in Ghana: Power, Ideology and the Burden of History, 1982–94*, London: Pinter, 1993, 18–23 and works cited there. Nugent concludes: 'Private accumulation had traditionally been lauded, and even the milking of political office had been tolerated as long as there was some expectation of wider community benefits. But by the end of the 1970s accumulation had become clandestine and seemed to be directly correlated with mass misery.' (ibid., 269) For Africa's 'Big Men' see Blaine Harden, 'The Good, the Bad and the Greedy', *Africa: Dispatches from a Fragile Continent*, London: Harper Collins, 1991, 217–70.

[45] Gyekye, *Corruption*, 19–22.

This case of the media calls for particular mention. There had been private (as opposed to state-controlled) newspapers in Ghana since the onset of constitutional rule in the early 1990s, and some (at no little risk) were vehemently anti-Rawlings and anti-NDC (and vitriolic about Mrs Rawlings, sometimes referred to as 'Lady Macbeth' or 'Jezebel'; the *Chronicle* once carried a picture of her with the simple caption: 'Mrs Rawlings: a Symbol of Evil'). Kweku Baako Jr, editor of the *Crusading Guide*, and Kwesi Pratt Jr, of *Insight* had spent spells in gaol—Pratt fourteen of them—and Eben Quarcoo of the *Free Press* and Kofi Coomson of the *Chronicle* had a long lawsuit dismissed only after the change of regime.[46] Much of this comment in the independent press can only be described as speculative, but where accountability and transparency are so discounted, such speculation is inevitable.

However, 1996 saw the beginning of a veritable FM revolution. Although some of these new radio stations were government-connected and some were fairly bland, restricting themselves to playing music, others like Joy, Choice, Radio Univers (of the School of Communication Studies at the University of Ghana) were remarkably courageous in covering public events and in comment. Since most of these radio stations were run on a very tight budget, a good part of their programming consisted of phone-ins, in which anyone with access to a phone could express personal opinions, denounce perceived abuses, publicise his plight, and in general raise issues that the state-owned media would never touch. Radio Univers broadcast a 90-minute 'Media Review' every weekday morning, in which panellists analysed the day's newspapers—even their most speculative stories—and then invited the public to phone in and comment. This programme deservedly won 'Best Radio Programme of 1999' from Ghana's Chartered Institute of Marketing. On such programmes, topics like the treatment of the ex-boyfriend of Rawlings's daughter and his parents drew enormous comment for days, almost all of it highly unflattering to Rawlings. The government was limited in the counter-measures it could take, since freedom of expression was guaranteed in the constitution and such freedoms were monitored by the countries whose aid kept Ghana afloat.

One cultural factor often said to be significant in Ghanaian politics is Ghana's endemic factionalism, which is of some importance now that 'social capital' is hailed as a key element in development. In Ghana the relative lack of social capital is most clearly seen in the matter of chieftaincy. Rathbone has shown in an important study of the Nkrumah period that 'despite the romantic essentialism of some colonial assumptions of a

---

[46] They had alleged that the NCC government dealt in drugs and used the proceeds to purchase arms and ammunition to create chaos in the country if it lost the 1996 elections.

rural harmony orchestrated by the uncontested legitimacy of "natural rulers", virtually every chieftaincy, virtually every stool, was in reality a tense political cockpit.'[47] This is equally true today. Not a week goes by without the media carrying reports of yet more fighting over stools, much of it quite serious, some involving deaths, and a good deal of it almost certainly detrimental to development.[48] In early 2002, at the time of the assassination of the Ya Na or Dagbon Paramount Chief (probably Ghana's second most important traditional ruler after the Asantehene) and the killing of about fifty others at Yendi, it was said that there were about 200 chieftaincy disputes in the Central Region alone, some of them reaching back thirty years.[49] Rathbone shows how Nkrumah had originally set out to abolish the institution of chieftaincy: 'It was hard to conceive of agencies less adapted to the work of what was now called development... than the organs of chiefly rule.'[50] But Nkrumah came to realise that the institution of chieftaincy could be used to his political advantage, and it was thus changed to serve another purpose, becoming another cog in the machinery of neo-patrimonialism.[51] Rathbone does not labour the comparison, but no one living in Rawlings's NDC Ghana could fail to see the close parallels.[52]

The significance of this debate about political culture as a factor in development will become clearer below, especially in Chapter 5.

---

[47] Richard Rathbone, *Nkrumah and the Chiefs: the Politics of Chieftaincy in Ghana 1951–60*, Oxford: James Currey, 2000, 34.

[48] 'The resources of the area, far from being channelled into productive ventures, are wasted on conflicts and this only contributes to the stagnation and even retrogression of the area. This is not to mention the effect of the prolonged conflict scaring away investors who can contribute to develop the area and improve the well-being of the people.' (editorial, 'End the Wa Chieftaincy Dispute', *Graphic*, 31 May 02, 7) Likewise the Western Regional Minister lamented that he had to spend 'most of his working hours resolving chieftaincy matters and claimed these disputes were retarding its development'. (*Chronicle*, 19 July 02, 8)

[49] *Graphic*, 1 April 02, 13. In the space of two months government spending required to handle this Yendi dispute and others at Bawku and Bimbilla totalled 3.3 billion cedis ($500,000)—as one minister explained, an amount comparable to what is required to build over 30 basic schools or 20 clinics for these districts: 'All three administrative areas are among the most deprived of the 110 districts in the whole country.' (*Graphic*, 5 June 02, 1)

[50] Rathbone, *Nkrumah*, 17.

[51] Under Nkrumah, as Dunn and Robertson wrote, 'Tenure of chiefly office was undoubtedly dependent on political party affiliation', *Dependence and Opportunity: Political Change in Ahafo*, Cambridge University Press, 1973, 204, cited in Rathbone, *Nkrumah*, 143.

[52] See also Sandbrook and Oelbaum, *Reforming*, 16–17; T. Peter Omari, *Kwame Nkrumah: the Anatomy of an African Dictatorship*, London: Hurst, 1969, repr. Accra: Sankofa, 2000: 'Truly not much has changed.' (new preface, xi)

Transition

One particular aspect of this general context calls for more detailed discussion. This research was conducted around the time of the general election in the year 2000, and since this election focused the public involvement of the churches, it is significant for what follows.

After two terms in office Rawlings was constitutionally required to step down, and to his credit (since at the same time President Frederick Chiluba in Zambia was trying to engineer another term for himself) he abided by the constitution. He obviously thought that he could continue to exert control from behind the scenes, and to this end hand-picked his successor, the law professor John Atta Mills (a choice which alienated many of his long-term supporters who soon broke from the NDC to form a Reform Party).

The NDC used the advantage of incumbency for all it was worth. For months before the election Atta Mills was on the TV news almost every night opening or commissioning new projects, some of which had been opened or commissioned before, even more than once. Government vehicles constituted an enormous advantage, and the public media were used to the maximum. The Electoral Commission was still far from transparent, although an improvement was apparent compared to previous elections. Intimidation was used; some weeks before the election, both in Accra and Kumasi, the army stormed positions like the airport and key city buildings in what they said were just routine exercises but were widely seen as attempts to cow opposition. In the last quarter of 2000, the government stopped borrowing and just printed money—it was rumoured that this amounted to 900 billion cedis.[53]

In the parliamentary elections of 7 December 2000 the NDC lost 41 of its 133 seats, and its majority in parliament. The NPP made all the gains, and took 100 of the 200 seats. In the presidential race, no candidate reached the 50% required to win outright, but the NPP challenger Kufuor took 48% of the votes, to 43% for Atta Mills. All the other parties together polled only 9%, which many saw as a good sign for Ghana, with a gradual shake-down into two dominant parties. In general the elections were peaceful, with only one major outbreak of violence, in the extreme northeast constituency of Bawku Central, where over fifty died.

Immediately after the first round, all five eliminated candidates (even of the avowedly 'socialist' parties) threw their support behind the neoliberal Kufuor for the re-run scheduled for 28 December. The NDC

[53] *The Economist*, addressing the issue of 'Ghana as Economic Model', notes that economic reforms were greatly undermined by the NDC's fiscal irresponsibility before the elections of 1992, 1996 and 2000. (27 Apr 02, 62)

began claiming that they had 2 million voters who had not turned out for the first round, and whom they intended to mobilise for the second; many took this as an ominous sign that the NDC was determined to raise its tally by any means. The media campaign stepped up several gears.[54] The NDC realised that Rawlings himself was coming to be perceived as something of a liability, and he was kept more in the background, with Atta Mills given space to show himself as his own man. The ethnic factor was played up; in some areas of Accra dominated by the original Ga inhabitants, loudspeaker vans broadcast that the Asante were coming to dispossess the Ga.[55] The judiciary ruled that students would not be able to transfer votes in constituencies other than where registered, thus preventing those home for Christmas from voting.

On 28 December itself there was a heavy military presence, particularly in the Ashanti Region, Kufuor's stronghold, but not at all in the Volta Region, Rawlings's home region and the NDC heartland. One factor that surprised everyone in the election, particularly the rerun, was the role of the media.[56] During the elections some FM stations came into their own, especially Joy, Choice and Radio Univers, which carried the elections live. People who noticed irregularities would phone in and their observations would be broadcast live.[57] The day after the run-off when the votes were being counted, Radio Univers featured those students who had gone to the Volta Region as NPP observers. Here the military presence was nil, yet their tale was one of intimidation, exclusion of observers, multiple voting and distribution of books of ballot papers. The rigging was so unrestrained that some began to question the validity of the figures from the Volta Region in previous elections.

By the end of the day following the voting it was clear that Kufuor was in an unassailable lead. As the implications dawned, there arose a genuine and widespread feeling of pride and empowerment. The general euphoria was tempered with some apprehension about how Rawlings would accept the result. He had two official speeches to deliver between the second election and 6 January, the day of transition—one on December 31, the anniversary of his second coup annually celebrated with military parades, and the other at a farewell to him staged by the armed forces.

---

[54] For two different projects monitoring the evenhandedness of the media, see *Chronicle*, 1–5 March 01, 7; *Graphic*, 16 Nov. 00, 6; 21 Nov. 00, 8; 6 June 00, 11; and 7 Dec. 00, 4.

[55] *Mail*, 21 Dec. 00, 4; *Chronicle*, 8–9 Jan. 01, 3; *Guide*, 20 Dec. 00, 3 Jan. 01, 4.

[56] See *Media Coverage of the 2000 Elections, CDD-Ghana Research Papers 8*, Accra: CDD, 2001; D. A. Smith and J. Temin, 'The Media and Ghana's 2000 Elections' in Joseph R. A. Ayee (ed.), *Deepening Democracy in Ghana: Politics of the 2000 Elections*, vol. 1, Accra: Freedom Publications, 2001, 160–78.

[57] It was pointed out that the four regions which did not vote for NPP's 'positive change' were the regions where local radio had not been developed.

On 31 December he was at his worst—ungracious, divisive, ambiguous—and in his speech to the armed forces he again stated that he did not believe in democracy (contrary to what had been prepared for him in his set speech). In both, however, he reluctantly accepted the verdict of the polls.[58]

At his inauguration a few days later, Kufuor in an address argued that his accession, the first peaceful transfer of power from one regime to another in Ghana's history, was a victory for all Ghanaians. He pledged zero tolerance for corruption and promised that he would be an example of integrity. He asked Ghanaians to forgive—even if they could not forget—the injustices of the previous twenty years. He begged overseas donors for debt relief, warning that if Ghanaians did not see any democracy dividend, there would be an opening for unrest and more military intervention.

The election was a vote for positive change, for something different, for something better. A mood of euphoria was evident (which some likened to that after Nkrumah's overthrow in 1966 and even after Rawlings's 1979 coup). There was an immediate and palpable lifting of the sense of fear—three days after the re-run one TV news report referred to the 'total incompetence' of Ghana's police force, something that would have been unthinkable only a few days before. The transition was helped because the outgoing NDC administration in their last days engineered for themselves 'end of service benefits', including official cars at knock-down prices: the outrage this caused when so many Ghanaians could hardly feed themselves convinced many that these self-proclaimed guardians of the revolution were also driven by a large degree of self-interest.

Ghana has enormous problems, and is economically on its knees. Also the NPP in its bid for power made wild promises, and will have to repay all who helped it on its way. It is yet to be seen whether there will be any change in governance rather than merely a change in the names of the self-serving élite.

The above is the context within which the growth of a particular kind of Christianity needs to be explained. An outline of the current state of the debate about Africa's development has also been attempted because this provides criteria for assessing these churches' public role. Of all the ways in which these new churches might contribute to development, that in which they affect neopatrimonialism merits special attention.

---

[58] For the elections see Daniel A. Smith, 'Consolidating Democracy? The Structural Underpinnings of Ghana's 2000 Elections', *JMAS*, 40, 4 (2002), 621–50. Paul Nugent, 'Winners, Losers and Also-Rans: Money, Moral Authority and Voting Patterns in the Ghana 2000 Election', *African Affairs*, 100 (2001), 405–28.

2

PARADIGM SHIFT

The mainline or 'orthodox'

In 1980 there were at least four recognisable strands of Ghanaian Christianity. First there were the Catholics, the biggest single church; secondly the mainline Protestant churches—the Methodist, two Presbyterian (stemming from the Bremen and Basel missions) and the much smaller Anglican; thirdly the established Pentecostals (Apostolic Church, Church of Pentecost, Christ Apostolic Church and Assemblies of God); and fourthly the African Independent (or Initiated) Churches (AICs). The mainline churches have been of considerable significance in building the modern nation, particularly through their schools, to an extent probably unequalled in Africa. The schools—Mfantsipim, Adisadel, St Augustine's, Prempeh, with the government-founded but very Christian Achimota (for historical reasons nearly all in Cape Coast rather than Accra)—have created Ghana's élite since the nineteenth century. This is well caught by the title of a centenary book by the distinguished academic (and Rawlings' main challenger in the presidential elections of 1992) Adu Boahen, *Mfantsipim and the Making of Modern Ghana*. Ghana's most distinguished son, the UN Secretary General Kofi Annan, is a product of the Methodist Mfantsipim and, according to some public-school-conscious Ghanaians, 'head prefect of the world'.

The general cultural impact of Christianity is incalculable. It provided the images, metaphors and concepts for the independence struggle, most clearly in Nkrumah's slogans like 'Seek ye first the political kingdom'. Another example is the Creed of his 'Verandah Boys' (his followers, so called from the poverty of their living quarters): 'I believe in the Convention People's Party, the opportune Saviour of Ghana, and in Kwame Nkrumah its founder and leader, who is endowed with the Ghana Spirit, born a true Ghanaian for Ghana, suffering under victimisations, was vilified, threatened with deportation. He disentangled himself from the clutches of the UGCC and the same day he rose victorious with the

20

Verandah Boys, ascended the political heights, and sitteth at the supreme head of the CPP from whence he shall demand full self-government for Ghana. I believe in freedom for all peoples, especially the New Ghana; the abolition of slavery; the liquidation of imperialism; the victorious end of our struggle, its glory and its pride, and the flourish [*sic*] of Ghana, for ever and ever.'[1] Today it is impossible to begin or end meetings of any kind without Christian prayer (in which Muslims seem ready to participate). Christian, rather than specially African, metaphors occur in public discussion. Officers of the Ghana Journalists' Association are sworn in by a bishop.[2] Famously, Ghanaian shops are often given Christian names (Father, Son and Holy Spirit Ventures; For Christ We Live Brake and Clutch Linings; Lord of Glory Kebabs; By God's Grace Fresh Fish; Yahweh Fast Food; Holy Ghost Cosmetics; Sweet Jesus Hair Fashions). Slogans on vehicles are often Christian, even cryptic biblical references like 'Dt 8.1' or 'Is 41.10'. The independent *Chronicle* always ran a scriptural quote along the bottom of its front page, denouncing what it considered the latest aberration of Rawlings or the NDC with quotes like 'This son of ours is stubborn and rebellious. He will not obey us. He is a profligate and a drunkard' (Dt 21.20) or 'Woe to the wicked! Disaster is upon them. They will be paid back for what their hands have done.' (Is 3.11) The pervasiveness of this ethos was revealed at the Miss Ghana contest in 2001, where the contenders had not only to parade in their finery but to answer questions on 'health, education and religion', and debate 'among themselves that "Mission schools be handed back to the Missions"'.[3]

---

[1] Ebenezer Obiri Addo, *Kwame Nkrumah: a Case Study of Religion and Politics in Ghana*, Lanham, MD: University Press of America, 1977, 101. See also the rewriting of the Beatitudes (Mt 5,1–12): 'Blessed are they who are imprisoned for self-government's sake, for theirs is the freedom of the land. Blessed are ye, when men shall vilify you and persecute you, and say all kinds of evil against you, for Convention People's Party's sake. Blessed are they who hunger and thirst because of self-government, for they shall be satisfied. Blessed are they who reject the Coussey Report, for they shall know freedom. Blessed are the parents whose children are political leaders, for they shall be thanked. Blessed are they who took part in Positive Action, for they shall have better rewards. Blessed are they who now love CPP, for they shall be leaders in the years to come. Blessed are they who cry for self-government, for their voice shall be heard.' (published in Nkrumah's CPP newspaper *Accra Evening News*, 17 Jan. 1950) And the rewriting of the Lord's Prayer: 'O Imperialism which are in Gold Coast, his grace is thy name. Thy Kingdom go, our will be done in Gold Coast as it is done to you in Britain. Give us this day our full self-government, and forget about the infringement of charges against our leaders, as it was done to you when you advocated for independence from the Romans. And lead us not into fear, but deliver us from evil, For Ghana is a glorious land, for ever and ever.' (Addo, *Kwame*, 101–2)

[2] *Graphic*, 3 Feb. 01, 12.

[3] *Graphic*, 13 Mar. 01, 17.

Ghana's mainline churches have also produced some of Africa's best-known Christians internationally: Kwesi Dickson, theologian and President of the All Africa Conference of Churches; Kwame Bediako, a theologian well known for his argument that African Christianity is no longer an import, but has been thoroughly internalised; and Mercy Amba Oduyoye, for years at the World Council of Churches and now back in Ghana and the driving force behind the promotion of African women's theology.[4] Besides the mainline churches' network of schools and clinics, they have also been involved in development work.[5] Since independence they have been influential opinion-formers in political matters. They were probably most vocal against what were seen as the human rights abuses ('revolutionary justice') of the early Rawlings years. Their criticism was often sustained and courageous, and Rawlings did not disguise his antipathy towards mainline church leaders.

The mainline Protestants collaborate in a Christian Council, which is probably the best-run in Africa and as significant a national player as any such church body apart from the South African Council of Churches in the twilight of apartheid, and the Christian Council of Kenya. Even though donor funds are diminishing, this is not because of donor dissatisfaction with the Council. Through it in particular these Protestant bodies relate to and collaborate with the Catholics very closely. The Catholic-Protestant collaboration was evident in statements right from the early Rawlings years, and it gradually extended to Muslims, first the Ahmadiyya (particularly strong in Ghana) and then the traditional Muslims in FORB (Forum of Religious Bodies, very much a Christian-driven group).

If the development work of the mainline Protestants is considerable, it is dwarfed by the Catholic involvement which is incalculable. Besides the initiatives of each diocese, Catholic Relief Services (CRS), with access

---

[4] Kwesi A. Dickson, *Theology in Africa*, London: Darton, Longman and Todd, 1984; Kwame Bediako, *Christianity in Africa: The Renewal of a Non-Western Religion*, Edinburgh University Press, 1995; Kwame Bediako, *Jesus in Africa: The Christian Gospel in African History and Experience*, Oxford: Regnum, 2000; Mercy Amba Oduyoye, *Hearing and Knowing: Theological Reflections on Christianity in Africa*, Maryknoll, NY: Orbis, 1986; Mercy Amba Oduyoye, *Daughters of Anowa: African Women and Patriarchy*, Maryknoll: Orbis, 1995. For Oduyoye see Carrie Pemberton, *Circle Thinking: African Women Theologians in Dialogue with the West*, Leiden: E. J. Brill, 2003.

[5] They have long had systems of schools and Teachers' Colleges. Even though they lack resources properly to run these, they want to start universities. Some Ghanaians deplore this as illustrating a general Ghanaian trait towards status and prestige: appearances are more important than performance. The move on the part of Methodists to become episcopal also draws similar comment; it is more to do with the status of leaders, who felt themselves outranked by the Catholic and Anglican leaders. The *Methodist Times* (Jan. 00, 1) article announcing the change is all about their new titles.

to USAID money as well as American Catholic donations, is an important player on the national scene. The Catholics dominate many areas of development, from work with street children in Accra to health care in the Upper West. It must be said that development is the involvement that defines the Catholic Church in Ghana, not the human rights advocacy which characterises them in some other parts of the world. Despite the pronouncements of the hierarchy early in the Rawlings era (when the Catholic *Standard* was banned for three years for its human rights stance), by the late 1990s they were less vocal. Some claim that under Rawlings the attempts to contribute in this way were simply counter-productive (Rawlings let it be known that he did not want to appear on the same platform as Bishop Peter Sarpong of Kumasi, who in those early years was chairman of the Catholic Justice and Peace Commission).[6] Others say that it was becoming less necessary. Certainly, the Catholic Justice and Peace involvement is as weak as their commitment to development is strong.

The newcomers

These mainline churches ('orthodox' is their label in Ghana) remain significant bodies. Nevertheless, in the two decades we are especially considering (1979–2002) they have in many ways been eclipsed by something quite new, the charismatic sector (here we will keep to the term 'charismatic' although some in Ghana use the term 'neo-Pentecostal'). Precisely what this is and how it functions we need not resolve now because the rest of this book is concerned with describing and analysing the phenomenon.[7] However, nobody in Ghana is unaware of the shift. Everyone is aware of charismatic prayer centres, their all-night services ('All Nights'), their crusades, conventions and Bible schools, their new buildings (or the schools, cinemas and halls they rent), their car-bumper stickers and banners, and particularly the posters that every-

---

[6] In this running conflict with the mainline churches, too, Rawlings's similarities to Nkrumah are noteworthy; see John S. Pobee, *Religion and Politics in Ghana*, Accra: Asempa, 1991. It was much easier to coopt the non-mainline: John S. Pobee, *Religion and Politics in Ghana: a Case Study of the Acheampong Era*, Accra: Ghana Universities Press, 1992.

[7] Some studies use the word 'Evangelical' of these churches. Freston, following Bebbington, insists that Evangelicalism 'consists of four constant characteristics'—'conversion (emphasis on the need for change of life), activism (emphasis on evangelistic and missionary efforts), biblicism (a special importance attached to the Bible), and crucicentrism (emphasis on the centrality of Christ's sacrifice on the cross)' (Paul Freston, *Evangelicals and Politics in Asia, Africa and Latin America*, Cambridge University Press, 2001, 2). The term 'Evangelical' will be avoided here, in order not to presume that Ghana's new churches are necessarily characterised by any of these four qualities.

where advertise an enormous range of forthcoming activities. Everyone is aware of their media efforts. Above all, everyone knows of the new religious superstars—Bishop Nicholas Duncan-Williams, Pastor Mensa Otabil, Bishop Charles Agyin Asare, Bishop Dag Heward-Mills—and the prophets like Salifu Amoako. If these are the most prominent or the household names, it is just as obvious that they are merely the tip of the iceberg or (to change the metaphor) merely the 'premier division' in a multi-divisional 'national league'. There follow brief sketches of the men and churches that recur often in these pages.

Nicholas Duncan-Williams (it is reasonably common, especially along the coast, for Ghanaians to have European names, even hyphenated ones) had led a somewhat wild youth, even stowing away twice on ships to Europe, before being converted in 1976 while in hospital after something of a breakdown. In that year he went to Benson Idahosa's Bible school in Nigeria, and on his return in 1979 founded Christian Action Faith Ministries International (CAFM), and his church Action Chapel International (ACI). In 1992 he began holding services in his huge new building near the airport (still uncompleted in 2002). Duncan-Williams himself effectively moved to the United States in 1998, which led his critics to charge that the church was simply a means of bettering himself, and others to hint that his marriage was on the rocks. This latter was proved true when it was announced at a Sunday service in March 2001 that his wife had divorced him. His long absences and personal problems have affected the natural development of his church—at the time of his divorce about 3,000 attended the two Sunday services at his headquarters (down from 6,000 five years before), and the church has twenty-eight branches in Ghana and abroad.[8]

Pastor Mensa Otabil began his International Central Gospel Church (ICGC) in February 1984 in a rented hall in central Accra, and in December 1996 moved to his new church, still in the inner city. He draws about 7,000 on a Sunday to two services. His TV and radio preaching make him well known far beyond his own congregation; the church estimates that about 25,000 watch his Sunday evening 'Living Word' telecast. The church claims twenty-three branches in the neighbourhood of Accra and about 100 throughout Ghana.[9]

---

[8] Statistics from headquarters, 4 July 01; on the back of some cassettes CAFM is said to have 45 branches. In late 2001 it was announced that the Bishop and his wife had become reconciled (*Mail*, 26 Nov. 01, 1), and on 31 March 2002 Duncan-Williams spoke of this in an hour-long TV interview (see also *Guide*, 3 April 02, 1). For the divorce and reconciliation, see Francisca Duncan-Williams, *Reflections: the Untold Story*, Accra: Action Faith Publications, 2002.

[9] For Otabil, see Larbi, *Pentecostalism*, 335–63; Gifford, *AC*, 79–84; 237–44.

most on TV

Bishop Dag Heward-Mills, son of a Ghanaian father and Swiss mother, trained as a doctor, and his church grew out of his fellowship for medical professionals around Korle Bu Teaching Hospital. He left medical practice for full-time ministry in January 1991. His Lighthouse Cathedral is situated near the hospital, in inner Accra, but in the late 1990s the characteristic yellow signboards advertising Lighthouse Chapel branches began to appear all round the city. Most of his pastors are part time—he has only ten paid employees (on 25 December 2000 he compared this favourably to another charismatic church in Accra that employs ninety-five). He too has a big TV involvement, although for most of 2001 he simply disappeared from the screens, directing his resources instead to building a ministerial training school. He attracts about 3,000 to his four services at his cathedral every Sunday. He claims about 120 churches in twenty-five countries.[10]

Bishop Charles Agyin Asare was converted at the age of eighteen, attended Idahosa's Bible school in Nigeria, and returned to found in March 1987 his World Miracle Bible Church in Tamale, which had sixteen churches and an extensive ministry in the north before the ethnic disturbances there forced him in 1994 to shift his base of operations to Accra. He has a high-profile TV presence, his programmes often featuring his miracle crusades. He attracts about 4,000 to the four Sunday services at his headquarters, and the church (now the Word Miracle Church International, WMCI) claimed seventy-two branches in October 2000, eleven in Accra.[11]

more leaders

Prophet Elisha Salifu Amoako was born to a poor Muslim family in Kumasi and had virtually no schooling, but as a young man he was converted and introduced to the Resurrection Power Evangelistic Ministry of the controversial Evangelist Francis Akwesi Amoako in Santasi, working in the latter's house until the evangelist was killed in a car accident in 1990. Salifu claims his mantle—hence both 'Elisha' (to the evangelist's Elijah) and 'Amoako'. In 1994 he began his Jesus is Alive Evangelistic Ministry at the Orion cinema in the very centre of Accra, and in January 1998 inaugurated his church, Alive Chapel International. On a Sunday he attracts about 1,600 to his one lengthy service, where the sermon is in English but much else in Twi. Only in 2001 was Salifu seriously involved in establishing the structures of a church, and in advertising.[12]

---

[10] Larbi (*Pentecostalism*, 514) claims 250 Lighthouse churches.
[11] For Agyin Asare, see Paul Gifford, 'Ghana's Charismatic Churches', *JRA*, 24 (1994), 241–65.
[12] Some biographical details in Elisha Salifu Amoako, *Your Angel will Come*, Accra: Alive Publications, 1999, 49–55.

The other church in our premier division is Living Faith Church Worldwide, popularly known as Winners' Chapel. This is unlike the other churches just mentioned in that it was not founded by a Ghanaian, but is a branch of a Nigerian multinational based in Lagos. This was founded in September 1983 by Bishop David Oyedepo, and by 2000 had become active in thirty-eight African countries. Unlike the other churches mentioned here, Winners' in Accra is not identified with its pastor, who can be re-assigned as in a mainline denomination. The Accra church was founded in January 1997—crucially, on a former industrial site right in the middle of the city (close to Salifu's disused cinema). In late 2001 it attracted about 13,000 to its two Sunday services.

These churches are not all the same. This is both an important and a complicating factor for a study such as this, and one to which we will return regularly, but to identify at the outset some of the diversity within this sector of Christianity, consider the churches just mentioned. Duncan-Williams' ACI is most obviously a faith/prosperity/health-and-wealth church (a category to be explained later), even if the American faith origins were mediated through Nigeria's Idahosa, and Duncan-Williams has lately taken on a 'spiritual warfare' emphasis. In Winners' Chapel, a general faith or health-and-wealth orientation has undergone a mutation into a concern almost exclusively for financial success. Heward-Mills's Lighthouse Chapel is characterised by a stress on church planting and lay leadership. Agyin Asare's WMCI concentrates on evangelistic and healing crusades, and although the diseases cured at these crusades would certainly be understood in terms of demonic causality, this is not greatly emphasised. By contrast, in Salifu's Alive Ministry the stress is on the demonic causality for all ills, and the remedy is the gifts of Salifu himself. Otabil is almost exclusively a teacher, with no emphasis on healing, and the demonic is hardly ever mentioned. All these strands, with their different though often compatible emphases, are part of the new charismatic revival, and illustrate at the outset the considerable range involved and the difficulty in talking about 'charismatic Christianity' without qualification.[13]

Nor are these churches the same in their clientele. They attract different categories of people. I have developed my own wildly subjective grading system based on such things as the number of Mercedes, BMWs, Pajeros, Landcruisers and Patrols in the car park; the hairstyles and haircoverings of the women; the number of men in formal traditional cloth;

[13] Some in Ghana speak of a distinction between those (like Otabil and Heward-Mills) nurtured in organisations like Student Union with its holiness background and those (like Duncan-Williams and Agyin Asare) who lacked strong Christian roots before a conversion experience propelled them into full-time ministry. I have not considered this such a significant distinction.

the use of English; the obtrusiveness of mobile phones (Winners' has signs posted urging that they be switched off; Otabil's ICGC has computerised instructions flashing across a giant screen). A very rough guide to class (understood very loosely) is that if the affluent Catholic parish of Christ the King (President Kufuor's church) rates 10, Otabil's ICGC rates 9, Duncan-Williams's ACI 7.5, Winners' 7, Agyin Asare's WMCI 5.5, Heward-Mills's LCI 5, and Salifu's Jesus Alive 1.

Ghana's charismatic Christianity has not remained static. One can visualise developments in terms of waves. If for convenience we date the beginning of Accra's charismatic Christianity to around 1979, with Duncan-Williams leading the first wave, we can distinguish three further waves. The second is the teaching wave best illustrated by Otabil, the third is the miracle healing introduced by Agyin Asare, and the fourth and last the prophetic exemplified by Salifu.[14] A complicating factor is the tendency for each succeeding wave to affect all existing churches, making 'pure' or 'non-hybrid' types hard to find. For example, Duncan-Williams's ACI is still best seen as a faith-gospel church, but even it had to advertise its 2000 annual convention as a 'prophetic' convention—by 2000 *everything* had to be prophetic. Churches have not been influenced to the same degree, but the tendency is undeniable.

Services

All charismatic churches conduct services of three parts: 'praise and worship', offering, and sermon. We consider these in turn.

'Praise and worship' is carried by groups of eight to fourteen musicians, playing Western instruments like electric guitars and electronic keyboards; through the 1990s they came to use ever more brass—trombones, trumpets and saxophones. It is totally participatory. The songs are about 60% English (and imported, mainly from the United States) and about 40% Twi. These are simple and repetitive, although some churches, like Solid Rock, have their own hymnbooks which include old revivalist favourites. Some of the 'praise teams' are superb. Ola Williams of ACI has the congregation exhausted after about an hour; the team at Salifu's Jesus Alive is equally rousing, and brings considerable numbers dancing down to the front.[15] Not a few church singers and musicians have gone on to become professional artistes.

---

[14] Heward-Mills described the waves thus in a sermon 21 January 2001; for another treatment of these waves, see Susan Hanson, *A Nation Touched by the Fire of Heaven*, Accra: Journagraphx, 2000, 143–9.
[15] Salifu's praise team is often in effect the choir.

The taking of the offering sees the choirs in action, almost invariably facing the congregation from the back of the platform. They consist overwhelmingly of young women, and it is openly acknowledged (often in jokes) that most of them are looking for husbands. Their dress is normally uniform, with blouses and skirts of the same colour, often varied from Sunday to Sunday; they do not wear the gowns and mortar-boards that Ghana's mainline churches adopt from African American choirs. Some churches have more than one choir—Sam Korankye Ankrah's at RHCI has five—and more than one can 'minister' at a single service. Often the language is Twi. Less often an instrumental group ministers without singing (there is an outstanding flautist at Otabil's ICGC).

The sermon or 'message' is the principal focus. It usually lasts nearly an hour, and is never read, although the preacher can have notes on his lectern (some seem not even to have those). In the premier league the sermons are invariably arresting—because of the competition they have to be in order to maintain numbers. There is seldom any biblical reading as is usual in the mainline churches, but the message is considered 'the Word of God' and virtually identified with scripture. All messages relate in some way to a biblical text or texts, and most of the congregation bring bibles in which to follow (and underline or highlight) the main texts cited. When he is in town, it is normal for the founder or overseer to preach at all services—Heward-Mills and Agyin Asare at all four. Although these sermons do not invite the running commentary often heard in African American churches—'Amen!', 'Alleluia!' and 'Preach on!'—congregations are frequently called on to express agreement ('If anyone is here with me, shout "Amen"') and to interact with neighbours ('Turn to your neighbour and say....').

In keeping with the variety encompassed by these churches, their preaching styles differ considerably. Duncan-Williams is the most influenced by the African American scene—particularly by T. D. Jakes of the Potter's House, Dallas, as is evident in diction, dress, shoes and the way he strides upon the stage. Agyin Asare is characterised by enthusiastic intensity; the head pastors at Winners' by florid language combined with articulacy. Heward-Mills is more folksy, and Otabil more measured and restrained. Of others we will encounter, Sam Korankye Ankrah leads his congregation in unrestrained exuberance (to such an extent that once, on 12 July 2001, he even felt he had to turn to the camera and say to viewers 'Don't despise me'), and Lawrence Tetteh can break into a hymn every few minutes—many of his sermons thus consist mainly of singing (he also tends to become gratuitously short-tempered with assistants he regards as getting in his way). Individuality is a hallmark of this Christianity.

There are other features that all share. All welcome first-time attenders, who are asked to stand and be welcomed; they are given cards to fill in, and at Winners' they are sung to, brought to the front, each presented with a free cassette, and immediately led off for processing. All these churches have 'altar calls' for giving one's life to Christ, but some not every Sunday. All would have communion on some days, and this is obviously understood in different ways; communion can be very casual at Winners', but is taken more seriously at Otabil's ICGC. All have special activities (normally some kind of Sunday school) for children during the main Sunday service (ACI also has a special youth service for 13–19-year-olds running simultaneously). Some churches might have healings towards the end of a service, but this is not normal—Agyin Asare's fourth service is always a 'miracle service', something unthinkable with Otabil. Some make testimonies an important part of the service (at Winners' invariably six or seven, speaking for themselves; at Salifu's Alive Chapel up to thirty, but mediated through and abbreviated by pastors). Some have two offerings rather than one. Most would read announcements at some point. Most would introduce to the assembly couples about to be married, who would receive enthusiastic applause.[16]

There are several things an outsider cannot fail to notice. One of these is the youth of the congregation—and in some, contrary to much received opinion, the numbers of young men. Secondly, there is the sound system, without which the experience would be impossible. Banks of speakers are placed near the front and others as required. Because of the choirs and soloists and instrumentalists, there may be up to twenty microphones in play; wires run everywhere, and the mixing bay may resemble a broadcasting studio. Teams of assistants are involved, most obviously ushers (often called, as at ACI, the 'Protocol Department'), all stylishly dressed in matching uniforms. (At Winners' you may have shaken hands with as many as thirty people before taking your seat.) Although the words 'charismatic and 'pentecostal' most immediately relate to the gift of speaking in tongues or glossolalia, the latter in fact has hardly ever taken place. Many of the congregation may pray in this way at home, but it is not normally part of the service, even when the congregation is at its most exuberant. The Sunday service is not the only time for assembling. There are other activities on at least two evenings during the week, which there is heavy pressure to attend. These weekday gatherings essentially follow the same pattern as the Sunday service—especially their 'Bible studies'. In addition, all have daytime activities during the week, often run by

---

[16] Very frequently couples come from different churches; thus I am inclined to moderate my earlier view that an individual church itself acts as a marriage market (Gifford, 'Ghana's Charismatic', 254).

associate pastors. Even the smallest charismatic churches have assistant pastors, and the big ones have large teams of youth pastors, marriage pastors, premarital counsellors and so on. Besides the routine weekly activities, all—including the smallest—have annual conventions, and Easter is an accepted time for special programmes. These, too, essentially follow the three-part format of the Sunday service.

The liveliness of the worship and the sense of fellowship are important clues to the appeal of these churches. So is the quality of music. One must also recognise the importance of merely having somewhere to dress up to go to. Accra has some middle class suburbs (like Airport or East Legon), but most who attend these new churches come from areas where there may be several people sleeping in a single room.[17] In the evening or on Sundays, just to be able to go somewhere different in one's finery is of enormous importance. Cell groups can often add the intimacy of a close circle of friends. However, while the importance of these factors should not be underestimated, the case I argue is that it is the message of the pastor that is crucial.

The media

Accra's TV consists of three channels—GTV, the national network covering almost the whole country; TV3, available in the Greater Accra region; and Metro, available only in the city of Accra. It is hard to be exact in counting the Christian programmes because while some appear regularly, others come and go. It is difficult to find programme schedules, and where they exist they may not be adhered to; also reliable viewing figures are not available.[18] However, Christian programmes are equally prominent on all three channels, as much a staple as soap operas and European football, and some general observations can be made about this media involvement.

Nearly all programmes are videoed services. In content overall, about 85% of Christian TV would consist of teaching, perhaps 10% of healing, and about 5% of choirs and groups. Most of the music constitutes a sandwich around the message, which is overwhelmingly the important element, reinforcing the impression that these churches see themselves above all as providing answers. The sermons are overwhelmingly in English, although a few are in Twi and a few (like Kofi Danso's 'Impact Waves') in English translated into Twi after every few sentences (sometimes it is

---

[17] Heward-Mills remarked in a sermon (29 Oct. 00) that in a congested urban sprawl like Accra, it is difficult to take people to your house, because it is more than likely that you have converted the toilet and bathroom into accommodation.

[18] Attempts to establish viewing figures are tendentious: *Graphic*, 18 Dec. 00, 7.

vice versa); Agyin Asare has two distinct TV programmes on Saturday on different TV channels, one in English and the other in English translated into Twi. The teaching is given by the same speaker week after week, who is usually the head of the church producing the programme. Most of these programmes are made in Ghana and consist of sermons delivered at services in Ghana. Otabil's 'Living Word', Duncan-Williams' 'Voice of Inspiration', Heward-Mills' 'Mega Word', Agyin Asare's two series 'Your Miracle Encounter' and 'God's Miracle Power', Korankye-Ankrah's 'Power in His Presence', Isaac Anto's 'Let the Prophet Speak', Christie Doe-Tetteh's 'Solid Rock' and Gordon Kisseih's 'Treasures of Wisdom' are essentially all of this kind, and make up the majority.

However, a significant minority are not sermons delivered in Ghana. Of this minority some like Jason Alvarez's 'The Love of Jesus' and Barbara Ann Reis's 'Word Explosion' are North American imports screened by a local Ghanaian ministry or church which asserts its 'ownership' of the programme by flashing its name, address and contact numbers across the screen during the broadcast. Other American imports like Joyce Meyer's 'Life in the Word' and Randy Morrison's 'The Exalted Word' and 'The Ernest Angley Hour', have no local sponsor and are simply part of the worldwide outreach of the parent body (Joyce Meyer's heavy marketing of her videos and cassettes and literature directs customers to her African office in South Africa). The Nigerians Bimbo Odukoyo and T. B. Joshua screen their Lagos services in Ghana; Joshua has a branch of his Synagogue Church of All Nations in Accra, but this is not announced on the screen. Body of Christ Ministries of St Johns, Antigua, also transmit 'Restoration' with no host community. Matthew Ashimolowo, a significant figure in the development of Ghana's new Christianity, is a Nigerian who is the pastor at London's largest church; his 'Winning Ways' has been broadcast for three or four years on GTV, but only in 2001 did he open a Ghanaian office. (Gilbert Deya, a Kenyan operating from London, has functioned in the same way, although he is a far less significant figure than Ashimolowo.) There are also Ghanaians operating in London who broadcast their London services or crusades over Ghanaian TV—such are Lawrence Tetteh's 'Miracle Touch' and Francis Sarpong's 'Calvary Charismatic Ministry'. In some cases, what is essentially a Ghanaian ministry will fill in (when it has nothing of its own to screen) with American charismatic staples like Benny Hinn or T. D. Jakes. And all Ghana's new churches have crusades and national conventions, at which almost invariably some overseas celebrities speak; nearly all these churches (except Otabil's) would screen these overseas guests as well.

Thus there is a solid overseas component in Ghana's media Christianity. If we add the fact that Ghanaian pastors themselves (particularly the superstars) travel to overseas conventions, and that some of them have been trained overseas (particularly in Nigeria), it will be seen that drawing a line to distinguish Ghanaian Christianity from something more genuinely international is not a simple matter—something to which we shall return. There are obvious minor twists that do not fit the Ghanaian scene. For instance, Jason Alvarez occasionally fulminates against 'liberals' who are perverting the vision of America's founding fathers—hardly a Ghanaian concern. Similarly, some South American preachers on Heward-Mills's 'Mega Word' start to campaign for Christian radio stations, which is not a Ghanaian preoccupation. However, for reasons that will become clear, nearly all these programmes shed valuable light on Ghana's new Christianity,[19] although, as is maintained below, the reception of some may be different in Ghana from that in their country of origin.

Even if the technical proficiency of the Ghanaian programmes is not always high, and they are sometimes repeats of what was screened only a few weeks before, they generally score for spectacle, drama and performance. Whatever else they are, they are also entertainment and have to compete in a crowded field. The speakers, like their US models, are performers/entertainers, and the repeated screening of their programmes makes them to some degree media personalities and stars—thus, unlike the mainline churches, these churches are often personalised. This Christianity is a media phenomenon, to the extent that services are often built round the requirements of television. Many get more than one programme from a single service: for example, Otabil gets two 30-minute programmes from a single hour-long sermon. A consummate professional, he has little trouble in arranging his material appropriately for this purpose. Even the congregation in church probably do not realise that when he briefly recapitulates after about twenty-five minutes and then quickly outlines his thesis again, this is because of the two-programmes-from-one-sermon TV requirement.

[19] I will omit here some programmes. The 'Brotherhood of the Cross', from Nigeria's Brotherhood of the Cross and Star, consists mainly of homage to the founder Olumba Olumba Obu, and is so poorly produced it is almost unwatchable. The 'Ernest Angley Hour' is millennial, fundamentalist in a strictly American sense, defending biblical inerrancy, attacking evolution: 'If you love the truth, you'll love this service; if you are one of those sophisticated Christians you won't.' (*8 April 01*) Agape Mission's 'TV School of the Bible', produced by an American-led mission based in Accra, is millennial and seems very unrepresentative of Ghana's charismatic Christianity. I also omit the Sunday morning GTV SDA 'Voice of Prophecy', a sophisticated presentation of SDA morality and eschatology.

Media finances are important. Now that the airwaves are unregulated, any individual or any church with the money can bid for viewing time. Many churches spend considerable funds to get themselves on TV. Often the money is provided by 'clubs' within the church, groups of wealthy members who agree to support this aspect of its ministry. Otabil is able to find commercial sponsors because of his perceived ability to attract viewers or listeners (for his TV broadcasts a transport company and an Accra brewery in its capacity as producer not of alcoholic drinks but of the energy drink Vitamalt; his programmes on Radio Gold are sponsored by an aluminium roofing company).

What is probably most remarkable about all this media activity is that the mainline churches are simply not there (and of the classical Pentecostals only Christ Apostolic Church has a presence).[20] GTV, revealing its origins in a BBC-like public service ethos, still has a slot at mid-morning on Sunday where mainline churches take their turn, along with charismatics and other strands, to have a service screened, but otherwise the mainline have ceded the entire field to these new churches. The mainline churches utilise their considerable funds, gained both locally and from overseas, in development; it is the newer churches, which are hardly at all involved in education or development, that sink a large part of their resources in media.[21] Just as, in the computer age, value is given to what can be quantified, so in a TV culture it is what has dramatic or visual effect or entertainment value that matters. These media presentations are moulding what counts as Christianity, at least in Accra.

Because of its technicolour unavoidability television is the most high-profile media activity, but radio is perhaps even more significant—this is certainly the case outside Accra. We have mentioned Ghana's FM revolution and its politically empowering effect due to the scope the radio stations provide for individuals to make their voices heard. We mentioned how these stations are run on a shoestring and need filler programmes. Political and economic pundits can pontificate at length for little financial outlay, and they field questions and observations from listeners; but just as serviceable are pastors who can bring tapes of their sermons or, on phone-ins, accept requests for prayers or advise on spiritual problems. This involvement is simply too enormous to detail here in anything like the way just attempted for TV. In granting FM frequencies, the Rawlings government was careful to deny slots to churches. The standard response to the requests of the mainline churches was: 'We know you would be

---

[20] I leave aside the Lutheran (Missouri Synod) 'This is the Life', screened on GTV each Sunday morning. This is a (rather dated) drama with a Christian message.

[21] One 'multi-media crusade' claimed to break new ground by being covered by GTV and four different FM stations (*Pentecostal Voice*, vol. 2, 9).

responsible, but some of these newer aggressive churches might irre-
sponsibly stir up religious antagonism.' However, probably the opposite
was the case; the Rawlings government feared that the mainline churches
would raise issues of justice or human rights, whereas it sensed that it had
nothing to fear from the newer churches.[22] Thus there are no specifically
Christian radio stations (though Accra's 'Channel R' is Christian in all but
name[23]), but Christian programmes abound on nearly all, and these are
almost exclusively charismatic, of the kind discussed in the body of this
work. The charismatic pastors prominent on TV are also on radio, but
those who broadcast only on radio tend to be aspirants who cannot yet
afford TV (on radio, time is often free).

This proliferation of Christian programmes on FM radio has had a significant effect in promoting charismatic Christianity. This Christianity
puts great stress on the testimony—in Agyin Asare's words, 'When you
are healed, you must testify; if you don't, you don't keep your healing'
(28 April 2001). These phone-ins directly serve this purpose. People
phone in to tell what God has done in their lives, and since so many of
these testimonies effectively witness to what God has done through a particular man of God, these programmes serve as the best advertising a
church could have—at no cost.

The obvious dominance of the charismatics on both TV and FM radio
does not reveal the full extent of their media involvement: these same
churches place enormous stress on the buying of tapes, both video and
(more realistically) audio, and mostly the same tapes that are broadcast.
For example, Heward-Mills says (19 July 00) that he does not want to
deal with individuals for counselling; it is up to people to find solutions
in his preaching, his tapes and books—the solutions are there for all.[24] It
is quite normal in all these churches to be told before the service ends that
on leaving you must buy the tape of the sermon just concluded; all possess the technology to make this possible. The pastor in charge of tape
production told me that Heward-Mills preaches at four of the five Sunday
services. By the end of each service sixty tapes of that service's sermon
are on sale, and in the following days about 100 of each sermon are sold.

---

[22] The Catholics regard as an infringement of their fundamental human rights the prohibi-
tion on their church running a radio station (see *Pastoral Guidelines for National Pastoral
Congress, 7–14 April 1997*, 150); the new Kufuor government seems just as resolved not
to grant frequencies to religious organisations, although by early 2002 sixteen religious
bodies had applied for a licence to operate a radio station (*Standard*, 4 Feb. 02, 1).

[23] A letter in *Graphic* (4 Sept. 00, 9) accuses it of being 'entirely a religious FM station, contrary to the regulations of the National Frequency Control Board'.

[24] Another indication that these churches see their message as their contribution. Heward-
Mills also: 'People who follow me buy my books, buy my tapes.' (1 March 01) He continued, significantly: 'I've followed Hagin by his books and tapes.'

In all, they sell about 1,000 sermon tapes each week—which at 7,000 cedis a tape amounts to 7 million cedis ($1,000) a week. Many pastors say it is only after a message has been heard about six times that it can be understood and 'owned'.

Another aspect of this media dominance that is of profound cultural significance is that of musical creativity. Ghana has had its own particular form of popular music, called Highlife. This was a popular form back in the 1920s, and has been a thriving cultural phenomenon since the 1950s. It peaked in the 1970s, since when its supremacy has been challenged by 'hip-life' (a fusion of hip-hop/rap with traditional Highlife melodies). Under Rawlings, however, two important things happened. First, the years of curfew (1982–4) after his second coup curtailed live entertainment, and secondly, the straight entertainment business was heavily taxed—e.g. up to 160% for importation of musical instruments. Such taxes virtually forced the Highlife industry into the only field free of taxes—the churches. Overnight, the Highlife artists that did not emigrate (one superstar, Daddy Lumba, lives in Germany where the form has evolved into 'Burgher Highlife') became the vocalists and instrumentalists and groups carrying charismatic worship. Highlife in its new setting became Gospel Life (or 'G-life'). It is in worship and particularly during the choir or group ministry time at these new churches that G-life flourishes. Similar economic factors influenced gatherings of the young. To stage a dance required an entertainment tax of 12.5% to be paid up-front to the Internal Revenue. Because dances were so expensive, few could hold them any longer. Gospel revivals or crusades were held instead, where the same music featured, but out of reach of the tax authorities. The top exponents of G-life are given prominent billing for any special service or crusade or convention. The Tagoe Sisters, Pastor Joe Beecham, Cindy Thompson, Bernice Ofei, Suzzy and Matt and the Daughters of Glorious Jesus are given equal billing with the preachers on fliers for many crusades. Their cassettes and CDs top the national charts, and are given extensive airtime.[25] All three TV stations use such promotional videos as fillers between programmes, and there are TV programmes (like TV3's 'Songs of Praise' and GTV's 'Gospel Trail') consisting of just these videos. A whole cultural form—a whole industry—has been carried by these new churches and has increased their enormous appeal. Thus reasons for their growth are not exclusively religious.

Not as obvious as the visual and aural aspects, but significant nonetheless, is the change in the balance of published material. Publishing has

---

[25] Cindy Thompson won not just Gospel Song of the Year, Gospel Album of the Year, but the Female Voice of the Year at the Ghana Music Awards for 2001: *Mirror*, 12 April 01, 13.

been hard hit in Ghana under structural adjustment, particularly with the collapse of the cedi after 1998. Of course, textbooks are required for schools (contracts in this area are much sought after, and power to award them has been a source of considerable income for senior officials in the Ministry of Education), but otherwise publishing has suffered drastically. The one area where publishing seems to flourish is the charismatic churches. Most of the pastors we will consider have written several books, most published by their personal publishing house.[26] Heward-Mills, whose bookshop is the most elaborate, has a publishing empire; in April 2002 he had thirty-four of his own titles on sale, most of them handsomely printed in London. Why is publishing profitable here but nowhere else? Pastors, especially the super-pastors, have a captive market; they require no advertising and no distribution network—Eastwood Anaba, launching a Duncan-Williams book, announced that 'a presiding bishop' should be able 'to sell 2,000 copies on the first Sunday' (7 April 2002). In a church of several thousand, half might buy the pastor's book. Many may not read it—one is often told that 'Ghana has no culture of reading'—but just possessing a copy functions as a badge of membership. Anyway, they may well have heard the message before, since these books tend to be recycled sermon tapes.[27] Publication increases the pastor's status and spreads his name—another effective form of

---

[26] Stephen Adu-Boahen of the Universal Gospel Centre has published thirty (*Mirror*, 5 Aug. 00, 4).

[27] The only obvious exception to this is Agyin Asare's *Rooted and Built up in Him* (Accra: Miracle Publications, 1994, 2nd edn 1999), which is a 489-page 'systematic theology' (p 11). This is a remarkable book, and its treatment of topics like marriage (307–75) and ministerial ethics (218–20) must be of considerable help to students in Bible schools. It consists of countless points with biblical references, culled indiscriminately. Agyin Asare does not cite authorities or other books; there is a short bibliography, and the names referred to in the text are: Miller, Finney, Moody, Cerullo, Bob Gordon, Hagin, Kumuyi, Copeland, Maria Woodworth Etter, Luther, Wesley, Adeboye, Rebecca Brown, Dakes, Ussher and Alex Ness. These give some indication of his sources. The fact that he refers (p 411) in a complimentary way to Ussher, who dated the creation of the world to 4004 BC, indicates that some of his sources are American fundamentalist; and the examples he cites (411) for the benefits of tithing (including Rockefeller, Penney, Kraft, Proctor, Colgate, Hershey, Kellogg, Heinz) would support this impression of American influence. Words like 'Romanist' are not Ghanaian, either. Parts of the book seem very formalised; some of the material, e.g. on the last things (433–69) and total depravity (63), sit uncomfortably with Ghana's charismatic Christianity as it is in fact experienced. I have seen Agyin Asare giving out this book at pastors' conferences.

Another book not adapted from tapes is Agyin Asare's *New Testament Minister's Manual*, which again meets a real need in providing an order of service for various ceremonies, such as weddings and funerals, that a pastor may be called on to conduct. This is evidence for the routinisation of the charismatic movement.

advertising.[28] It can also increase his income.[29] Ghana has a practice of 'launching' a book, inviting friends and admirers (and church members) to outdo one another in donating to the author's cause; in effect it is a grand auction. This practice at least enables the author to recoup some of his expenses, and at best it brings in considerable funds. At the launching of Duncan-Williams's *Destined to Make an Impact* at Accra's most luxurious hotel, on 6 April 2002, the first three copies were auctioned for 10 million cedis ($1,500) each, the next three for 5 million. After the launch and after both church services the next day, 600 books (out of a print-run of 2000) had been sold, producing revenue of 100 million cedis ($15,000).[30] When a pastor can take his book overseas, where bids are made in dollars or pounds, he benefits accordingly.

These books are not always quite what they seem. Some are not strictly 'written' by the author himself, as we shall see below. Salifu, for example, is largely uneducated; his books are written by a 'theological consultant' from tapes of sermons and from discussions. They are self-consciously edited, and—as we shall also see—his books do not fully represent the Christianity he really stands for. Even Duncan-Williams does not necessarily 'write' his books; most are ghosted by the same consultant who puts together Salifu's books, and another was written by Eastwood Anaba after a conversation with Duncan-Williams. At least two of Ampiah-Kwofi's books are so dissimilar in viewpoint that it is extremely unlikely that he could be the author in the accepted sense of both.

One effect of the depressed state of the local publishing industry is to increase the significance of outside forces. We shall meet below the American Mike Murdock, who boasts that he gives away one million of his books a year. Even if, say, only 20,000 find their way to Ghana, they stand a good chance in such an artificial market of profoundly affecting the entire way Christianity is viewed—or at least affecting it in a way that would not happen where a wider range of approaches is to hand. It is significant that in this whole field of Christian publishing the mainline churches are almost totally absent.[31]

---

[28] The magazines produced by some ministries, usually containing testimonies, are another form of effective advertising.

[29] James Saah of CAFM let slip in a sermon (13 Dec. 00) that in three months he sold 8,000 copies of his book: in Germany they were selling for 60,000 cedis (nearly $10), and one woman gave 5 million cedis ('I read your book and God told me to give you…') for one copy.

[30] See *Graphic*, 8 April 02, 3, where it is claimed that the first six were sold for 10 million cedis each; it might be wondered whether this was a genuine mistake or a deliberate attempt to puff the book even further.

[31] Challenge Bookshop, Ghana's biggest Christian book distributor, was founded by the Sudan Interior Mission (SIM, more recently Society for International Missions) and best

[handwritten margin notes: 1990s / new / Christ / rules?]

Hence, by the end of the 1990s, Christianity was as dominant in Ghana as it had been twenty years earlier—indeed more so—but it was no longer the recognisably mainline (or 'orthodox') Christianity of old. Ghana has more accurate Christian statistics than any other country in Africa. They provide incontrovertible evidence of the charismatic upsurge. The Ghana Evangelism Committee conducted a survey of the entire country, counting attendance at Sunday services in 1986–7 and again five years later. A comparison of the two sets of findings reveals that over those five years the traditional AICs lost members, sometimes up to 20%. The mainline Protestant churches overall held their own, although their increase of 7% over those five years is well below the 17% increase in the population generally over the same period. The Catholic Church, though still the largest single denomination, decreased by 2%. The growth occurred mainly in the Pentecostal churches (both the older-established ones and the newer kind that are the focus of this book), some increasing over the five years by figures between 30 and 80%. Those surveys support our contention that recent years have seen the collapse of the older AICs, the relative decline of the mainline churches, and the explosion of the charismatics.[32]

The flourishing of this charismatic Christianity has had a significant effect on Ghanaian Christianity more widely, beyond the strictly charismatic fold. One of these is the 'charismatisation' of other churches. The mainline or 'orthodox' churches have been stung into adapting if they are to retain their following—after all, these charismatic churches have grown not by converting non-Christians but by attracting members of the mainline and AICs.[33] Out of sheer self-preservation, the mainline churches have tried to incorporate elements which will stem the flow. One loyal

---

represents that conservative Evangelical strand. Every year they run a National Prayer Conference which puts together ten or twelve books for about 2,000 pastors. Every ten years or so they run what they call a 'Pastors' Book-Set' conference, in which they distribute (with the help of sponsors) a set of books for give-away prices at week-long conferences in the country's major cities. In 2001, 2,400 pastors attended, paying the equivalent of $75 for a set of books worth $700. The books generally represent the Evangelicalism associated with Zondervan, and IVP. These conferences attract predominantly mainline churchmen (which helps explain the Evangelical rather than liberal character of Ghana's mainline churches), not the charismatic type. Challenge, through such conferences, played a role in fostering deliverance among pastors (see Asamoah-Gyadu, *Renewal*, 244).

[32] See Gifford, *AC*, 62–3 where these surveys are analysed in some detail.

[33] This is queried in Aylward Shorter and Joseph N. Njiru, *New Religious Movements in Africa*, Nairobi: Paulines, 2001. But cf. Archbishop John Onaiyekan of Abuja: 'These churches are getting most of their members from us', cited in Kenneth L. Woodward, 'The Changing Face of the Church', *Newsweek*, 16 April 2001, 66.

Methodist explained to me why Methodists are no longer leaving for the Charismatics—'because we are now doing all they do.' The Catholics have the Catholic Charismatic Renewal which is encouraged to different degrees in different dioceses. The Accra Catholic Archdiocese had a priest who was in many ways the equivalent of a charismatic leader; he had considerable following, but was suspended in mid-2000, more for his attitude to authority than because his charismatic Christianity could not be accommodated. The Presbyterians and Methodists both now have their charismatic wings, and the Evangelical Presbyterian (EP) Church actually split over (among other things) this issue of charismatisation.[34]

Moreover, an element of defensiveness seems evident in the mainline churches. In an Anglican pastoral letter of August 1992 the bishops invited help in seeking answers to questions: 'Why do you feel unfulfilled in the Anglican Church? What changes would you like to see in the Church, and in what specific areas?' This element is expressed in bumper stickers with slogans such as 'I am a Methodist: I love my Church', 'I love being an Anglican' and 'I am a Catholic, I will remain a Catholic, and I will die a Catholic.' The sense that the initiative has moved from the mainline churches was evident in March 2001 at the launching of the Agyin Asare Gospel Crusade when Methodist and Anglican bishops took the platform to endorse his initiative, the latter in his capacity as chairman of the Christian Council.[35] Similarly, at Easter 2001 Lawrence Tetteh, a Ghanaian based in London who frequently runs high-profile miracle crusades in Ghana, was joined by the Methodist Church to conduct a crusade at Madina, the first of many such combined crusades to be held across the country.[36] When Bishop Duncan-Williams consecrated a deputy 'resident bishop' of the ACI, he was assisted by both the Methodist and Anglican bishops of Accra.[37]

The effects on the mainline churches are thus obvious, but perhaps less attention is given to the effects on the established Pentecostal churches.

---

[34] Cephas Omenyo, 'The Charismatic Renewal Movement within the Mainline Churches; the Case of the Bible Study and Prayer Group of the Presbyterian Church of Ghana', M. Phil. thesis, University of Ghana, 1994; Birgit Meyer, *Translating the Devil: Religion and Modernity among the Ewe in Ghana*, Edinburgh University Press, 1999.

[35] Agyin Asare had long been conducting crusades in Ghana and abroad; this function was to establish a legal entity separate from the church specifically for crusades.

[36] The Methodist bishop was 'convinced that a partnership between the Methodist Church and Dr Tetteh's World Miracle Outreach would undoubtedly be a formidable one that could be of great benefit both to Christians and to the nation as a whole.' Tetteh had the Methodist Bishop admitting, that, 'contrary to popular belief, the Methodist Church does believe in miracles: "Brother Lawrence, I want to assure you that the Methodist church fully supports your ministry."' (*Mirror*, 28 April 01, p 4)

[37] *Graphic*, 12 Dec. 01, 28; *Spectator*, 15 Dec. 01, 8.

These still tend to separate the sexes in services; their music is character-ised more by drums and tambourines than guitars and trumpets; and at the appropriate time they may have individuals 'prophesying' from the congregation (this is not characteristic of the new charismatics). The chairman of the Church of Pentecost has claimed that a distinction can be found in that Pentecostals restrict themselves to scripture whereas the charismatics are prepared to go beyond it,[38] but for reasons discussed in chapter 3 too much weight should not be placed on that distinction. The differences are probably not great. For example, the views of the CoP Chairman on prosperity seem almost indistinguishable from those in the charismatic churches.[39] We will return to this.

Even it one suspects that much of this paradigm shift could be paral-leled in other African countries, some factors of this charismatic explo-sion are unique to Ghana. We have already mentioned music and tax; another factor is Rawlings himself. As noted above Rawlings developed considerable antagonism to the mainline churches; he could expect little validation from them. So to some degree he consciously courted these new churches for the support and legitimisation they could provide. This is best seen in the annual 'national thanksgiving service' inaugurated by Rawlings. For the first of these services, held in 1993, the mainline chur-ches could not be persuaded to take part; thereafter they did, but were very circumspect, insisting on a celebration of democracy rather than of Rawlings. The new charismatic churches were far less critical, particu-larly Duncan-Williams, often turning these services into cheerleading for Rawlings.[40] The level of legitimisation given to Rawlings by these chur-ches will be considered below, but it may be said that this was not neces-sarily consciously political, but that they were flattered by recognition which had hitherto been reserved for the mainline churches. So the NDC regime helped give these churches status. Here again we find a non-religious factor contributing to the place they have acquired in Ghanaian society.

Reaction

The new charismatic Christianity is an unchallengeable fact of Ghanaian society, but not all observers see this development as healthy. The chair-man of the National Commission on Culture has said that the rate at

[38] Michael K. Ntumy, *Pentecostal Voice*, vol. 2, 12.

[39] Michael K. Ntumy, *Financial Breakthrough: Discovering God's Secrets to Prosperity*, Accra (1993?).

[40] Gifford, *AC*, 86–7. For similar co-opting under Acheampong, see Pobee, *Religion and Politics...Acheampong Era*.

which churches are springing up, 'with all kinds of people, including drug dealers and rapists becoming bishops, apostles and right reverends overnight... [they] could undermine the developmental progress of the country.'[41] The chairman of the National Commission on Civic Education has said that the phenomenal proliferation of churches is 'a threat to national development'.[42] A columnist wrote in an open letter to the incoming President J. A. Kufuor that 'three prominent landmarks dominate the landscape' as he came to power, the second being an 'ostentatious display of often ill-gotten wealth' and the third 'bankrupt management' within the civil service, government and state corporations. However the first and most obvious was a 'proliferation of religious organisations professing the Christian faith', full (of women), loud, and in competition 'for the limited and not so limited wealth of very often their gullible congregations'.[43] We return below to the frequently adverse judgement on this phenomenon, and evaluate the reasons adduced.

Above all, perhaps, the rise of this new Christianity has played a large part in the revival of Afrikania, an organised form of African traditional religion, which has attracted some academic interest.[44] Afrikania was founded by a former Catholic priest, Vincent Kwabena Damuah, who for a time was a member of Rawlings's PNDC. This political dimension is significant. Part of the PNDC strategy was to set up parallel structures—people's tribunals alongside the courts, workers' defence committees alongside the trade unions—and there was an attempt also to set up religious structures alongside the churches. This was not very successful, but when Damuah left the Catholic Church his championing of Afrikania was thought to serve just as well.[45] After he died in 1992, Afrikania effectively collapsed. Two leaders had brief spells in charge, but then the leadership fell to Osofo Kofi Ameve, a prosperous building contractor. Under his leadership Afrikania revived considerably. Ameve tried to gather all the separate shrines, particularly among the Ewe in the Volta Region, into a self-conscious religion like Christianity or Islam.

The big issue in the Volta Region is that of *Trokosi*, often described as 'religious slavery'; families who are convinced that some misfortune is caused by offending a local deity make amends by giving a young daughter to the god at a shrine. This effectively makes her a slave of the priest there. As human rights have become a more important issue in Ghana, this practice has drawn much condemnation, and led NGOs, particularly

[41] *Times,* 23 Nov. 00, 1.
[42] Ibid.
[43] K. Gyasi, in *Spectator,* 20 Jan. 00, 3.
[44] Bediako, *Christianity in Africa,* esp. 17–38.
[45] See Okomfo Damuah, *Miracle at the Shrine,* Accra: Afrikania, n.d.

an Evangelical Christian organisation called International Needs, to attempt to abolish the practice.[46] This campaign amounts to a concerted attack on traditional Ghanaian religion, and Afrikania has set itself to combat this, not least by denying that the practice exists.

Afrikania is linked with a tabloid publication called *Love and Life*, which along with some near-pornography carries every week an article of the wildest Afrocentrism written by H. M. Maulana, an African American heavily involved in the movement to win reparations for the slave trade. It is obvious that Afrikania's agenda is linked to the African American agenda, and the Afrikania service held every Sunday is invariably attended by visiting African Americans. This service is a most interesting construct, with many parallels to a Christian service. Readings from Afrikania's scriptures are followed by a sermon.[47] There is a communion (a remembrance of ancestors 'who died for us. Eat and remember their sacrifice'), and an offering. At appropriate times, the congregation shout 'Amen Ra!' just as charismatics may interject 'Alleluia!' Afrikania claims that it is not anti-Christian, but its concerns reveal the degree to which it is reacting to the born-again explosion.[48] Afrikania was just completing its new headquarters/training centre for the priests and priestesses of the shrines when the NDC lost power. The Volta Region was the NDC heartland, particularly its villages, and traditional priests were a factor in controlling the people and their vote.[49] It remains to be seen what will happen to Afrikania without government patronage.

---

[46] 800 *Trokosi* were freed in a ceremony carried by news broadcasts on 30 July 2000, during which it was said that 5,800 have been freed, and 2,000 remain to be freed. A slightly different figure was given in the *Standard*, 8 April 01, according to which there were 4,714 females in bondage at 51 shrines (43 in Volta Region, 5 in Greater Accra, 3 in Eastern Region); 2,800 had been freed, leaving 2,021 still in bondage. See the First West African Regional Workshop on Female Ritual Servitude, 6–8 Feb. 2001 (sponsored by Anti-Slavery [UK] and Global Ministries of the United Methodist Church [USA]). Participants report in *Mirror*, 17 Feb. 01, 22.

[47] Kofi Ameve, *The Divine Acts: Holy Scriptures for Sankofa Faith*, Accra: Afrikania, n.d. 'Every word and every sentence in this book contains great truth which we must decipher.' (p. 72)

[48] See Kofi Ameve, *The Origin of the Old and New Testament*, Accra: Afrikania, 3rd edn 1991, esp. 1–40.

[49] For the alleged use of juju in the 2000 elections in Cape Coast and the Volta Region, see *Chronicle*, 15–17 Dec. 00, 1, and 12–13 Dec. 00, 1, and 13–14 Dec. 00, 5. According to these accounts, chiefs, backed by religious leaders, had informed the electorate that 'a terrible misfortune would befall anyone who voted for' a particular candidate. An insight into voting in some rural areas is afforded by the General Secretary of the National Catholic Secretariat in his urging people to accept bribes politicians offer them: 'It's your money… It was taken in one way or another from services you render to this country, and it is being given back to you by a politician who wishes to exploit you… So take it… I understand that when you are given such monies you are made to swear some oath, or

In this chapter we have traced the shift in Ghana's Christianity, and noted the preoccupation of the newer charismatic churches with media. We will next attempt to establish in more depth the characteristic features of these churches.

---

other things are done so that if you do not vote for a particular person you are made to suffer the wrath of some spirits. Because of this you fear and you forfeit your right to exercise your God-given freedom in elections. On this day, by the authority given me by the church as a priest, I have exorcised in advance the machinations of any spirit that anyone may invoke to force you to vote against your conscience.' (*Standard*, 17–23 Sept. 00, 5)

3

RECURRING EMPHASES

In describing Ghana's new churches it is advisable to avoid talking of their 'essence' because of the genuine variety that exists. However, some generalisations are possible. The first is that for these churches Christianity has to do with success, wealth and status.

Success

This emphasis on success is found everywhere. It is found in the names of the churches themselves: 'Winners' Chapel', 'The Triumphant Christian Centre', 'Power Chapel', 'Victory Bible Church International'. Size, numbers and expansion are tangible signs of success, and the word 'International' which so many include in their title, and the flags adorning the platforms make the same point. Heward-Mills's Lighthouse Chapel calls itself simply 'the Megachurch'.

It is found in the bumper stickers prevalent in Ghana: 'Unstoppable Achievers'; 'I am a Winner'; 'The Struggle is Over'; 'I will make it in Jesus' Name'; 'I am a Stranger to Failure'; 'The Favour of God is upon Me'; 'With Jesus I will always Win'; 'My God is able; more than able'; 'There is Power in the Blood'; 'Being a Covenant Child you are Seriously Blessed'; 'I am a Child of the Covenant; I can't be Down'; 'God is in Charge; your Struggles are over', 'Your Success is determined by your Faith'; 'I have a very big God—he is always on my Side'; 'I am a Product of the Covenant; I am smelling Success'. Then there are the biblical snippets: 'More than Conquerors (Rom 8.37)'; 'If God be for us who can be against us? (Rom 8.31)'; 'I can do all things in him who strengthens me (Phil 4.13)'; 'The Blessing of the Lord maketh Rich and he addeth no Sorrow with it (Prov 10.22)'.

There is a special category of bumper sticker, proclaiming a particular church's label for the current year, like '1999, My Year of Dominion', '2000, My Year of Enlargement' or '2001, My Time to Shine'. Other labels given by various charismatic churches to recent years are 'My Year

44

of Glory', 'My Year of Divine Intervention', 'My Year of Newness and Fulfilment', 'My Year of Expectation', 'My Year of Impact', 'My Year of Exploits', 'My Year of Achievement (Dt 1.7)', 'My Year of Answered Prayer', 'My Year of Taking Territories', 'My Year of Excellence and Divine Upliftments', 'My Year of Double Blessings', 'My year of Advancement', 'My Year of Transformation', 'My Year of Greater Works', 'A Year of God's Grace and Establishment'.

The same emphasis is found in the themes of their crusades and conventions: 'Taking your Possessions', 'Winning Ways', 'Experiencing Open Heavens for Divine Blessings', 'Stepping into Greatness', 'The Force of Divine Progress', 'Be a Winner in Jesus Christ', 'Come and Possess your Promised Land', 'From Captivity to Restoration', 'The Best is Yet to Come', 'Highway to Success', 'Dawning of a New Day', 'Taking New Territories', 'I will restore unto You', 'Breaking your Barriers', 'Breaking the Yoke', 'Abundance is My Portion', 'Going Up to Higher Places'.

It is found in their hymns: 'Jesus is a Winner Man'; 'I cannot fail/I am destined for greatness/I'm a stranger to failure/born to win'; 'Abraham's Blessings are Mine'; 'I'm a Winner in the Lord'; 'You have a God who never fails'; 'This Mountain shall be Removed'; 'There is Power, Power, Wonderworking Power in the Blood of the Lord'; 'You will really be Blessed'; 'I can see Him Now/I can see God moving mightily in my Favour'; 'I am on the winning Side'; 'My miracle has come, my Breakthrough is here/Jesus has given me a Testimony, my Miracle has come'; 'Lord, lift us up where we belong/where the Eagle flies, on the Mountain high'.

It is evident in advertising slogans. ACI advertises itself in bus shelters round the city as 'Where Overcomers never Quit'. Agyin Asare's headquarters proclaims 'Where Jesus makes Everybody Somebody'. The titles of books, magazines and TV programmes convey the same message: 'Power in his Presence'; 'Winners' World'; Agin Asare's *From Nobody to Somebody*; Heward-Mills's books *Solomonic Success, Secrets of Success* and *Principles of Success*; and Duncan-Williams's *You are Destined to Succeed*. This is also true of the banner headlines of the monthly *Winners' World*: 'Covenant Prosperity is Real' (August 2000), 'Success made Easy' (September 2000), 'Making it Big on all Fronts' (March 2001, which also has the centrespread: 'Success without Sweat'), 'Breakthroughs All the Way!' (May 2000), 'Your Breakthrough is Now' (December 2001), 'God's Secrets for Surplus' (March 2002).

In enumerating these examples, the data have not been skewed: examples of other emphases that do not fit our argument have not been left out. Banners or bumper stickers reading 'Take up your cross daily (Lk 9.23)', or 'I am crucified to the world (Gal 6.14)', or 'Blessed are the Poor

(Lk 6.20)' or 'My Year of Self-Denial' have not been ignored or over-looked; they simply do not exist and are impossible in this Christianity. This writer saw one sticker with a millennial message, 'Behold he com-eth soon', and another sticker stressing morality, 'He who loves Jesus obeys his teachings', but these are noticeable only because they are so exceptional. It is success, victory and wealth that matter. Talking to charismatics corroborates this point. The key words are progress, pros-perity, breakthrough, success, achievement, destiny, favour, dominion, blessing, excellence, elevation, promotion, increase, expansion, plenty, open doors, triumph, finances, overflow, abundance, newness, fulfilment, victory, power, possession, comfort, movement, exports, exams, visas, travel. The negative things to leave behind are closed doors, poverty, sick-ness, setback, hunger, joblessness, disadvantage, misfortune, stagnation, negativities, sadness, limitation, suffering, inadequacy, non-achievement, darkness, blockages, lack, want, slavery, sweat and shame. These reali-ties are understood in a fairly commonsense way.

Some students of Christianity might be perplexed. Didn't Nietzsche see Christianity as a religion for losers, glorifying virtues that fostered weakness? Similarly, liberation theology, a form of Christianity that has attracted much scholarly attention, makes much of a 'preferential option for the poor'; poverty is not glorified, but there is a certain value ascribed to it. Ghana's new Christianity is different, and Ghanaians are aware in particular that it is different from what was brought by the missionaries who, it is widely argued, did not bring the complete gospel. Duncan-Williams echoes a widespread view when he writes: 'The traditional and orthodox churches we grew up in held many views which were diametri-cally opposed to God's word.... They preach a doctrine which says in essence—poverty promotes humility. But you all know this is not true.... The missionaries erred tragically by not teaching the Africans God's Word and laws regarding sowing and reaping.... Thank God he has called us to declare his full counsel to our generation. I preach and teach pros-perity like any other doctrine of the Bible.'[1] Otabil has said of the missionaries: 'They gave us the limited knowledge of their time... conse-quently their content didn't wholly address the needs of our society. Sometimes we [must necessarily] negate what they sowed.' (31 March 01) This charismatic Christianity is about success and wealth, which is a Christian's proper state. If a Christian is without them, something is very wrong.[2]

---

[1] Nicholas Duncan-Williams, *You are Destined to Succeed*, Accra: Action Faith, 1990, 145–50. This book was reissued in 2002 as *Destined to Make an Impact*.

[2] Shorter and Onyancha's view that 'self-denial and altruism [are] the heart of the Gospel message' would not be shared by this Christianity, nor would these Christians endorse any

It will be argued here that this message has fallen on very receptive ground, because it embodies the traditional orientation of African religion. However, the way it is expressed is profoundly influenced by developments in the United States. For convenience, let us distinguish different ways in which Christianity has been associated with success.

First consider Russell Conwell, from 1879 pastor of Grace Baptist Church in Philadelphia. His 'Acres of Diamonds' sermon was delivered more than 5,000 times across America. In it he stated: 'Never in the history of the world did a poor man without capital have such an opportunity to get rich quickly and honestly as he does now in our city.... I say that you ought to get rich, and it is your duty to get rich.... To make money honestly is to preach the gospel.' This theology was at one with the Spencerian thinking of the age, the age of the Robber Barons, of Rockefeller and Carnegie. It was effectively a blessing of the American dream; a Christian should become rich by looking round for needs and providing for them—in other words, by initiative and enterprise, by becoming the entrepreneur of the American dream.[3]

There is a second form. In the post-war years before the first OPEC oil price-hike in 1974, while the world led by America was undergoing a period of growth never before experienced in recorded history, Norman Vincent Peale, a Presbyterian, likewise formulated a version of Christianity well suited to his time, to which he gave definitive expression in his *The Power of Positive Thinking*. His basic message was very American: this is the land of opportunity, so get out there and win through self-confidence and a positive mental attitude. 'Attitudes are more important than facts,' he insisted;[4] thoughts create circumstances, not vice versa.[5] Because of the practical nature of the book, an acknowledged 'self-improvement process',[6] Peale recapitulates regularly, and a close reading of the points summarising his chapters shows that well over half of them are not specifically Christian and have nothing to do with God. The Bible functions as a mine of positive thoughts; you apply positive thinking techniques (which often include reciting biblical texts) but the Bible is not unique here—Emerson, William James, Thoreau and even Euripides, Socrates and Marcus Aurelius will do just as well. There is a good deal about a 'Higher Power', but this is deliberately left vague. Of course

---

'hermeneutical privilege of the poor'; Aylward Shorter and Edwin Onyancha, *Secularism in Africa: a Case Study*, Nairobi: Paulines, 1997, 46–8.
[3] See Gifford, *Christianity and Politics*, 182–5.
[4] Norman Vincent Peale, *The Power of Positive Thinking*, Lagos: Blessed Family Publishing, n.d, 22.
[5] Ibid., 169.
[6] Ibid., 77.

Christians are quite free to understand this power as the Christian God, but Christianity is not necessary (for Peale Judaism will do just as well). There is nothing here about any pastor or spiritual guide being necessary (except perhaps, for motivation, a guide like Peale himself); it is all up to you. Peale's books, in pirated Nigerian editions, are commonly found in Ghana, although the economic differences between the post-1945 United States and Rawlings's Ghana are not adverted to.

A third form of this 'Christianity entails success', which arose within Pentecostal Christianity, is called the Faith Gospel, the Gospel of Prosperity, or the Health-Wealth Gospel. According to this, God has met all the needs of human beings in the suffering and death of Christ, and every Christian should now share in Christ's victory over sin, sickness and poverty. A believer has a right to the blessings of health and wealth won by Christ, and he or she can obtain these blessings merely by a positive confession of faith. This thinking is inevitably linked with the names of the Americans Kenneth Hagin and Kenneth Copeland. Obviously this faith gospel is much more theological than the first two views outlined above, since it propounds the view that the human condition of the born-again believer has been profoundly altered by the work of Jesus.

In theory this faith gospel is distinguishable from Pentecostalism; faith gospel churches thus form almost a sub-set within Pentecostalism generally. In some places—as Coleman has shown in the case of Sweden—considerable tension exists between established Pentecostal churches and new churches propounding the faith gospel.[7] However, it seems that in Ghana almost all charismatic churches (and indeed many beyond them) would hold some form of the faith gospel, even though a few might cavil at the lack of subtlety of some of its expressions.[8] It can be argued that this ready acceptance can be traced back to the traditional African religious worldview according to which religion has to do with achieving material well-being. However, if the faith gospel is almost ubiquitous in Ghana, one will also meet the first two attitudes—that a Christian's success is linked to entrepreneurship and to unquestioning faith in oneself—and sometimes all three motifs are found together.

Some observers of the African religious scene are uncomfortable when links are suggested to Western developments, as if it devalues Africa to admit any such influence from outside. Most Ghanaians involved feel no

---

[7] Simon Coleman, *The Globalisation of Charismatic Christianity: Spreading the Gospel of Prosperity*, Cambridge University Press, 2000, 27–47.

[8] Hanson makes the point that, in Nigeria, Benson Idahosa with his 'revelation of prosperity and total well-being' definitively shifted perceptions: Idahosa's position is now 'generally accepted'. (Elkanah Hanson, *Understanding the Holy Spirit in Politics*, Port Harcourt: El Shaddai, 1999, 10)

such embarrassment. Those close to these churches in the early 1980s admit the pervasiveness of Hagin's and Copeland's literature—it was a time when few other books were available. Many of the main figures openly admit this influence. For example, Heward-Mills publicly acknowledges that the person who has had most influence on him is the founder of the faith gospel: 'I listen to his tapes all the time... I have Kenneth Hagin tapes like this [opening arms wide]... Yesterday, as I was flying back, I was reading his books, feeding, feeding, feeding' (*19 July 00*)[9]; Agyin Asare is open about his debt to Cerullo.[10] Kofi Banful, preaching at Robert Ampiah-Kwofi's Global Revival Ministries convention (3 April 01), acknowledged his dependence on another giant of the faith gospel, Fred Price of Los Angeles: 'I listen to his tapes all the time.' Ralph Osabutey, supervisor of a district of eleven of Otabil's ICGC churches, can advise: 'Read books on faith, e.g. books by Kenneth Hagin, Fred Price etc.'[11]

The success which is the right of a Christian covers all areas. God is to meet you, in the standard phrase, 'at the point of your need'. As the theme for an October 2000 Heward-Mills convention expressed it, 'Whatever your need, come and receive more than you can carry.' However, if in theory it applies universally, in practice the success means primarily financial prosperity (something Power Chapel suggests with its home page: www.financeword.com). This is not surprising since for most Ghanaians this is their biggest problem. In a sermon entitled 'The Road to Financial Blessings', Heward-Mills justified talking about finances in church by describing the joy of a woman hearing her most pressing needs addressed for the very first time, 'the first time anyone dealt in church with the biggest thing in her life.' (29 Oct. 00) This prosperity can be understood in a minimal way. In the words of an African American preaching at ACI, 'It's his will that you prosper—not a million cedis in the bank, but my needs are being met—that's prosperity.' (26 Nov. 00) Otabil insists: 'Prosperity is not the same for everyone... a bicycle for one who walks, that is prosperity.' (18 Aug. 02) It is far more common, however, to hear things like Ebenezer Markwei: 'I hear the sound of cars, new cars, luxury cars' (7 Nov. 00), and Adamson Aromaegbe, a Nigerian preaching at WMCI: 'Get ready to prosper; you haven't seen anything yet.' (27 Oct. 00) Or even Otabil, whom we have just cited in a minimal sense: 'God desires to bless you beyond your wildest dreams and wildest expectations' (16 Aug. 01),

---

[9] Also *18 July 00*; and his *Lay People and the Ministry*, Accra: Lighthouse Chapel Publications, 1999, 140, where he acknowledges Fred Price also. See also above, p. 34, note 24.

[10] Agyin Asare, *It is Miracle Time, 1 & 2*, Accra: the author, 1997, passim.

[11] Ralph Osabutey, *How to Receive Bountifully from God*, Accra: the author, 2001, 31.

and Dele Bamgboye of Winners': 'Before the year comes to an end, there are people here who will be counting millions of dollars in their accounts... the money is already there in my account now, millions of dollars. You are that person, in the name of Jesus.' (11 June 00) On 13 May 2001 Bamgboye's successor at Winners' claimed: 'Between now and next December, some people here will own their own aircraft.'[12]

If it is the case that the ordinary Christian should be rich, it goes without saying that the pastor should be even richer: 'When people see your church and pastor, they should say: "Their God is rich."'[13]

There is a theological vision here. There is an understanding of God— as Joyce Meyer expressed it, that he is 'El Shaddai, the provider, not El Cheapo'; or, in Ashimolowo's words, 'God is in the business of addition and multiplication; Satan is in the business of subtraction and division.' (*13 Jan. 01*) There is also a vision of the human condition: in Duncan-Williams words, 'You were born to have everything' (23 July 00). In the words of an assistant pastor at the Living Light Chapel, 'What is yours will come to you' (21 Oct. 00). If you don't have everything, the fault is yours. As Apostle Ntumy, head of the CoP, expressed it, 'God has signed a blank cheque for you through the blood of Jesus', and if we haven't cashed it, there is something wrong with us (12 Nov. 00). I have heard in a Presbyterian church in Ghana the view that 'God chastises' (*23 July 00*). It is almost unthinkable for that view to be heard in a charismatic church, where no positive value is given to suffering.[14]

This victory or success must be proclaimed in a testimony. All these churches tend to give considerable space to testimonies, not as optional extras but as necessities. To cite Agyin Asare again, 'You must testify; if you don't you don't keep your healing' (28 April 01); again, your healing 'only becomes permanent when you testify' (22 Oct. 00). The role of this witnessing as continual and free advertising cannot be discounted in explaining the growth of these churches; this seems to be the main reason for newcomers attending. It is sometimes claimed that these testimonies centre round deliverance from sin and vice,[15] but in my experience they

---

[12] I therefore tend to disagree with Larbi, for whom prosperity teaching in Ghana 'is simply having a decent or comfortable living' (*Pentecostalism*, 313, see all 312–15); also with Elom Dovlo, in *Graphic*, 14 July 01, 11.

[13] Agyin Asare, *Rooted*, 406.

[14] I have heard Otabil (26 June 01) teach that God tests character in this way, but no others.

[15] Asamoah-Gyadu, *Renewal*, 200, 339. Elom Dovlo writes: 'The desire for supernatural help to overcome destructive habits, weaknesses, difficulties in one's life such as promiscuity, smoking, alcoholism, anger, fear and all sorts of human foibles finds answers in many New Religious Movements' ('The Church in Africa and Religious Pluralism: the Challenge of New Religious Movements and Charismatic Churches', *Exchange*, 37 (1998), 62).

invariably focus on material things. Agyin Asare's are overwhelmingly about healings; Korankye Ankrah's about finances; and Deya's about finances, marriage and visas. In the magazines of Jesus Connection, Bethel and other prayer camps the testimonies focus on children, jobs, finances, husbands; only very few on deliverance from vices like drunkenness. At Jesus Connection services only about 10% of testimonies were ethical in content—deliverance from laziness or drink.[16] Winners' has about seven testimonies every Sunday; only very rarely are they not exclusively concerned with material things, and the testimonies in its *Winners World* are generally headed 'Open Heavens!', 'I'm a Millionaire Today!', 'Jobs started coming in!', 'A Miracle Car!', 'Now they pay me in Dollars!', 'Orders Galore!', 'My Own Choice Car!', 'Two Cars in Two Days!', 'Overflowing Supply of Money!', 'A Baby, Two Cars and Promotion!', 'Triple Promotion in One Year!'[17]

A particular characteristic of the success guaranteed in these churches is that it is to occur 'today', or 'now', or 'before I finish'. In the words of a preacher at ACI: 'I speak a promotion to you this morning. I empower you this morning by the Word of God to leave your lowliness and to rise to the level you belong.' (22 April 01) At Duncan-Williams's 2000 convention the talk was of a '24-hour miracle' (28 Nov.–2 Dec. 00). Lawrence Tetteh always speaks in this way. At one crusade: 'If you are not married here, take your miracle today', whereupon he broke into Wagner's Bridal March (11 Nov. 00). A Nigerian warming up a Lawrence Tetteh crusade expressed it in memorable pidgin: 'Poverty, I depart you: today I be moneyman. My room key, my car key, my suitcase key [for travel?] they follow tonight.' (15 Sept. 2000) A Nigerian at WMCI claimed: 'Wonderful things have happened tonight. When you wake up tomorrow you will find pain gone, business turned around, husband fallen in love with you again.' Agyin Asare added: 'This week you will find debts

---

[16] The same is true of the testimonies in Tackie Yarboi's *Voice of Victory*; the mainly Jesus Connection testimonies each week in the tabloid *Anomaa Nsem*, and those in 'From the Church House' in *Newsmaker.*

[17] The testimonies in Oyedepo's books are invariably material and usually financial: see *Breaking Financial Hardship*, Lagos: Dominion Publishing House, 1995, 153–62. See *Winners' World* every month and the weekly *Signs and Wonders Today*, from headquarters church. In fact, many testimonies are not primarily to the goodness or power of God at all, but rather to the exceptional gifts of the particular man of God. At RHCI the culmination of one testimony to a miraculous healing was the astounded doctor's question: 'Where do you worship?'—i.e. only a great man of God could have achieved this (7 Nov. 2000). Another long testimony ended with the young woman being transformed from squalor to adoption by the church, even to scholarships for her children 'from nursery to university'. The pastor exclaimed: 'She shall be in RHCI until she flies off to Europe, and it shall certainly come to pass.' (6 Nov. 00)

abolished, people will give to you that you don't even know, those who owe will repay, and finances will be turned around.' (22 Oct. 00)[18] The fact that it is impossible for many of these things to be accomplished in the time prescribed shows that these claims are rhetorical devices rather than needing to be meticulously verified; in this Christianity verification counts for little. This, of course, is not a criticism; the genre has a long history in Christianity, and much of the Old Testament prophetic literature has a similar status in logic.

The relentless stress on victory means that negative realities can only be rejected. One must not only reject them but refuse even to speak of them, for 'you get what you say'—a recurrent theme in the faith gospel. One preacher at ACI urged the congregation not to pray about a problem, which only increases it: 'When you pray a negative prayer, you have agreed with Satan. When you agree with Satan it increases the power of Satan... We don't pray our situation; you pray your desire.' (2 Dec. 00) Hence some of the churches refuse to use the phrase 'for better, for worse' in the marriage ceremony, preferring 'for better and better'. Duncan-Williams explained to his congregation how he refused to sign a will his lawyer had drawn up for him, because it used the phrase 'after my death'. Using the word 'death' was an open invitation to the 'Spirit of Death' to hover around in wait: 'There are all sorts of things we do professionally that can bring all sorts of serious problems.' He insisted that the wording be changed to 'when I have finished my course' (29 July 01).

The focus on victory and rejection if not denial of evil has affected the way these churches deal with funerals. When the churches first arose, members were overwhelmingly the young, so funerals were not a pressing issue; but they were all influenced by the faith gospel, according to which no one should die in less than the biblical span of seventy years. As a result, death has always been something of an embarrassment in these churches. At Winners' the pastor cheerfully claims: 'Every member of this assembly should live to 100.' (18 Feb. 01) In February 2001 Winners' advertised a 'Covenant Winners' Family Day, featuring Victory over Untimely Death, Releasing the Covenant of Long Life'. At Otabil's ICGC the deaths of members were never announced in services, but less publicly in cell groups. Funerals would be arranged at home; only in 2000 was it decided that bodies could lie in church. All this was taking place at a time when funerals were increasingly assuming such cultural significance that

---

[18] Sometimes the fulfilment is to be understood spiritually: Agyin Asare, at RHCI, spoke of your bills 'being settled not tomorrow, but tonight' but 'in the spirit' (7 Nov. 00). Lawrence Tetteh claimed: 'In the spirit you are going to get your marriage partners [now].' (3 March 01)

the time and resources devoted to them has come to constitute a serious hindrance to Ghana's development. These churches have not dealt with this aspect of life at all, because they are ill equipped to do so; the only way to deal with negative realities is to repudiate and reject them. That explains the reaction of his church to Duncan-Williams's divorce; the only way of dealing with it was to deny it.

'Winning Ways' Convention

To illustrate some of the points made above we will outline in some detail the 'Winning Ways' convention brought to Ghana by three internationally acknowledged charismatic stars— Matthew Ashimolowo, Myles Munroe and Mike Murdock—in early 2001. This convention makes the international character of this Christianity easier to grasp, but it also starkly focuses some of our issues, for it was both presented and received as almost a distillation of this Christianity; the essence in concentrated form.[19]

Let us consider Myles Munroe's sermon on the first morning entitled 'Understanding the Power of Purpose': 'I was a victim of colonialism; I thought white was better.... I know what it's like to have rats and cockroaches crawling over you sleeping. I know what it is to sing "Rule Britannia"... and tell the Queen of England "You were born to rule over me". Well, the British were wrong about me. I am not a half-breed, retarded... Our Sunday afternoon tour was to go and see houses where [the British] lived. Today I live in a house on the beach better than theirs. The house is paid for. All my cars are paid for. I'm worth a few million in US dollars... They thought I was a dummy at school. I've written textbooks. I used to be a zero, now I'm one of the 10%. I didn't have to leave my island to be successful... You don't need to become a British citizen to be successful.'

He said that the British had taught him never to begin a sentence with 'I'. 'That psychologically damaged me'—self-confidence is 'a gift from God'—and Jesus was always saying 'I am'. 'I wasn't born successful—I *became* successful. No one gave me a break; I broke the forces of darkness.' He told his audience that he owns 57 acres of beachfront property; has built a resort hotel; now he is building a shopping mall and a second hotel. He has an International Leadership Training Institute. His success is based on the 'principles of this book'—the Bible. He has read it twenty-seven times. He urged his audience never to let anyone categorise them. 'To be a winner you have got to declare independence from Ghana

---

[19] This convention was given unprecedented publicity: *Graphic* 17 Feb. 12; 28 Feb. 9; 3 March, 12; 5 March, 17; 6 March, 17; 8 March, 17; *Chronicle*, 7–8 March, 1; 8–12 March, 1; 9–11 March, 1 (all in 2001).

[this was Ghana's Independence Day]. I am an international citizen, a global citizen. I just happen to have the Bahamas as my base. The Bahamas are privileged to have me, honoured. I bring dignity to the Bahamas... One of my books sold one million copies. I still live on an island 21 miles by 7. My books make bestseller lists. Now people come from all over the world to see where I live.... The minute they think you African, they classify you: "You can't speak, you can't do chemistry, just dance and sing."' He urged, 'Tell your neighbour: "Neighbour, if you knew who I was, you'd invest in me,"' and later, 'Tell your neighbour: "You ain't seen the best until you've seen me."' He kept relating his message to Jesus: 'Archaeologists say Jesus came from Nazareth, a town of one street and eleven houses. Now, that's what I call winning!' He concluded: 'If you didn't know what Jesus is saying, you'd think this is positive thinking. This is not positive thinking; this is revelatory reality!'

The following day he spoke again on 'the Power of Personal Purpose', basing it on Proverbs 19.21: 'Many are the plans in a man's heart, but it is the Lord's purpose that prevails.' He that said 99% of people die without living; he hoped his audience would not be among them. They had to find their purpose. 'The greatest tragedy in life is not death; it is life without a purpose.... You were not born just to make a living; you were born to live, and live abundantly.' Jesus was only thirty-three when he died; at his death he said 'It is finished', meaning he had fulfilled his purpose. When we die we must make sure we have completed our purpose. God gave each of us a purpose before creation of the world—'I chose you before the world began.' (Eph 4) 'Whenever God begins something it's already finished. The fact that you exist is evidence that there is something finished already that you were born to start.' (At this point each listener had to tell his or her neighbour: 'What you see is not who I am yet. You are going to be glad you knew me.')

'Once you have seen your end, and believe it, you become dangerous. Most of you have seen your end, but don't believe it. You are thinking like an African, not a Son of God.... Why did God make sure the inn [in Bethlehem] was full? Because he wanted to cancel your excuse for [failure]. You were not born lower than Jesus. Look where he is today—on the throne! Why were you not white? [Because] what you were born to do does not require a white man.... Some of you are ashamed of what you are. I have come to rebuke you. You are exactly what is required for your purpose.... Where you live right now is not what God showed you [in your vision]. If what you see [around you] is not what you saw [in your dream], then what you see is temporary...what you see is not permanent... You're coming out of where you are; your success is coming!' (shouted three times)

inspiring speeches

Obviously this is highly inspirational—Munroe is a skilful speaker, and his message of purpose and vision, even for those who right now are nothing, and in a peripheral country like Ghana, really enthused the thousands in his audience. In such a message he obviously brings in much of himself ('You can become like me'); but this made it even more effective. Much of this is the approach found in Norman Vincent Peale: have confidence, ambition, motivation (and Munroe took it to a higher degree than is usual in Ghana). Munroe christianises the rationale for confidence— because God decreed your unique role before the foundation of the world. He also skilfully links his message at critical points with the scriptures, especially the words and deeds of Jesus.[20]

Munroe's sermons concentrated in this way on vision and motivation. However, as we noted above, there is another, slightly different route to achievement (also to be found in Peale): this is success through various laws of self-help. At 'Winning Ways' this approach was more characteristic of Mike Murdock, as shown in his talk on the first morning entitled 'Twelve Characteristics of a Winner'. A winner organises his life around dreams and goals; creates a climate that feeds his passion for those dreams and goals; chooses a mentor; solves problems closest to him first; packages himself; recognises greatness in those closest to him; creates a daily routine; studies and documents the results of his own efforts and the efforts of those under his supervision; knows the legacy he wishes to leave; sees his adversaries as providing opportunities for promotion; and recognises God as his true source of money. Obviously many, if not all, of these characteristics have nothing specifically Christian about them, although with a little ingenuity a biblical example can be found for each (e.g. David using an encounter with his adversary Goliath as an opportunity for promotion). Some are rules of organisational efficiency and productive time management and indeed both Murdock and Munroe double as purely secular business consultants, the field in which they admit they have made most of their wealth.[21]

help yourself

— not Christ's message really!

These are ways in which Christianity is deemed to bring about success. 'Winning Ways' illustrates them all. The ways to success are through

[20] An example of a Ghanaian equivalent: Michael Essel, *The Treasure Within You*, Accra: Essel Library Publications, 2000. Everyone has a gift; find it, develop it to the point of excellence, and you will bring prosperity, favour, promotion, and a position among the great. His big examples are Thomas Edison, the biblical Joseph (pp. 51–6) whose gift was interpreting dreams, and David (pp. 57–63) whose gift was playing the harp.

[21] Murdock's 'School of Financial Success' videos, on sale in Duncan-Williams's bookshop, include titles like 'Solomon's 17 Secrets for Achievement'; 'Paul's 26 Principles of Successful Negotiations'; '25 Steps to Abundance'; 'The Winner's Guide to a Financial Harvest'; 'Seven Ways to stay Motivated'; 'Five Keys to achieving Goals'; 'Ten Steps for overcoming Financial Adversity'.

faith or through motivation, through habits (like those advocated by Murdock), through inexorable laws, or even through God's unmediated miraculous intervention. However, in Ghana in the late 1990s ever more emphasis came to be placed on the role of a special individual in the achievement of victory and success. Besides those other means, the gifts of a 'Man of God' can bring about success in one's life, often through ritual and above all by anointing with oil. Indeed, throughout the charismatic sector 'the anointing' is now a key concept, used in expressions like 'imparting an anointing to prosper', or in Korankye Ankrah's claim that he has a 'visa anointing' that enables his church members to move all over the globe (10 Nov. 00). Many churches sell small bottles of olive oil, a commodity which is not easy to find in Accra's supermarkets, the staples being vegetable and sunflower oil; it may be that sales of olive oil in Accra are centred on the churches.

Winners' Chapel

At this point we will consider Winners' Chapel in a little more detail. Winners' began in Lagos on 17 September 1983; by 2000 it had spread to thirty-eight African countries, with 400 branches in Nigeria and proudly boasting in Lagos the biggest auditorium in the world, seating 50,400 ('Watch for the 2001 *Guinness Book of Records*: it will be there,' the congregation was told on 17 September 2000). It establishes only one church per city, and so far in Ghana it has them only in Accra, Tema, Takoradi and Akosombo. Its Accra church had a congregation of about 13,000 at the end of 2001 and was increasing like wildfire, with almost 300 first-timers every week, of whom about half stayed. However, in early 2002 Winners' experienced a split. The Nigerian senior pastor was redeployed to Nigeria; he obviously felt he had not been given a post commensurate with his merits and he resigned from Winners' and returned to Accra to establish his own 'Triumphant Global Ministries'. At Winners' he was replaced, in an exercise of damage limitation, by a Ghanaian, Bishop George Agyemang. This split has reduced numbers, but the church is still growing. Its growth may be helped through its location on a disused industrial site near Nkrumah Circle, one of the city's biggest transport hubs. Of all these churches Winners' certainly extends the biggest welcome to first-time worshippers (bringing them to the front, singing to them, presenting them with a cassette). Members of Winners' are dedicated to evangelism, and in 2001 stepped up their advertising on billboards and on TV. Unlike the other churches we are considering, this is a Nigerian creation, and its founder, David Oyedepo, is based in Lagos. Loyalty to him is marked, and nearly every sermon cites him as a model for something (he is actually called 'the visioneer' [13 May 2001], a word I have heard used only within the Disney organisation). The senior pastors during the period of this research—two Nigerians and one Ghanaian—have been superb speakers, in a repetitive, orotund style. Winners' does not cooperate with other churches for anything, but single-mindedly pursues its own vision, demanding attendance not only on Sunday but also on Tuesday and Thursday evenings.

At Winners' Chapel the stress is all on success. 'Success is our birthright' (18 Feb. 01)—'If you won't succeed, go to another church.' (1 Oct. 00) 'Very soon I am going to inspect people's shoes before they enter church. When your shoe is opening its mouth [developing holes] I will tell you to go to the next church. Amen. Then my wife will be checking people's shirts. If your shirt is white and under the armpit is brown, you are going back home. This is the home of signs and wonders. No dead is permitted here.' (23 June 00) Success extends to all areas of life—Winners' provides 'a supernatural financial, social, spiritual, marital, academic, business takeoff'. (1 April 01) 'When you enter a covenant with the Lord, then war, hardship will cease around you and you will see "rest" run about [reference to II Chr 15.15]. "Rest" means rest financially, socially, health-wise, in the family, everywhere.' (23 June 00) However, in practice success relates overwhelmingly to wealth. Typical titles of sermons are 'Prosperity is my Identity' and 'Prosperity is my Heritage'. In the latter sermon it is called (in a reference to Proverbs 10.22) 'sorrow-free Kingdom prosperity', and each member of the congregation tells his neighbour: 'Supernatural prosperity is my heritage.' (1 June 00) 'Financial hardship is an insult to your identity, your location, your position, your kingdom', and arises only because 'people have broken covenants.' (23 June 00) This focus on financial prosperity is perhaps to be expected from the account which the founder of Winners', Oyedepo, gives of his calling by God. His experience is obviously modelled on the call to Moses, but whereas Moses in Midian was commanded 'Go and set my people free', Oyedepo in the United States was simply told 'Get down home quick and make my people rich.'[22]

The change begins right now; incessantly results are proclaimed 'now', 'today' or 'this morning'. 'I see somebody exploding into his destiny this morning' (10 Sept. 00) or 'Many of you are beautiful, but no man has asked to marry you. Today, after the anointing, ten people will rush to you.' (18 Feb. 01) 'As you depart from here today, you will be receiving phone calls, for a new job, a new business, new opportunity.' (11 June 00) 'Within 30 days from today your life will be dramatically changed. By the end of this week your crisis will be gone.' (1 April 01) First-time attenders are told: 'If you don't see a miracle in two weeks, you can go

---

[22] Oyedepo, *Breaking Financial Hardship*, 51.

back [to your previous church].' (13 May 01) 'This month, no accident, sickness, stagnation [will affect me]. Every attempt to block my way this month is frustrated. No evil reports, no bad things... I am moving forward this month. It shall be better for me this month than last month. All things are working in my favour. Enter the realm of plenty, open doors... Turn to someone and say "Happy New Month".' (1 Oct. 00) In keeping with this sharp sense of time, every week is different, and every service is advertised with a special theme, e.g. 'Winners' Covenant Day of Power', 'Covenant Day of Success' or 'Covenant Winners' Family Day' with the slogan 'Fruitfulness All Round'. Every month has a new theme, blazoned across the auditorium: 'I am a Child of Destiny' and 'More than a Conqueror' in September and October 2000 respectively, 'Success is my Birthright' in August 2002. A branch of Christianity that has no concept of the traditional Christian liturgical cycle of Advent, Lent and Easter seems to be developing its own particular scheme of linear progression.

The church would see itself as creating entrepreneurs (in May 2001 it held a mini trade fair, which attracted about 120 businesses, and began a businessmen's fellowship for members). Still more important is the motif of motivation. A sermon on 3 September 2000 on Jeremiah 1.5 insisted: 'You are not a biological coincidence. Heaven planned a destiny for you... God has programmed you. You are designed according to his purpose, foreknown, predestinate... You are the apple of God's eye.' The pastor had the congregation shouting: 'I am special, I am peculiar, I am different.' A week later the preacher proclaimed: 'You are not a mistake, a biological error, an environmental animal. You are here to fulfil a divine agenda. There is a heavenly timetabling over you. You are important to God, this country, the world. You are part of the divine programme. If you had not been born, the body of Christ would have been missing something... You are not a nonentity, you are not programmed by governments, parents, witches, demons, but by God... You are a first-class creation of heaven.' Much is made of one's vision: 'What you dream is what you will experience. Don't leave your future a blank. Expect something, or you will be a victim of anything. Carry a dream, of the task, assignment. See it, carry it, be pregnant with it, and you will give birth to it.' The following week's sermon reinforced the message further: 'Every part of your destiny is assured by God, insured by God.' Members are regularly invited to say to each other things like 'I am bound for the mountain top, and nothing will hold me back' and are urged 'Touch three people, and tell them "See you at the top".' The message is relentless.[23]

---

[23] There is much practical instruction, too; advice about handling delicate matters of the extended family (22 Oct. 00), and even how to find a marriage partner at a forthcoming service ('So dress appropriately').

So Winners' encourages entrepreneurs and gives motivation. However, even more significant, and underlying everything, is the faith gospel—not surprising, given his links with the giants of the faith movement; the Lord has told Oyedepo that Hagin's 'baton has been passed' to him, and he received Copeland's anointing by sleeping in a bed once slept in by Copeland.[24] But the most notable characteristic is the shift beyond the faith gospel to a stress on the Man of God's gifts for producing the victory. The preacher is likely to say: 'I stand in the fullness of the commission to declare to you...' and then pronounce the blessing, shouting 'Receive it!' with the entire congregation repeatedly shouting back 'I receive it!' 'Marriages don't collapse here, businesses don't collapse here, nobody fails here. Nobody is stagnating here. Receive it!' There follows the programmed response: 'I receive it!' (17 Sept. 00) At Winners' the climax of the service is not the sermon but rather a ritual reinforcement of the blessings promised, which can continue for more than an hour. For example, after a sermon about boldness ('If you look cheated you will be cheated, our world does not respect sheep'), the congregation were made to roar like lions while shouting: 'The boldness of my countenance is changed today. My sheep nature is changed to a lion nature. Every feebleness [is gone] from today. This is the dawning of a new day.' (13 May 01)

Winners' has developed its own characteristic rituals of reinforcement. A white handkerchief is called a mantle; every congregation member waves one, and the Man of God blesses it, and imbues it with double anointing (the reference is to Elisha inheriting the mantle of Elijah, with its double portion—II Kings 2.11–14). Oyedepo explains: 'The mantle ministry is not given to everyone; it is the preserve of those who carry transferable unction. The demand on these men is so much (more than they can be available to deliver physically) that they are gifted by God to be able to distribute themselves into men. So the honour on them is now available for others to carry just as in the case of Moses (Num 11.17).' He then reports how one of his Bible school students, with a mantle from Oyedepo, raised the dead.[25]

All members are also told to bring along their own particular 'instruments of destiny'. At services, members of the congregation hold up scissors (dressmakers?), pens (teachers or office-workers?), pliers (electricians?), pharmaceuticals (chemists?), video camera (photographers?), bars of Sunlight soap or bolts of cloth (market women?) to have them prayed over. On 10 September 2000, while holding the instrument of

---

[24] Oyedepo, *Riding on Prophetic Wings*, Lagos: Dominion Publishing House, 2000, 103, 121 and 124. His early books are pure faith gospel.

[25] Oyedepo, *Prophetic Wings*, 106–10.

rituals

destiny in the left hand, each hit the instrument with her 'mantle' three times; again, the ceremony was orchestrated and enacted with wild exhilaration. (In a similar way, members bring along documents or deeds to home or land or cars, for a thanksgiving ritual.)

Several times a year Winners' conducts a washing of the feet, another ritual proper to itself. It is built on the example of Jesus at the Last Supper (Jn 13), but also on Joshua 14.9: 'Whatsoever your feet tread upon shall be given unto you for a possession.' Hence it is yet another encouragement to possess: 'Everywhere you step after (the foot-washing) you will enter.' (18 Feb. 01) Another ritual is the 'covenant handshake', with which, for example, every newcomer is greeted. 'It is not my hand, but the touch of God', the senior pastor said on 28 January 2001. 'It looks like the hand of a man, but as I shake your hand, the right hand of God will find you and give you your miracle.' (18 Feb. 01) Again, 'I will give you a covenant handshake. I will pull down the miracle you are wishing for. It looks like the hand of Abraham [the pastor's Christian name], but behind it is the hand of God.' (1 April 01)

power

Winners' most characteristic ritual involves oil. It openly claims to have introduced this modern stress on anointing to Christianity (17 Sept. 00). Anointing in Christianity has traditionally been related to healing sickness, and linked to texts like Mark 6.12–13 and James 5.14. Winners' anointing is about power, and linked to texts like anointing Aaron's family (Ex 30.30–31) and Samuel's anointing of Saul (I Sam 10.1–7) and the miraculous stories of Elijah and Elisha, 'so we know from Scripture that power comes with anointing.' (19 Nov. 00) The anointing ceremony brings about 'a transfer of unction' (1 April 01). Many testimonies specifically proclaim the role of the oil; one testimony claimed that after a pair of shoes belonging to a lost child were anointed, the child returned within seven days. Another testified that his car would not start, but the application of some anointing oil to the engine brought it to life immediately.[26] In the service, after oil is rubbed over head, hair, face and arms, as the pastor shouts 'Receive husband!', 'Receive baby!' and so on, the congregation cries 'I receive it!'

Another ritual is 'the impartation', named from Romans 1.11–12 (KJV), and referring to Moses' laying hands on Joshua (Dt 34.9), and II Timothy 1.6–7 and 14. For example, on 1 April 2001 after a sermon on 'The Hand of God', every single member of the congregation wrote on a

---

[26] Oyedepo himself recounts many such stories; in one, fibroid in a woman's womb was transformed into a baby by anointing, and when born this baby had an oil mark on its head (*Prophetic Wings*, 75). Other treatments of anointing include Eastwood Anaba, *The Oil of Influence*, Bolgatanga: Desert Leaf Publications, 2000; Samuel Martey, *Understanding the Mystery of the Anointing Oil*, Tema: Resurrection Publishers, 1999.

piece of paper the precise area in which he or she particularly wanted an impartation ('financial, social, spiritual, marital, academic, business'—it is unremarkable that at Winners' the financial area is mentioned first), filed forward to the pastor who anointed each person with oil, and placed the paper in a basket. While this was happening (it took an hour and a half for about 10,000 to be anointed) the congregation sang hymns like 'Just one touch from the master's hand...I'll be whole again' and 'He touched me...and made me whole.' When all had been anointed, the pastor poured more oil on the papers and prayed that 'no lack or scarcity in any such area persist; nothing negative persist, all hindrances and yokes be destroyed.' All these rituals (which together constitute a certain re-sacramentalisation reversing the Reformation) bear witness to this increasing emphasis on the gifts of the specially 'anointed' 'Man of God' in achieving the success this Christianity proclaims.

The final way in which Christianity brings success is related to finances. However, this is such an important area that it is dealt with here in some detail, in a wider context.

Finances

The charismatic Christianity we have been studying is closely adapted to its context. It addresses marginalised people (even Ghana's educated can be considered marginalised) and tells them that change is possible. In the later Rawlings years when illness, deprivation and poverty became major issues, any Christianity that purported to address questions of poverty was sure to flourish. But there is another, closely related way in which this message is equally adapted to its context. The mainline churches had missionaries and resources and were well established with school and health systems (often with subventions from the colonial government), even if their numerous properties and institutions are too expensive to maintain now. But this new charismatic Christianity did not have access to such foreign resources to establish itself. Nevertheless, all the new buildings, cars, electrical equipment, programmes (like crusades and conventions) and foreign travel—and indeed the huge number of new religious professionals—all had to be paid for. A theology was to hand. The faith gospel in the United States had quickly formulated its theology of giving in order to receive. There was probably no necessity for this development; faith could have been considered to lead by itself to prosperity. But the faith gospel as it evolved took hold because it was eminently tailored to the needs of its original exponents, the big televangelists whose expenses were astronomical. It met their needs, because it became linked to the seed faith idea, originating with Oral Roberts, according to

which one prospered by first giving to God or his representative.
A. A. Allen is said to have been another pioneer of such divine fundraising.[27] Ghana's new pastors are not media evangelists in the American
sense, but they are religious entrepreneurs where general economic circumstances are difficult.

In Ghana it is widely accepted that to prosper the first requirement is to
give (to God or to the nearest representative, the Man of God). Thus
Lance Johnson: 'God is waiting for you to bless him before he blesses
you.' (*30 July 00*) And Korankye Ankrah: 'If we take care of God's business, he takes care of your business.' (12 Nov. 00) Also: 'Give to the Lord
and see prosperity in your life.'[28] Agyin Asare illustrates this point. On
31 Dec. 2000 he gave two different sermons at the one service (required
by TV commitments), the first entitled 'Possess the Land'. From the
beginning, he argued, God declared something to be special to him,
namely the tithe. God has always forbidden mankind to take everything.
God has given us everything, but he sets limits. Achan (Josh 7.21–25)
brought trouble upon Israel by taking what was God's: 'If you don't pay
your tithes you are bringing trouble on yourself... When you take God's
tithe you bring yourself under a curse. You prevent God from being able
to bless you... If you tithe, you will succeed (where others don't). As you
pay your tithe, people will look at you and say "You are Blessed" ... If
people are going to give a job, you are the one they look for because you
are not taking what belongs to God.' He went on to give a second method
of 'possessing the land', but it is unremarkable that the first way is to give
to God.[29]

Agyin Asare can preach sermons on holiness, but even here the divine
fundraising element is seldom far beneath the surface. In a sermon on the
anointing, the first requirement was to serve; but the second was to 'pro-
voke the anointing by giving'. The woman in II Kings 4.8 provided for
the prophet, and even though she had forgotten she wanted a child, she
had her needs met. Similarly, to meet 'even those needs you have forgotten about...it is very important to sow in anointed ministries.' (*7 April 01*)
Similarly, in a sermon on consecration, Agyin Asare made four points:
first, that God owns everything; second, that all we have comes from
God; third, that 'you need to give it back to God'—and this includes
finances; and fourth, the need to surrender to God's will: 'Live for God's

---

[27] See A. A. Allen, *The Riches of the Gentiles are Yours*, Benin City: Calvary Publications,
n.d; on p. 66 he seems to imply that this teaching is new.
[28] Sam Korankye Ankrah, *God's Favour: Operating through Covenants*, Accra: Journa-
grafx, 1998, 71–6.
[29] According to Oyedepo, 'There is only one way to get money. This is by giving away what
you have.' (*Breaking Financial Hardship*, 105)

Kingdom and the extension of his Kingdom… If God tells you to give all your salary for crusades, can you do it?' (*12 May 01*)[30]

Let us consider some examples of this divine fundraising. Robert Ampiah-Kwofi of Global Revival Ministries hosted in April 2001 a four-day revival 'Experiencing Open Heavens for Divine Favours', at which the preacher was the Ghanaian Kofi Banful of Praise Chapel, London. The four days were unadulterated faith gospel; 'I'm teaching you principles so you have money in your pocket so your needs can be met.' 'The only thing that touches or pleases God is faith.' The convention finished with a massive fund raising, for the church was buying thirty-two plots in the exclusive suburb of East Legon, at an estimated cost of 410 million cedis, to start a university, medical centre and so on. On the Thursday night Ampiah-Kwofi urged those attending to sell cars, houses and property and close bank accounts, before the fundraising on Sunday, and give to the church (it was hard to tell how this was received).

Ebenezer Markwei, at the opening of Korankye Ankrah's new premises, began his sermon by noting that because the latter was so obviously blessed, his congregation would benefit from his anointing; 'In one year's time [shouted three times] I see people carrying gold they never carried before, houses they never carried before, bus, cars, transport…. Because you gave him a house, [to] everyone who contributed, God has to give houses cars, gold, silver.' He told them: 'The time of your renting your house is over, the time of driving a tro-tro [public taxi] is over… I hear the sound of cars, new cars, luxury cars… by virtue of the fact that you associate yourselves with this man… The people of God who can tap into God's plan, they shall blossom. Give a powerful offering you have never given before. If you need to borrow, go and borrow.' (7 Nov. 00)

The Jamaican Paul Lewis spoke at Markwei's Living Streams convention in November 2000, and ended his sermon with the announcement that he so loved Markwei that he was donating $1,000 to him, because it was not right that he did not have a proper church (Living Streams meets in a pavilion in the Trade Fair grounds). Lewis announced that he wanted to raise 200 million cedis at the service on the following day; but that night thirty-eight people were to 'obey the prophet' and give one million cedis each. They were to give even if they had nothing, for 'In the midst of your famine, that's when God works.' They were to bring their savings if they were saving, borrow if they had to ('I wish I had the opportunity

---

[30] 'We also honour our leaders by giving them our substances. … We also honour the great by contributing to make them even greater. Add to the great man. Do not withhold from him. To him that has, more is added.' (Duncan-Williams, *The Price of Greatness*, Accra: Design Solutions, 1999, 45–7, esp. 45)

you have'). Only two came out: 'Who will be the next one? I wouldn't say this unless God had revealed it... This is the only way out of their poverty. I could pick you out [i.e., name the other thirty-eight], but I won't.' He asked the congregation if they were putting aside for a rainy day, but promised: 'If you give [to this cause], you won't have a rainy day.'[31]

When advertising his 2000 Convention, Duncan-Williams stated that one of its aims was 'Economic Empowerment'. He promised some new thinking: 'Do you know the difference between a white man and a black man? The white man doesn't spend his money, he spends the profit on his money.' Thus, 'We must employ new techniques and methods.' (26 Nov. 00) But the main speaker on this topic, Marcus Hester, a white American from Chicago, simply refined this faith gospel motif of giving to receive. His topic was 'Releasing the End-Time Secret Weapon of God', and he disclosed that the end time weapon was money. 'America is the most prosperous nation in the world because it gives.... We are here to break the Spirit of Poverty here in Ghana.' He had the congregation shouting six times: 'Money, come to me!' Hester insisted: 'I'm here to say "The sky's the limit."' And of course, the method was 'the more you give, the more you receive'. He explained how he had owned two successful companies, but had lost everything in bankruptcy. Then he 'started giving 10% to the church, and in the last ten years [God] restored everything I got and doubled it. Say to your neighbour "If it happened to him, it can happen to me."' In a subsequent talk entitled "Satan is driving my Car" (i.e. Satan is in possession of what is rightly mine), he dealt with the problem arising when giving does not produce what it theoretically should, and moved on to the subject of curses, which is discussed below, but the message reinforced his earlier one, in that the principal reason why you do not have the car is that you are not giving; 'It's not the only reason, but it is the biggest.' (1 Dec. 00)

James Saah, Duncan-Williams's deputy, spoke at this same convention on 'Economic Empowerment'. He stated: 'The first key to kingdom prosperity is giving.' He went on to outline (more briefly) other keys—working, thinking, trusting, waiting, talking (the faith gospel idea of 'proclaiming')—but it is unsurprising that giving to God comes first and is the most important.

On a more theological note, it is often possible to detect the idea that one buys one's prosperity with what one gives to the church, and thus a certain 'Catholicising' tendency. Agyin Asare writes in a section entitled 'He Deserves a Miracle', 'Do not leave yourself out when pledges are

---

[31] I could not attend the following day, so cannot reveal how successful his fund-raising was.

taken as contributions for church projects, for God is not unjust to forget your labour of love.'[32] Duncan-Williams (with his notoriously uncompleted church) argues: 'Some of you have not done anything for the house of God. Some of you [have put] no money in your account in heaven... What have you put in your account, so that in time of need you can withdraw?' (3 Dec. 00) At a Gilbert Deya crusade (6 Sept. 00) there was actually a role-play showing that you can withdraw from a bank only what you have deposited; if you have paid in only $5,000, you cannot withdraw $6,000. The lesson was made explicit: 'The worship, tithe, offering, sacrifice of time... you are depositing in your account. In time of trouble Jesus looks in your account and [judges accordingly].' This was also the logic of the sermon at Winners' on assurance (19 Nov. 00). Using Psalm 20.1 ('The Lord will hear you in your day of trouble'), the pastor stated: 'The Lord will remember your offering; it is comprehensive assurance.'

We have already discussed the visiting 'Winning Ways' convention in some detail, because it well illustrates the centrality of success in this Christianity, and argued that the convention was an important event for Ghana, not least because it was acknowledged to be staged by charismatic stars, sanctioned by all significant Ghanaian pastors, and calculated to further entrench this stress on winning. However, it had another message beside winning, namely giving. Perhaps the giving is not so much a second message, as an integral element of this single emphasis on success, because giving was presented as the main—if not the only—way to win.

Mike Murdock is unashamed about this. Consider his talk of 7 March 2001, entitled 'Wisdom Keys for Uncommon Success'. He began with eleven points of organisational efficiency, some of which, as noted above, are not specifically Christian, but would be acceptable in a talk to management trainees of any big firm. But with his twelfth and last point, on which he spent as much time as on all the others combined, he moved to a new plane altogether. This point was that in the quest for success, 'If you insist on taking something God did not give you, he will take back everything he gave you.' He gave biblical illustrations: Adam and Eve were given everything in the garden but the tree; because they took the tree, they lost the garden as well. Ahab was given the nation of Israel, but not Naboth's vineyard; he took the vineyard, so lost the nation (I Kings 21). David was given the favour of all Israel, not Bathsheba; he took Bathsheba, so he lost the favour of all Israel. In this way, Murdock explained, God has given us 90 per cent of our income, not the first tenth

---

[32] Agyin Asare, *Miracle Time II*, 83, see all 81–3.

or the tithe. 'If you take the tithe, he will take back the 90%.' He asked for a rough average monthly wage in Ghana, and was told 200,000 cedis. 'The tithe then is 20,000; the tithe must be paid before the offering is given.' 'If a couple bring out of 200,000 [only] 15,000, [what] is it? A tithe? No! Is it an offering? No! What is it? It is nothing, neither tithe nor offering. It's an attempt to bribe God. They go back [home]... Nothing happens. They are not blessed. Really, why would God bless a thief? But if they give 20,000, now the 90 per cent is ready for reproduction.' He then prayed for three miracles for new tithers: uncommon health, uncommon financial ideas, and uncommon favour.[33] It is the third reward of tithing that is of most interest: if you pay the tithe, others come to bless you. Murdock explained how this had worked in his own life. One birthday he played a video cassette he had received and it told him to look outside. 'I went outside, and there was a $65,000 Corvette.' A few weeks later a woman gave him a vintage Corvette (Murdock added, 'I gave it to a friend'). Just a few weeks before he had come to Ghana, he had driven into his drive, and there was a beautiful yellow Corvette for him; a friend explained: 'I just wanted to give it to you.' Murdock admitted that he has 'to stop to think how many cars' he has received in this way. Then he asked if any in the congregation had missed any week's tithe of the past year. 'If you are willing to make a new vow, on the count of three, stand, because I want to release the most fabulous twelve months you have ever experienced.' Almost all stood. Murdock insisted that it had cost his ministry $150,000 (in lost revenues?) for him to travel to Ghana for this convention. 'I didn't come here to make money; I came to sow seed. I'm going to release the greatest twelve months of your life; this will be a turning point. *Today is the poorest you will ever be the rest of your life.*' He had the congregation repeat this last sentence three times. He then asked everyone to hold up his or her wallet, and asked every pastor to come out and stand with him. He addressed the pastors singly: 'Pastor, if you don't mentor your people on the power of the tithe, the holy part, who will?' He continued: 'Pastors, look at these people, [at their] incredible honesty. Stretch forth your hands; release the greatest twelve months in their life.' Then he addressed the spirit of poverty: 'Spirit of Poverty, Go! I command you to leave this nation, this city, our churches... I release uncommon health, uncommon financial ideas, uncommon favour.' He explained how he had asked God to raise up 300 millionaires under his ministry: 'So far we have twelve.' He continued: 'I want everyone here

---

[33] The second, the miracle of uncommon financial ideas, builds on Deuteronomy 8.18, that God will give an idea to create wealth. Murdock said: 'I've had ideas that have brought me half a million dollars. Lord, show them the methods to start them on the way.'

to sow 400,000 cedis... If I'm saying this for personal gain, may my tongue cleave to my mouth. I ask for 300 who will [go further and] plant 400,000 cedis for every member of their family. I release that harvest for the glory of God. It is done.' And beginning the collection, he had everyone repeat to her neighbour: 'Today is the poorest you will be the rest of your life.'

Murdock's third and final sermon was about the three most important things in his life. The first was the realisation that wisdom is everything; the second, that one must find one's 'assignment' or purpose in life (for one thing, 'Financial provision is only guaranteed at your place of assignment'); and third, the principle of the seed—'My whole life is run by the principle of the seed.' He defined the law of the seed as 'something you have been given will create something else you have been promised'. The remainder—indeed the greater part—of the message was his testimony (which he revealingly described as 'the story of the financial changes in my life'). He is the son of a poor Pentecostal preacher, and became a poor preacher himself—in one month his income was $36, in another $90, and for one year it was $2,263. His break came when a preacher asked him to make a 'faith promise', defined as a 'promise that if God gave you so much you would give it back to him'. Murdock made a faith promise for $100. The next Sunday morning he was preaching for his father, when a man stood up and declared that God had been so good to him that his pocket was full of $100 bills: 'The Holy Spirit told me to give Mike one now.' (At this point Murdock turned to Matthew Ashimolowo and remarked: 'Pastor, I've been everywhere—to the Pyramids, Kilimanjaro, Switzerland—and there is nothing more beautiful than a $100 bill!'.) As he had promised, Murdock sent the $100 to the South Texas Assemblies of God mission department. He then drove to preach in another town, and passed a trailer which he needed, on sale for $100. The Devil said to him: 'See what you could have bought!' Murdock was playing the piano before his service, when a woman came in and gave him a cheque for $150 (he realised: 'This is God'). So he went back, bought his trailer, and wrote a second cheque for the remaining $50 for the Assemblies of God missions. The next week he was at another church when a very meanlooking individual came up, very reluctantly gave him a $100 bill, and said: 'Don't thank me, thank God.' The lesson: 'I'd sowed out $100, I'm reaping $100s' (or in the words of Jesus, 'The measure you give out is the measure you will receive', Lk 6.38).

On another occasion, he was listening to a preacher when the Holy Spirit told him to give to that particular man. All he possessed was 500 record albums (but 'everything you have is seed if you sow it, harvest if you keep it'). Murdock gave the preacher these albums, and the result was that not long after, when he was preaching in Nairobi, he was called to the phone to be told that Jimmy Swaggart wanted to buy 40,000 of his records (Murdock is a composer and recording artist as well). With the proceeds from that 'I bought a big white Lincoln.'

Similarly he gave money to another preacher for a suit. Seven days later a couple whose son he had helped came up to him and said: 'The Holy Spirit told us to buy you some clothes.' They bought him four suits, and six months later another four, and since then another four every six months. Others have given him suits up to a value of $3,200; 'I couldn't begin to tell you how many clothes I've been given. *What you can walk away from determines what God will give you.*' His aim has been to sow himself out of trouble. One preacher to whom he gave later presented him with a car, explaining: 'Only nineteen cars of this special make were ever made. I have serial number one. While preaching the Holy Spirit said give it to you.'

There were other stories teaching the same lesson, and 'In Ghana if God invites you to sow everything you've got, he will open the windows of heaven.' Because Murdock gave to another, he received the idea of an invention that brings him royalties every ninety days that have enabled him to 'build me a gym, with an NBA basketball court; one bought me a Rolls Royce, cash.' The message? 'God has blessed my socks off.' He told of once being seated next to Oral Roberts, when the Holy Spirit told him to give Oral Roberts $25,000. 'I said *he* should be giving *me*... but then I remembered that I am going to need more...' He sowed into Oral Roberts's ministry, and within two days he was asked to speak to managers of a multinational firm: 'I've been paid $40,000 for one hour; $100,000 for one day. An uncommon seed creates an uncommon harvest. I have bought my sister a car. I have bought my brother a Porsche. It's working in my life. If I keep what I've got it's harvest. If I give it away, it is seed... I've flown here to tell you that this principle of the seed will work in Ghana as it does in the USA... God has blessed me beyond measure. [I've received] $25,000 Rolexes—I couldn't begin to tell you how many I've got. I don't ask for these things; I just sow. If I can't trust God for my money why would I trust him for my salvation?'

Then he returned to his idea of $58 seed; Murdock has calculated that there are fifty-eight blessings in the Bible—by giving $58 one enters a covenant to receive these blessings. 'I'm asking everyone here to sow [its Ghanaian equivalent] 400,000 cedis—that's two months salary, but I felt [driven] to ask everyone here. If you never do it again, you should have one opportunity.'[34] He had flown twenty-two hours to Ghana, after a

---

[34] For this, see Mike Murdock, *The Covenant of Fifty-Eight Blessings*, Denton, TX: Wisdom International, 1994.

gruelling trip through many cities, to deliver this message. He addressed God: 'I ask you, within 58 days, to explode this place with... uncommon favour. Let someone rise up to provide and bless us. He will do for us in a day what we haven't been able to do in a lifetime.' He then addressed God again: 'Father, there are eight people in this crowd who can give $1,000.' Even if they had been saving for something special, they should give the money. 'Put a Boaz anointing [named from the Book of Ruth] on them, taking the anointing that is on me, and give the same to them. Every time someone gives me a car, let them get one. Everything you do for me, do the same for them. Be it done.'

Ashimolowo then took the microphone, urging everyone to bring the 400,000 cedis immediately. 'This is your connection point with a change in your destiny. Come forward; this is your break with the past. A prophet is in the house. This is your season. You might not get this opportunity again... You are building a bridge. You are saying bye-bye to what you used to be.' Obviously it was financial lack to which one was saying good-bye, since no other dimension of life had been mentioned. Ashimolowo had earlier described Murdock as his mentor, and told his hearers, in a reference to Murdock's worldwide influence in this charismatic Christianity, that if they had ever heard a sermon on sowing, the ideas in it probably originated from Murdock. Ashimolowo had twice before in this conference observed that his London church members often asked when Murdock was coming back so that they could benefit from giving him $58. On this evening, after Ashimolowo's praise, the Californian gospel singer Helen Baylor (billed on the posters with Ashimolowo, Murdock and Munroe) prefaced her performance by saying: 'Oh the Man of God has spoken tonight! That message which just went forward was awesome. It has changed my life... Give glory for Mike Murdock. As we step out in obedience, God is going to fill our gaps.'

The message of this 'Winning Ways' convention was twofold: <u>Christianity means success, and this success depends on giving to God</u>. My argument here is not that advanced by, for example, Asamoah-Gyadu in his *Renewal*—that there is a huge revival in Ghana, which in some areas is, perhaps regrettably, influenced by the prosperity gospel; it is rather that <u>the prosperity gospel is an integral part of Ghana's charismatic revival.</u> It is left to the Worldwide Church of God, which most of these churches would label a 'sect', to protest that 'the symbol of Christianity worldwide is the cross, not the cedi or the dollar sign.'[35] These

[handwritten margin note: the Prosperity gospel]

---

[35] On their radio programme 29 Oct. and 24 Dec. 00. Herbert Armstrong's Worldwide Church of God came to Ghana in the mid-1970s and now has about 500 members. Through the 1990s the parent church changed a great deal, giving up its characteristic

charismatic churches have grown by claiming to have the answer to
Ghana's poverty.

This insistence by visiting speakers on giving is not unconnected with
the readiness of Ghana's charismatic leaders to welcome such foreign
stars. Outsiders greatly help their host-pastors by raising up tithers in a
way that might possibly be thought excessively self-serving if the local
leaders had to exert such pressure. We have noted this dynamic with
Markwei at Korankye Ankrah's RHCI; the Nigerian Adamson Aromaegbe
at WMCI; the Jamaican Lewis at Markwei's Living Streams and Bamful
at Ampiah-Kwofi's GRM. It was evident too with the American Randy
Morrison at Otabil's ICGC and the Nigerian Elkanah Hanson at Duncan-
Williams ACI.[36]

The serviceability of this faith message is thus evident. In Ghana this
was a time when industries were collapsing; capital was simply not available, with interest rates rising to 46%. The aggressive, theologically driven
quest for funds is the salient characteristic of many churches.[37] This has
given rise to the image of the money-grubbing pastor, someone who had
gone into religion for the money when other avenues of accumulation
were drying up. Certainly the backlash against these churches has been
fuelled mainly by this perception. Kumah laments that only a few observers have 'recognised that the prosperity they were hearing about was
affecting only the Pastors, the new Bishops and a selected few'.[38]

Another reason for the readiness to contribute in this way may be
sought in African traditional religion. Suppliants at a local shrine expect to
pay, and to pay handsomely, for services rendered.

Anglo-Israelite theology and now arguing that tithing is not part of the new covenant—as
a result their incomes have dropped dramatically. Because of their rethinking, splits
occurred; two of the splinter groups are also found in Ghana: the Church of God International and the United Church of God.

[36] Hanson offered the refinement of offering an amnesty for those who had been remiss in
tithing. 'Whatever reproach and disaster is meant to come on you, by the authority conferred on me [as] an ambassador of Christ, we declare you forgiven, discharged, acquit-
ted… You won't withhold tithes any longer. Go and sin no more.' He insisted that the
Bible teaches that 'three things you must be careful with: the glory of God, tithing,
revenge.' (6 May 01)

[37] Some of them, like LCI and ACI and Korankye Ankrah's RHCI also have thank offerings
within the service, when people have read out how much they have given to the church for
favours received.

[38] Kumah, *Is Ghana under a Curse?*, Accra: SonLife, 2000, 98. It is not irrelevant to note
that when Britain's Charity Commissioners took control of Ashimolowo's 8,500-member
church in December 2002 because of supposed irregularities affecting its charitable status, it was announced that Ashimolowo was receiving about £70,000 a month from his
church. (*Chronicle*, 6 Dec. 02, 1)

Biblical

All these churches would insist that they are 'biblical' in a hard sense, and in a way no longer found in the mainline churches. Many churches present this as the first thing you should know about them. Thus every Sunday at Otabil's ICGC a statement of faith is read, beginning: 'We are an evangelistic Bible-believing charismatic church....' Similarly the WMCI announces itself as 'a pentecostal, charismatic, Bible-believing church...' Many adherents, when asked why they have left a mainline church to join a charismatic one, reply 'Here they teach the word.' Not all the leaders use the Bible in the same way: Otabil can preach an entire series from one text, e.g., his sixteen-programme 'Principles of Effective Living' from the first chapter of Genesis, or his ten-programme 'Pulling Down Strongholds' from II Corinthians 10.4. At the other pole Agyin Asare most nearly adopts a 'concordance' approach, introducing many texts that deal with the same topic or use the same word. There are all manner of possible positions in between, although most would fall towards the Otabil end of the spectrum.

[margin note: Bible use diff by leaders]

The Bible is understood to tell *my* story; it explains who I am. Jason Alvarez speaks for them all when he says: 'I am what the Bible says I am; I can do what the Bible says I can.' (*28 April 01*) Likewise Agyin Asare: 'I don't know what your situation is, but I know what the Bible says.' (24 Sept. 00) The Bible is much more authoritative on me and my future than what others, or school reports, or medical bulletins, or bank statements, or the visa section of the US embassy, might say of me. The Bible is much more authoritative about me and my destiny than my present circumstances. This Christianity puts great stress on not being influenced by what you see or feel around you. Ignore your situation; you must rather believe what the Bible says. There is a hymn which I have heard sung by Lawrence Tetteh, Korankye Ankrah and Christie Doe-Tetteh, to the tune of 'Michael Row the Boat Ashore', with the following words: 'I'm not moved by what I see, Alleluia/I'm not moved by what I hear, Alleluia/I'm not moved by my circumstances, Alleluia/I'm only moved by the Word of God, Alleluia.' This is a stock motif in the churches studied here. Thus Jason Alvarez: 'If I were to ask my body, it would say "You are sick", but if I were to ask the Word, it would always tell you that "by his stripes you are healed". Who are you going to believe?' (*13 Jan. 01*) And Korankye Ankrah: 'I will hear what God is saying, and not look at situations.' (*13 Jan. 01*) All subscribe to this understanding of the Bible.[39]

---

[39] Here follow other expressions of this key idea. Chris Oyakhilome of Christ Embassy: 'I'm broke; you are looking at the wrong things, for the scriptures say, "my God supplies all things".' (*31 Mar. 01*) Isaac Anto: 'Never see the problem, but see the solution... don't

Agyin Asare expresses the same idea through his distinction between speaking intellectually and speaking spiritually (16 Sept. 00). He also makes a distinction between what is 'real' and what is 'true': 'Some things are real but not true. Reality is not the truth. The fact on the ground is that you feel sick, but "By his stripes you were healed." The fact on the ground, you are economically challenged, but "The Lord is my shepherd, there is nothing I shall want." The fact on the ground is that you have no money, but the Bible says, "My God shall supply all your needs according to his riches in glory"… Maybe the doctor says you are too old to have a child… but my Bible says "None shall be barren".' (9 Sept. 00) Tackie Yarboi of Victory Bible Church also makes the same point with his distinction of 'fact, not truth'.[40]

The Bible functions primarily as a repository of narratives, overwhelmingly of the miraculous, about (in what appears to be their order of importance) Abraham, Joseph, Elijah and/or Elisha, David, Daniel, Joshua, Moses and Job—effectively the champions of faith mentioned in Chapter 11 of the Letter to the Hebrews. The crucial element is not the miraculous in itself but that the narratives illustrate God's desire and ability to intervene to prosper his chosen followers. Thus the Bible is no mere historical record. It is addressed to *me* and to me *now*. 'If we come as they did in Bible days, we will receive as they did.' (Agyin Asare, 28 April 01)[41]

---

look at the situation. I will never allow the situation to bamboozle me' (*17 March 01*), and again 'Don't believe in your five senses; believe in the Lord Jesus Christ.' (*30 Dec. 00*) Ashimolowo: 'Speak God's word, not what you see. Don't pray the situation, pray the Word' (*28 Oct. 00*), and again: 'No longer be led by what you see', for 'what you see in spirit is what you get in reality.' (*17 Feb. 01*) Adamson Aromaegbe at WMCI: 'God, my body says I am sick, but I have received thy Word, and that Word is working right now.' (30 Oct. 00) Somuah Dapaah of Living Light Chapel: 'I'm not moved by what *they* say, I'm moved by what *God* says.' (*12 Aug. 00*) Agyin Asare: 'Don't look at your situation, look at Jesus.' (3 Feb. 01) Randy Morrison at Otabil's ICGC: 'Revelation knowledge has nothing to do with what you receive through your senses. We are taught to respond to what we see, hear, feel, [but] whatever God says to me, I'm going to believe it… What you see are facts. Facts can change; truth can never change.' (12 Sept. 00) Otabil deplores the situation when 'instead of walking by faith, you walk by what you see.' (4 March 01)

[40] Murdock actually claims that 'the essence of the entire Bible is Numbers 23.19' (Murdock, *31 Reaon People do not receive their Financial Harve$t*, Dallas: Wisdom International, 1997, 216). The text reads: 'God is not a man that he should lie, nor a son of man that he should change his mind. Does he speak and then not act? Does he promise and not fulfil?'

[41] The use of the Bible is thus performative, transformative, effective and effectual; see Coleman, *Globalisation*, 117–42. Oyedepo expresses it: 'The Bible is a Prophecy Bank. Anything said in it is directed at "*whosoever*". When you receive it, it becomes your own prophecy, surer than anything anyone else can prophesy. It is not only a Prophecy Bank, the Word is also a fountain of living waters, containing answers to all situations. All you

These biblical personages are used to illustrate various points. In the case of Abraham it is a vision or promise fulfilled, a covenant observed, faith rewarded with wealth. Joseph illustrates the need for a vision, but particularly the rapid transformation of fortune, so that in twenty-four hours one can go from being a nobody to a somebody—even to number two in the country. In referring to Joseph, phrases frequently heard are 'from prison to palace' and 'from pit to palace' (as at Winners', 'Don't mind where you are now. You may be in Potiphar's house today. Tomorrow you will be raised to your throne.' 24 Dec. 00). Elijah and Elisha routed enemies and performed miracles, and Elijah passed on a double anointing. David overcame odds, most spectacularly against Goliath, and was raised from shepherd boy to king (his transformation is often enhanced with the claim that he was an illegitimate son of Jesse—hence not worthy of consideration for the kingship). Daniel remained faithful through all trials and was brought safely to glory. Joshua miraculously crossed the Jordan which barred his progress, brought down the Walls of Jericho, and took possession of the Promised Land. Moses confounded Pharaoh and destroyed his persecutors at the Red Sea. Job, despite his trials, remained faithful and therefore was doubly rewarded. These are the major motifs that recur incessantly, although such a figure, once established as paradigmatic, can be used to illustrate related if subsidiary points. Other examples are Gideon, Samson, Hannah, Esther and less celebrated figures from the books of Kings; Jabez who prayed that his 'boundaries be increased' (I Chron 4.9–10) is a favourite. That they come predominantly from the Old Testament is obvious. When the New Testament is used, there are some miracles of Jesus that are particularly apposite, but probably more important than the Gospels are the Acts of the Apostles, with Peter's deliverance from prison (Acts 12) and the freeing of Paul and Silas (Acts 16) being particularly significant.[42]

Normally, too, the stories are taken in a fairly plain or commonsense understanding, although occasionally one finds more symbolic interpretations. At the opening of Korankye Ankrah's new premises Markwei preached such a sermon, even finding meanings in numbers.[43] Similarly Winners' Dele Bamgboye showed, through other texts, that five stones in

---

have to do is come and drink freely.' (*Prophetic Wings*, 56) Miller has noted that in what he calls North America's 'New Paradigm Churches' (e.g. John Wimber's Vineyard) the Bible similarly functions as a repertoire of life-changing experiences. (Donald E. Miller, *Reinventing American Protestantism: Christianity in the New Millennium*, Berkeley: University of California Press, 1997, esp. 123–33)

[42] James Saah's *Finger*, 74–93, contains a list of things to pray for, with their related texts; this well illustrates the overwhelming OT dependence in this Christianity.

[43] As, in his book, he finds meanings in colours; Markwei, *Silver Stones*, 31.

David's sling represented the Word of God, as did both the wood and the water of Elijah's altar (5 Nov. 00), thus proving that the Word of God can solve all our problems. These were virtuoso allegorical treatments of which the Alexandrian fathers would have been proud. Thus figurative interpretations can be found, but they are certainly not representative.

A standard example of charismatic use of the Bible is this Christie Doe-Tetteh sermon screened on 4 March 2001. Her theme was 'Who will not serve a God like this?' God gave Abraham a child when he was old. Moses could not speak but God used him to confound Pharaoh. God brought Joshua across the Jordan; he used Gideon, although from a small tribe, to break the altars of Baal; he raised up Jephthah, Deborah and Rahab; he made Joseph prime minister of Egypt; then (from the New Testament) he miraculously changed water to wine at Cana, and protected the woman taken in adultery. After dwelling on each example she repeated her refrain 'Who will not serve a God like this?'[44]

Ashimolowo used a similar list in a sermon entitled 'Praying to Get Results'. (*31 March 01*) Rebecca, Daniel and Hannah prayed successfully; Peter had iron gates opened for him (Acts 12); Samson prayed and killed more people in his death than when alive (Jg 14–16); Elijah prayed with spectacular results (I Kings 18); Nehemiah prayed and moved a king to supply him; Esther fasted and prayed, and thereby delivered a people; Job prayed, and his 'latter days were better than the former—that's your story!' This is an almost ideal type, in its heavy reliance on the Old Testament, with the New Testament illustrations coming from Acts and not the Gospels.

We can note other examples, offered almost at random. Agyin Asare, at the watchnight service on 31 December 2000, which he argued would be the year of divine intervention, used Sara, Moses, Ruth, manna in the wilderness (Ex 16. 12–35), Samson, Elisha, Peter finding tax money in the fish's mouth (Mt 17.24–27), and Paul on Melita (Acts 28. 3–5). Similarly Jason Alvarez treated Abraham, Moses, Joseph, Joshua, David, Elijah, Daniel, Paul, Peter and finally Jesus in a sermon on 'the Power of God to get up and keep going'. 'The key element that stands out; they learned how to persevere, get up and go again until they received their promise.'

Of course, there is a range of non-narrative passages (again, often used with considerable ingenuity) to impart the success or victory motif. The recurrent non-narrative passages include Ezekiel's vision of the dry bones (Ez 37), which unsurprisingly is not used to refer (as in the spiritual) to resurrection after death, but to the resurrection of dead finances, businesses, marriages here and now. Another is I Corinthians 2.9 'Eye

---

[44] See also her book, *Who would not Serve a God like This?*, Accra, Dot Publications, 1999.

hath not seen, nor ear heard... what God has prepared for those who love him', again reworked to apply to this life rather than to the next. There are frequent texts of encouragement: 'I know the plans I have for you, declares the Lord, plans to prosper you and not to harm you, plans to give you hope and a future' (Jer 29.11); 'Open your mouth wide and I will fill it' (Ps 81.10); 'He takes delight in the prosperity of his servant' (Ps 25.27); 'I will restore to you the years which the locust,... canker worm have eaten. You shall eat in plenty and be satisfied' (Joel 2.25–26); and 'There is hope for the future, declares the Lord.' (Jer 31.17)[45]

Other texts stress the need to look to the future, not to the past: 'Forget the former things; do not dwell on the past. See I am doing a new thing' (Is 43.18–19) and 'The latter glory shall outshine the former' (Hag 2.9); 'I press on...' (Phil 3.12–14) Texts emphasising the power and will of God to intervene are frequently cited. 'I am the Lord, the God of all mankind. Is anything too hard for me?' (Jer 32.27) 'God is not man that he should lie... Has he said it and will he not do it?' (Num 23.19)

God's covenant promises are recited, with the hearers the current recipients. Besides the classic faith gospel texts,[46] the following are frequently cited: 'If they obey and serve me and do what he commands, then they will spend their days in prosperity and pleasure' (Job 36.11); 'You shall serve the Lord your God and I will bless your bread and your water, and I will take sickness away from the midst of you' (Ex 23.25); 'He brought them forth also with silver and gold and there was not one feeble person among the whole people' (Ps 105.37); 'God will give power to get wealth' (Dt 8.18); 'It shall be a jubilee for you...' (Lev 25.8 10)

Many phrases are constantly invoked to reinforce the status of the Christian. 'God will make you the head not the tail... the top not the bottom' (Dt 28.13) is almost a mantra, which the congregation will take up after the first few words. Other frequent texts make the point that those who are lowly today will have a glorious future: 'The first shall be last and the last shall be first.' (Mk 10.31) Phrases can be wrenched wildly out of context if they can be forced into service to prove that the hearer will now move to another level: 'This is your time' (II Sam 18.21), 'Your servants will pass over' (Num 32.27), 'A thousand times more' (Dt 1, 11), even a merely geographical expression like 'To the other side' (Mk 6.45).

Jesus is obviously not as prominent as several OT figures, but some Gospel narratives such as the resurrection of Lazarus, the curing of the woman with a flow of blood, and the cure of the Syro-Phoenician woman's

---

[45] Otabil makes much of this text: 'This is the verse God wrote for me.' (*23 Aug. 01*) His radio programme is entitled, 'Believer's Voice of Hope'.
[46] These are Dt 28; Mk 11.23–24; Ps 103.1–3; Is 53.4–5 (= I Pet 2.24), Mk 10.29–30; Phil 4.19; III Jn 2; all are regularly heard in Ghana.

daughter are particularly apposite. The disciples' fruitless fishing until Jesus told them to 'put out into the deep and let down your nets for a catch' (Lk 5.3–6) is often cited. The parables of Jesus are not particularly significant (although that of the talents is used), nor is the Sermon on the Mount;[47] of Jesus's sayings 'I came that they might have life and have it more abundantly' (Jn 10.10) is probably the most significant. It is important that Jesus must not be understood to have been poor. Thus Christie Doe-Tetteh: 'Jesus was born in a manger, but didn't remain in a manger—so let your ideas of Jesus born in a manger change and grow.' (*27 Dec. 00*) Agyin Asare, alluding to the Magi bearing gifts, expresses it thus: 'Joseph and Mary may have been poor, but as soon as Jesus came into their lives money started coming in.' (Mt 2.10–11)[48] Owusu Bempa makes a distinction between John the Baptist and Jesus. The former did not eat properly, and was clothed in mere skins, but he 'pointed the way to Jesus, who lived well, was well dressed, and fed and clothed his workers well.' (31 Jan. 01)[49] This writer heard in a Catholic Church in Accra an attempt to capture the liberation theology motif that 'Jesus identified with the poor and hungry. Jesus shared the situation of the poor people of his day.' It would be almost unthinkable for this to be heard in a charismatic church.

Skewing message of Jesus

In such an eminently pragmatic Christianity texts are applied to the believer's life rather than used for speculation. Philippians 2.5–11 has been an important text in the history of Christianity for speculation on the nature of Christ. Bamgboye at Winners' interpreted the 'Every knee shall bow' of Philippians 2.10 to mean that 'the knee of accidents, financial disaster, lack, want etc.' would bow to the believer in Jesus. (19 Nov. 00) Otabil applied 'Let this mind be in you' (Phil 2.5) to the 'winning mind' of Jesus, for 'Christ was the greatest winner in life'. The statement that he 'emptied himself' (Phil 2.7) shows that winners can get down from their position to 'where the real action is'. 'Therefore God exalted him' (Phil 2.9) shows that 'you will succeed' here (*19 July 01*). Agyin Asare, preaching at Christmas on the Incarnation, uses it to stress that 'If God [could do that], then everything you design could be [accomplished] for you.' (30 Dec. 00) Korankye Ankrah uses the fact that 'You are sons' to show that, just a son has access to his father's fridge, you have access to the power and blessings of God. 'God gave us his son' (Jn 3.16) is used to show that if he gave us this, he will give us everything. Even the

---

[47] Although Otabil preached a whole series (of sixteen broadcast programmes) on the Beatitudes (Mt 5.1–12) in mid-2001.

[48] Agyin Asare, *Rooted*, 406, where the reference is given as Mt 1.10–11—a misprint.

[49] Although cf. J. Alvarez on II Cor 8.9: 'The blessings of Abraham are yours, because Jesus became a curse for me; He became poor so that you (through his poverty) might become rich.' (*18 Nov. 00*)

resurrection is not dwelt on as such; it is used to make the point 'You cannot keep a good man down'; he will rise to the top, very much like Joseph. (ACI, *22 April 01*) And at Winners': 'This is the month of the Resurrection. You can have a financial resurrection this morning. Before a pump begins to flow, you need to prime it to get free flow. By your tithes and pledges you will roll away your stone.' (1 April 01)

Not only are texts selected to expound the message of success and victory, but others reinforce the need to give. The text enjoining tithing is crucial (Mal 3.10). Further incentive is provided by texts emphasising that all we have was given to us by God anyway (Hag 2.8; I Chron 29.14). Texts emphasising the building of the first temple are frequently cited: the biblical play on words 'You build me a house [temple] and I will build you a house [dynasty]' (II Sam 7.5–16 and parallels) is often heard, given the meaning that if you give to the construction of the church, you will soon move out of rented accommodation in to your own home.[50] Great importance is placed on Solomon as someone who gave unstintingly to the construction of the temple, and was therefore rewarded with great wisdom and wealth. The value of Solomon's temple is often calculated: Agyin Asare variously estimates it at perhaps US $2 billion (12 May 01), or 'about $100 billion according to today's estimates'.[51] Elkanah Hanson at ACI estimated it at $700 billion (6 May 01) and Mike Murdock at $500 billion.[52] David, too, gave $32 billion for its construction, according to Adamson Aromaegbe at WMCI. (27 Oct. 00) Oyedepo calculates that David gave about $600 million of his own money to the temple.[53] Heward-Mills estimates that Solomon's annual income was $19 million.[54] If we are to honour God and therefore succeed like Solomon and David, our duties are clear—and the existence of all the new churches around Accra testifies to the effectiveness of this message.

Obviously one of the major problems for this Christianity is God's seeming delay in intervening on behalf of his faithful, and, as might be expected, texts are used to address this issue. The woman with the issue of blood (Mk 5.25) had been afflicted for twelve years before her fidelity brought her cure; the disciples had been fishing all night (Jn 21.1–4) before Jesus appeared; the man lying by the pool at Bethesda had waited thirty-eight years (Jn 5.5); and Lazarus was actually allowed to die (Jn 11.14) before Jesus intervened—which shows that no situation is irredeemable. At the wedding at Cana (Jn 2), 'Jesus kept the good wine

[50] The collection envelopes at ACI are inscribed with I Chron 29.3 and Eccles 11.6.
[51] Agyin Asare, *Rooted*, 406.
[52] Murdock, *Secrets*, 8.
[53] *Breaking Financial Hardship*, 68.
[54] Dag Heward-Mills, *Solomonic Success*, Accra: DgTP, 1997, 10.

till last. God has kept it for you this morning.' (Winners', 24 Dec. 00)
The Syro-Phoenician woman shows that persistence and patience will
even get the rules changed for you (Mk 7.24–30). Paul and Silas were
'praising God' in prison at midnight (Acts 16.25), the darkest time, when
their chains were struck off. The midnight motif is quite common, as is
its corollary 'Joy comes in the morning'. (Ps 30.5) Hannah is an OT figure whose patience similarly paid off. (I Sam 1)

text to calm womes

Other texts also deal with this issue of delay in various ways. Daniel
(Dan 10.10–14) is used to show that in fact our prayers have already been
answered, even if the result is not yet visible. (Otabil, *16 Aug. 01*) The
cursing of the fig tree, which needed a lapse of time for the results to
become evident (Mk 11.21), is sometimes used to make the same point.
The idea of God's good time, the proper season (Eccles 3), dovetails with
the Ghanaian traditional motif of 'God's time'. Joshua is told (Jos 1.10)
to prepare because 'in three days' his plan will take shape. A warning is
seen in Saul's impatience; his failure to wait (I Sam 12.8–14) meant that
he lost his kingdom. A significant related text is Joseph's words: 'You
meant it for evil, but God used it for good' (Gen 50.20), to make the point
of Romans 8.28: 'All things work together unto good.'

We could not leave the subject of recurring biblical motifs without noting how in the Bible the fate of enemies receives prominence. Esther is a
great text; not only are enemies routed and the righteous vindicated in
glory, but Mordecai is promoted Prime Minister and Haman is executed—Esther even inherits the house.[55] Similarly, Daniel is not only res-
cued from his fiery furnace and ennobled, but his enemies are cast into
the furnace in his place. (Dan 6.25) Psalm 23 ('The Lord is my shepherd')
is a staple, not only for the protection extended while walking through
'the valley of the shadow of death', but also just as much for the banquet
prepared 'in the presence of my foes'. Their being ultimately discomfited
is almost equally significant.

The biblical text itself is rarely read at any length. In fact, Catholic and
Anglican services would contain far more biblical reading, although
Korankye Ankrah and Christie Doe-Tetteh do have set readings like the
mission churches. Where the Bible is read, even when the sermon is going
to be given in Twi, it is surprisingly often read in English, mostly from the
King James Version.

These new churches are quite un-influenced by the historical (or criti-
cal) reading of the Bible, usually said to have begun with Strauss's *Life of
Jesus* (1835), which has profoundly affected mainline Christianity in the
West. The implications of this historical approach and its 'assured

---

[55] Saah, *Finger*, 22–53.

results' have been enormous: it has come to be accepted, for example, that the gospels are not eye-witness accounts but second- or third-generation faith testimony; that the Pentateuch is composed of different strands from different ages and authors, and thus reflecting various viewpoints which may or may not cohere; and that the prophets were not predicting the events of the Christian era but rather *were so understood* by the early Christians. The effects of this revolution have little or no influence in this charismatic sector of Christianity; narratives are assumed to be historically factual, texts are understood atomistically, and there is a presumption that all texts agree and cohere.

This absence of historical or 'critical' perspective does not make these churches 'fundamentalist' (a term best avoided, because of its special link with particularities in the North American scene), but it gives their use of the Bible a particular character, one very different from that characteristic of mainline churches of the West.[56] One way to highlight the characteristics of this approach is to note that it is almost the diametrical opposite of the liberal Protestantism associated with Adolf Harnack and strong in Europe up till the First World War. As the historical reading of the Bible became accepted, miracles and prophecies were downplayed, and Jesus came to be seen as a great teacher. In Ghana's new churches this writer has never heard Jesus presented as a teacher, and the Sermon on the Mount is only infrequently mentioned. The stress is on the miraculous, and the miraculous as it is available to the reader or hearer of today, in exactly the same way as the Bible recounts.

There is one insight of modern religious studies that this Christianity well illustrates. Scripture is a relational term; like husband or mother it has meaning only in relation to another. It is the community's persistence in according it an authoritative position in its life that constitutes a text as scripture. Thus 'scripture' is not an attribute of texts, but 'a human activity', one that is ongoing. 'No doubt their scripture to a mighty degree makes a people what they are. Yet one must not lose sight of the point that it is the people who make it, keep making it scripture.'[57] The implications of this realisation are coming to be acknowledged for all religions. For example, the Mishnah and Talmud have been almost universally viewed as commentaries on the Jewish Torah, whereas on deeper inspection their secondary or derivative appearance is revealed as just that—an *appearance*

---

[56] Of course, many Ghanaian charismatic leaders, when they descend to detailed biblical exposition, *are* fundamentalist in their interpretation—see Heward-Mills on the curse of Noah (*Unbeatable Prosperity*, Accra: Parchment House, 2000, 41–7) or Apostle Ahinful on prophecy (*Mirror*, 22 Dec. 01, 18), but the term is still best avoided.

[57] Wilfred Cantwell Smith, *What is Scripture? A Comparative Approach*, London: SCM, 1993, 18–19.

arising from the framework imposed upon them. In fact both the Mishnah and the Talmud are deeply original works, their novelty in some
cases quite startling. It is the prior assumption that they must be expounding the 'more authoritative' Jewish scripture that has obscured this. 'The
bulk of Jewish literature is in the form of commentary on scripture,
whether this form is always justified or not (often the pretence of commentary disguises a full-fledged original personal viewpoint).'[58] In fact,
in the case of both the Mishnah and the Talmud, 'Rather than seeing these
new works as commentaries on a preceding scripture, one might suggest
rather that each of them in its own way presents as it were the preceding
scripture, if at all, as a commentary on itself.'[59] So the 'scripturalising' of
a text has in many cases obscured, as much as it has revealed, the dynamics operative in the life of a religious community. Barton has written of
sacred texts that they 'tend to be semantically indeterminate, for they
have to be read as supporting the religious system to which they belong,
even at the expense of their natural sense.'[60] That insight helps us understand Ghana's charismatic Christianity less as a timeless distillate from
the scriptures than as a form of Christianity related specifically to certain
people in certain social conditions, who have tried to cope with those
conditions through a particular reading of the scriptures, just as every
other body of Christians has done before them.[61]

Summary

The issues raised here will recur below, but at this point some observations can be made. First, the pervasive emphasis on victory or success is
not simply to be identified with another debate on the 'victorious Christian life' which characterised some sectors of nineteenth-century Protestantism in the United States; that was a debate about the possibility of
living a sinless life.[62] In Ghana's new Christianity the 'victory' is above

---

[58] Moshe Greenberg, 'On Sharing the Scriptures' in Frank Moore Cross *et al.* (eds), *Magna-
lia Dei: the Mighty Acts of God: Essays on the Bible and Archeology in Memory of
G. Ernest Wright*, New York: Doubleday, 1976, 462, as cited in Smith, *What?*, 117.

[59] Smith, *What?* 114.

[60] John Barton, *People of the Book?* London: SCM, 1997, 61.

[61] I therefore find only minimally helpful such statements as: 'In the present day, it may be
that it is only in the newer churches that the Bible can be read with any authenticity and
immediacy, and that the Old Christendom must give priority to Southern voices', Jenkins,
Next Christendom, 217.

[62] See George M. Marsden, *Fundamentalism and American Culture: the Shaping of Twenti-
eth-Century Evangelicalism 1870–1925*, Oxford University Press, 1980, 72–80. On Easter
Sunday 2002 Otabil preached a sermon asking 'Can we live a sinless life? I believe we
can', which could be considered as joining that debate, but that is the only time I heard
such issues raised.

all in the economic sphere. It is justifiable to call this faith/prosperity gospel pervasive because it is not an incidental or an optional extra to this Christianity—it has been indispensable, for the seed faith element ('give and you will receive') has been the motor that has powered this entire explosion. All these buildings, pastors, programmes, vehicles, instruments and sound systems have had to be paid for, and in a situation of economic crisis. Van de Walle noted that, after the state, the aid business is now the biggest single employer in most African economies.[63] It may be that in Ghana Christianity is now the next biggest, and it is the faith/prosperity gospel that has made it all possible.

Secondly, it is apparent that healing has been displaced in importance by this shift to economic success. Naturally, healing forms part of the overall well-being—victory is over sickness as well—and services like Agyin Asare's can be devoted to it, but it is noticeable that specifically physical healing has become subsidiary.

Thirdly, this new Christianity is not marked by millennialism. There is almost no mention of the end times. Sometimes someone will refer to 'these last days', but more often this is meant in a restorationist sense (these are the days when signs and wonders or—as we see in the next chapter—the 'prophetic gifts' more generally are restored to the church) rather than alluding to the end of the world that we know. In fact, there is very little focus on heaven or hell, and no one I interviewed spontaneously mentioned them. Ghana's new Christianity bears on this world. Above all, no pre-millennial dispensationalism could be detected. Accra's Challenge Bookshop, founded decades ago by the Sudan Interior Mission, does stock books by dispensationalists like Ryrie and publishers like Eerdmans, Tyndale, Moody and Baker, and in mid-2002 was planning a major promotion of the LaHaye and Jenkins 'Left Behind' series which has become such a publishing phenomenon in the United States that it warranted a cover story in *Time*.[64] Pre-millennialism is not, however, a preoccupation of Ghana's charismatic Christians.[65]

---

[63] Van de Walle, *African Economies*, 58.

[64] The series by Tim LaHaye and Jerry B. Jenkins has sold 36 million copies: see *Time*, 1 July 2002. Marsden notes 'In the 1970s most fundamentalists, holiness groups, pentecostals and other evangelicals held some form of these premillennial views' (*Fundamentalism*, 239, n. 11), but despite the LaHaye and Jenkins phenomenon, it may be that even in the United States Pentecostalism is now jettisoning this premillennialism (see Margaret Poloma, 'The Millenarianism of the Pentecostal Movement' in Stephen Hunt (ed.), *Christian Millenarianism: from the Early Church to Waco*, London: Hurst, 2001, 169).

[65] Otabil (*20 Aug. 02*) referred to the early 1970s, when Ghana's Christians used to greet one another with 'Maranatha' ('come, Lord' from Rev 22.20) as part of a general millennial consciousness; he implied that that consciousness was a thing of the past.

Fourthly, evangelism or <u>soul-winning</u> does not receive <u>equal emphasis</u> <u>in all these churches</u>. Winners' regularly has evangelism drives, and Agyin Asare conducts crusades characterised by both evangelism and healing, but others are not noted for this. When Otabil mentions mission it is more in the sense of 'mission statement', such as would be produced by Unilever or General Motors.[66] Perhaps this is not unrelated to the previous point. Over the last century, zeal for mission has been particularly linked to pre-millennialism; where the latter weakens, the missionary drive has been hard to sustain.[67]

---

[66] See his sermon 'Mission Mindedness' in 'Becoming a Leader' series (*29 Aug. 02*).
[67] Marsden, *Fundamentalism*, 166–8.

4

DELIVERANCE AND THE PROPHETIC

African religion

We have argued that Ghana's new Christianity, as pioneered by Duncan-Williams, was the Nigerian form of the faith Gospel, and—allowing for variations—this is still the underlying orientation. However, before long other strains became important. Before we proceed, something must be said about the pre-Christian religious orientation and ritual process characteristic of southern Ghana.

In this pre-Christian religion reality consists of beings and objects charged with varying degrees and qualities of supernatural power.[1] There is a supreme being (*Onyame*) and lesser deities (*abosom*). Ancestors too are honoured; and other spirits dwell in rocks, rivers, trees, animals and various objects. In daily religious life more attention is paid to the lesser deities than to the supreme being, but all spirits have powers which in certain situations can be dangerous to human beings. Talismans (*asuman*) are also important. These gain their power from the deities and spirits, and are sometimes considered magical objects charged with personal forces that can be manipulated by secret formulae. The physical realm and the realm of the spirit are not separate from each other but are bound up in one totality: nothing is purely matter, since spirit infuses everything and changes occur as the result of one spirit acting upon another.

In this understanding causality is to be discerned primarily in the spiritual realm, although natural causality is not entirely disregarded. Destiny or fate (*nkrabea*) is important, as are all kinds of spiritual influences.

[1] For studies in the religion of southern Ghana see M. J. Field, *Religion and Medicine of the Ga People*, London: Oxford University Press, 1937; M. V. Gilbert, 'Rituals of Kingship in a Ghanaian State', PhD thesis, University of London, 1981; R. S. Rattray *et al., Religion and Art in Ashanti*, Oxford: Clarendon Press, 1927; Abamfo Ofori Atiemo, 'Mmusuyi and Deliverance: a Study of Conflict and Consensus in the Encounter between African Traditional Religion and Christianity', MPhil thesis, University of Ghana, Legon, 1995; and Kofi Asare Opoku, *West African Traditional Religion*, Accra: FEP International, 1978.

'A man's trading ventures may succeed as the right forces aid him, or be unsuccessful because someone is "spoiling" his work by using charms against him. It is impossible to turn in any direction and say of any matter that the gods and spirit-ancestors, or witches and bad *suman* (magical objects), have no part in it.'[2] This world is one of action and counteraction of potent forces; spirit acting upon spirit. A stronger or higher being can easily destroy or impair the weaker or lower; since humans are low beings, they can be controlled by the former.

A stronger or higher spirit acting negatively upon the spirit of man may affect the whole family, clan or state. It therefore becomes a central concern to avoid this or, where it is suspected to be imminent, ward it off quickly. The absence of such negative forces forms the idea of the good life. 'For the common man, religion is very largely the means of reinforcing life, of proper precautions against the powers which might destroy him.'[3] Deities are consulted to ward off this negative influence in important matters, but consultations are also used for lesser evils like failure to find a husband, infertility, giving birth to unhealthy offspring, and failure in business and education. Of course, deities may be manipulated by others, particularly to inflict evil; hence the preoccupation with witchcraft. Consulting at shrines serves normally to discover why individual persons or communities are suffering particular afflictions; the causes are usually divined in specific terms, and are almost always connected to the supernatural.

In religious rituals the concern is to preserve a cordial relationship with the supreme being, the deities and the ancestors. The belief underlying these rituals is that the destructive evil condition, event or action of a person or community is caused ultimately by supernatural forces and can mainly be restrained, corrected or totally eliminated by appropriate contact with these forces. The healthy individual or community is one that maintains this appropriate contact. Good behaviour is behaviour that ensures the continuing flow of positive influence from the benevolent supernatural forces; this influence will ensure prosperity and protection from evil. This prosperity includes long life, healthy offspring, and a good death. Conversely, evil deeds leave one open not only to the anger of good spiritual forces and the withdrawal of their benign influence, but to the actions of evil spiritual forces and one's physical enemies. In all this the extent of human responsibility is not perfectly clear.

[2] Williamson, *Akan Religion and the Christian Faith* (Accra: Ghana Universities Press, 1974), 96–7, cited in Atiemo, *Mmusuyi*, 17–18.
[3] Williamson, *Akan*, 105, cited in Atiemo, *Mmusuyi*, 29.

Deliverance

Much more could be said about pre-Christian Ghanaian religion, but even such a brief outline makes the deliverance phenomenon that became very prominent in the 1980s and early 1990s easier to understand. In one form, the preoccupation with evil forces gives paramount importance to Satan—who as the preceding outline indicates, is not part of Ghanaian religion. Satan is a Western missionary import, but one which, as Birgit Meyer has well shown, became central in much Ghanaian Christianity, often being considered the prince of all the negative spiritual and witchcraft forces of local religion.[4] This apotheosis of Satan is well exemplified in the continent-wide best-seller, Emmanuel Eni's *Delivered from the Powers of Darkness*.[5] Eni claimed to have been sucked down into the undersea life of evil spirits by marrying a woman from the spirit world. He became a ranking agent of Satan, performing all kinds of wicked deeds including several murders, until he met Jesus, when his life was transformed. Such confessional literature has become less ubiquitous, although such testimonies are still heard. In mid-2000 a Ghanaian evangelist called Kwaku Anim claimed to have been such an agent of Satan, until the police, taking him at his word, arrested him for some of the murders he claimed to have committed in Satan's name, whereupon he swiftly recanted and admitted that his stories had no substance.[6]

Even while the popularity of these confessions was at its height, the more common form in which evil spirits were encountered was the 'deliverance phenomenon'.[7] The basic idea of deliverance is that a Christian's progress and advance can be blocked by demons who maintain

---

[4] Meyer, *Translating*.

[5] Emmanuel Eni, *Delivered from the Powers of Darkness*, Ibadan: Scripture Union, 1987.

[6] Opong Agyare Checheku, 'From Witchcraft to Priesthood', *Pentecostal Voice* 1 (April–June 2000), 29–31; *Graphic*, 29 July 00, 1; 'Newsfile', Metro TV, 29 July 00. For a similar case of a self-confessed murderer at a crusade of Evangelist Emmanuel Apraku, see *Newsmaker*, 28 Aug.–4 Sept. 00, 3. (At the same Apraku rally two children, aged six and eight, confessed to killing 128 people by the use of witchcraft.) A self-professed witch at JCPC (19 Dec. 01) explained how she used her witchcraft to influence males to sleep with their own daughters; to cause infertility; to turn her brother into an elephant; and to change victims into fowls and pigs before killing and eating them; she confessed to killing over 300 people through witchcraft. She claimed to have received her powers from her paternal grandmother at the age of five (see *Spectator*, 29 Dec. 01, 12). Leonard Soku, *From the Coven of Witchcraft to Christ*, Accra: the author, rev. edn. 2000, is completely in the Eni mould (Soku is a graduate of Trinity, Accra's mainline seminary).

[7] See Gifford, *AC*, 97–109, and literature listed there. Additional books include Stephen Adu-Boahen, *Deliverance from Demons*, Kumasi: the author, 1999; S. Y. Kwami, *Deliverance; a Scriptural Approach*, Accra: the author, 1998; Wisdom K. Ayitey, *Broken Chains*, Accra: the author, 2001.

some power over him, despite his having come to Christ. The Christian may have no idea of the cause of the hindrance, and it may be through no fault of his own that he is under the sway of a particular demon; this can result from a curse on his ancestors or ethnic group. To diagnose and then to bind and exorcise the demon requires skill, and a special institution— the prayer camp or prayer centre—evolved to cater for this activity. Here the condition was normally diagnosed by means of a questionnaire. Supplicants were asked what dubious services they had attended; what talismans they had worn; what incisions they had received; what rites they had undergone; whom they had slept with; what shrines were in the family; what they had dreamed; what names they had received; what vows had been made on their behalf or that of ancestors—and so on, sometimes for pages.[8]

In the early 1990s such prayer camps cropped up everywhere, the best known being Owusu Tabiri's Bethel in Sunyani, and Macedonia and Canaan in Accra.[9] All were associated with dominant figures, but most were linked to classical Pentecostal denominations (most often the Church of Pentecost), though at their fringe rather than at the centre. The vast majority of those attending are women; they are from all denominations and none, and some researchers claim that they are from all social classes. Many draw attention to the fact that in the early 1990s user fees were placing health care out of the reach of most people, whereas these camps were free, but others do not consider that financial constraints are a significant issue.[10] Moreover, studies have shown that more important than health problems were business concerns. People flocked to camps for issues relating to marriage, children, visas, employment, lawsuits, education, accommodation, bad dreams, demons and witchcraft.

It is probably significant that in Ghana's economic straits the faith gospel by itself was not bringing the health and wealth promised, and therefore finding the blockages responsible for keeping one in poverty and sickness became very important. Besides, the religious mentality

---

[8] See Gifford, *AC*, 97–100.
[9] For Prayer Camps see Rita Acquah, 'The Church of Pentecost Prayer Camps: a Study of the Macedonia, Paradise and Salvation Prayer Camps', BA thesis, University of Ghana, Legon, 1997; Kwasi Addo Sampong, 'The Growth of Prayer Centres in Ghanaian Christianity: the Quest for Health and Wholeness', MTh thesis, Regents Theological College, 2000; J. N. Tetteh, 'The Dynamics of Prayer Camps and the Management of Women's Problems: a Case Study of Three Camps in the Eastern Region of Ghana', MPhil thesis, University of Ghana, Legon 1999; E. Kingsley Larbi, *The Search for Salvation: the Case of Pentecostalist Prayer Camps and Prayer Centres in Ghanaian Christianity*, Accra: CPCS 2001, 1–12; E. Kingsley Larbi, *Pentecostalism: the Eddies of Ghanaian Christianity*, Accra: CPCS, 2001, 367–418.
[10] Tetteh, *Dynamics*, 106.

underlying the camps, with its emphasis on demons and witchcraft, had always been resisted by the mainline churches; only now, with the acceptability conferred on this worldview by the charismatic explosion, could Christians flock to camps openly rather than going stealthily to traditional shrines by night. All commentators draw attention to the continuity between the camps and the traditional shrines, some virtually identifying them with each other.

At the same time as the prayer camps proliferated, videos manifesting similar thinking and concerns became very popular. Stories dealing with power, riches, beauty, supernatural forces (often Mami Wata, a deity half woman and half sea-creature, sometimes referred to as 'Queen of the Coast'), violence, ritual murder, dreams and communication with the dead all proliferated in cheap videos, which were sold on the roadside and screened in cinemas and on TV. Many of these were from Nigeria.[11] Lurid posters advertising them covered walls—competing for space with ones advertising charismatic crusades and conventions. Birgit Meyer has written illuminatingly of the link between these popular videos and Pentecostalism—and has often made the point that both deal with the same issues and respond to the same forces.[12]

As well as the popular videos, Ghana's tabloid press thrive on this religious imagination. Remorselessly *Flash, Love and Life, Anomaa Nsem, P&P (People and Places), Top Story, Newsmaker, Love and Joy, Top Model, Hello, Exciting Ebony* and *New Ghanaian* carry (though not all to the same extent) stories about spiritual forces and their pervasive influence. In these stories and in purported news items spirits force people to act in certain ways; supernatural powers enable special humans to perform incredible exploits; animals act under spiritual influence; juju ('African electronics', Ghanaians often call it) is used for all sorts of nefarious ends; juju men affect or even steal penises spiritually; killing is achieved by ritual means; women recount their exploits as witches; others covenant with or sleep with spirits, turn into animals, die from curses or are cursed so that they give birth to monsters; family members cause ills spiritually; dwarfs bring misfortune; people kill relatives for wealth or power; humans descend to the underworld. Whether these are serious reports or thought up in the newspaper office is beside the point. The tabloids sell, and both express and influence widely-held conceptions.

---

[11] One columnist complained that 85% of the Nigerian video films found on Ghana's TV stations were home-made videos not permitted on Nigerian TV; *Spectator*, 28 July 01, 9. See also Adewale Maja-Pearce, 'Onitsha Home Movies', *LRB*, 10 May 2001, 24–6.

[12] See, e.g., Birgit Meyer, 'The Power of Money: Politics, Occult Forces, and Pentecostalism in Ghana', *ASR* 41 (1998), 15–37.

Witchcraft remains a serious issue in Ghana. Often news items record punishments or death meted out to supposed witches; after the Accra stadium tragedy in May 2001 resulting in the death of 126 football fans a woman in Ho was lynched for supposedly using her witchcraft to cause the disaster.[13] Camps exist where witches are banished, often for life— Gambaga (dating back to 1870), Duabone, Tendang, Kukuo, Ngani and Kpatinga.[14] Concerned Ghanaians themselves speculate on the modern spread of belief in witchcraft and its baneful influence.[15] It is common for political figures to be rumoured to use spiritual means to achieve or preserve power. Many are mere rumours, but interestingly the dismissed Minister of Youth and Sport, at his trial in mid-2001 for misappropriating US $46,000, tried to accuse members of the Ghana Football Association of setting him up; three had come to him asking for 20 million cedis for 'juju' to beat Sudan in a World Cup qualifying match; he had given them only 5 million, which he claimed had turned them against him.[16]

The rise of deliverance thinking did not go unchallenged within the charismatic churches. Many thought it easily led to extremes, but the pressure was so strong that all had to go along with it. So Duncan-Williams's ACI has deliverance sessions every Tuesday and Saturday, and Otabil's ICGC has a 'solution centre' every Thursday—deliverance in all but name. Even the Catholics had their equivalent in Father Frempong, until he was suspended in early 2000 (although, as remarked above, not for his deliverance activities). The prayer camp phenomenon peaked about 1995, since when it has subsided somewhat; not all camps have survived. Many signboards advertising such camps can still be seen around Accra, and indeed one passes about fifteen on the road from Accra to Kumasi. The problem again seems to have been that they did not achieve the results expected, in the same way as the faith gospel earlier did not deliver but needed to be supplemented with deliverance. As Agyin Asare has remarked, 'How many times can you deliver someone?'[17]

---

[13] *Graphic*, 22 June 01, 17; see also *Times*, 19 Aug. 00, 1; *Mirror*, 21 April 01, 1; *Guide*, 18–24 Oct. 00, 1.

[14] *Mirror*, 5 May 01, 19 and 5 Aug. 00, 19; *Graphic*, 29 June 00, 32; *BBC Focus on Africa*, Oct.–Dec. 00, 24–25.

[15] A. Afrifa, 'Telling it Straight', *Chronicle*, 25–26 April 01, 2 and 2–3 May 01, 2; Tina Aforo-Yeboah 'Murder in the Name of Witchcraft', *Spectator*, 24 April 01, 13. In a seminar on witchcraft at the Tamale Institute of Cross Cultural Studies one of the participants, Jon Kirby, was reported to have stated that witchcraft accusations had become more widespread among the Konkombas and Dagombas since the 1950s (Roger Gocking, 'The Witchcraft Syndrome', *West Africa*, 16–29 March 1998, 366).

[16] *Daily Guide*, 10 July 01, 8.

[17] Chigbundu admits this problem with deliverance in *I Believe in Deliverance: Deliverance made Easy*, Benin City: Voice of Freedom, 1995, viii–ix, but hardly solves it.

However, although the religious imagination evident in Christian deliverance has close similarities to Ghana's pre-Christian religion, the way it was expressed was very much influenced by Western gurus—Derek Prince, Peter Wagner and Rebecca Brown—and by Nigerians like Abraham Chigbundu, whose books are found on stalls all round Accra.[18]

The deliverance phenomenon has not disappeared. It is noteworthy that on his return from studies overseas the ordained Presbyterian Dr Emmanuel Martey, author of *African Theology: Liberation and Inculturation*, set out to teach courses on deliverance at Trinity College, Ghana's mainline seminary, and instituted deliverance seminars for the Presbyterians, Methodists and Anglicans.[19] He would claim that he has not changed his focus, deliverance being for him just one aspect of holistic liberation. Yet it is legitimate to distinguish between a theology that uses socio-political categories to address structural and systemic ills, and one that stresses spiritual causality. The fact that Martey sees little difference testifies to the powerful and persistent pull which deliverance thinking exercises in Ghana.[20]

If deliverance thinking and activity persist, they have nevertheless shifted their institutional base somewhat, from the prayer camp to the prophet. The issues remain the same—husbands, children, success, wealth, jobs, promotion, visas—and there is the same understanding that their lack indicates demonic blockages. However, the blockages tend no longer to be identified by functionaries through questionnaires; a man of God is now able through his special anointing to identify and destroy your blockage and ensure your blessed destiny without your speaking— indeed some will not allow the supplicant to speak. Winners' founder,

[handwritten margin note: deliv thinkin shifts from prayer camp to prophet]

---

[18] Again, it may be that Africa influenced Derek Prince, who spent time in Kenya. Peter Wagner was obviously influenced by his sixteen years as a missionary in Bolivia. Tabiri is unabashed about his debt to Derek Prince, even stating that he 'got the idea' of 'breaking' (his form of deliverance) from Prince (interview, 26 Feb. 01). Challenge Bookshop, having done so much to spread deliverance (Asamoah-Gyadu, *Renewal*, 244), later refused to stock Rebecca Brown.

[19] Emmanuel Martey, *African Theology: Inculturation and Liberation*, Maryknoll, NY: Orbis, 1994; idem, 'Deliverance Ministry in the Church; a Theological Assessment', *TJCT*, IX (1999), 18–25; idem, 'The Importance of Fasting for the Deliverance Ministry', *TJCT*, VII (1997), 44–55.

[20] Pauline Walley, a Ghanaian based in New York, conducted a week-long ('certificate granting') School of Deliverance at Legon on 16–22 July 2001. Her book *Pulling down Satanic Strongholds: War against Evil Spirits* (New York: PWCC, 2000), about witches and witchcraft, has a foreword by Bill Hamon, one of the promoters of the new prophetic movement in the United States. The banner across the stage, at her Legon seminar, proclaiming 'On Mt Zion shall be deliverance… and the House of Jacob shall possess their possessions' (Obadiah 17), shows that this ministry at least has no difficulty in combining three of the most important themes of contemporary Ghanaian Christianity: possessing, deliverance and the prophetic.

David Oyedepo, exemplifies this shift to the prophetic. Earlier he would have presented himself as a faith teacher (we have already mentioned how he establishes his credentials by making his links to Hagin and Copeland explicit) but in 2000 he was repackaging himself as a prophet, and making this designation retroactive to 1981.[21] He writes: 'Whatever has come to a standstill in your life (just like the dry bones in the time of Ezekiel), it will not require anything more than a prophetic word to gain motion again.'[22] So the fundamental orientation is unchanged; Christianity is still about progress and success, but the crucial means now is prophetic gifts. The progress and success may be blocked demonically, but your 'instrument of release' is now the 'prophetic unction'. Indeed it now seems indispensable: 'Every act of release is committed to prophets to execute.'[23]

So by 2000 virtually everything in Ghana had to be prophetic.[24] But again the rise of the prophet in West Africa cannot be totally dissociated from wider developments. In charismatic Christianity worldwide there has been a significant move to the prophetic. Paul Cain (and 'the Kansas City prophets'), Bill Hamon, Rick Joyner and Peter Wagner are all names linked to the restoration (as they would see it) of the office of the prophet—although this author has not seen their books in Accra in anything like the quantity of those by Prince, Brown and Bubeck for deliverance.[25] Ghana's burgeoning prophets are not exactly the same prophetic figures as the Americans write about, but links exist, and 'prophets' from abroad come to Ghana to give workshops promoting the phenomenon.[26]

Prophet Salifu

In Accra, the movement to the prophetic is widely evident, but we shall deal with it by focusing on certain examples, Salifu in particular.[27] Elisha

[21] David Oyedepo, *Riding on Prophetic Wings*, Lagos: Dominion, 2000, 7.

[22] Ibid., 15.

[23] Ibid., 19–20.

[24] Apostle Kwamena Ahinful argues that congregations are now forcing their pastors to prophesy: 'Our African community wrongly equates "powerfulness" of a pastor with his "prophecies". So to be a "powerful" pastor is to be a "spiritual reader"' (*Mirror*, 4 Nov. 00, 16).

[25] Bill Hamon, *Apostles, Prophets and the Coming Moves of God*, Shippensburg, PA: Destiny Image, 1997; Rick Joyner, *The Prophetic Ministry*, Charlotte, NC: Morning Star, 1997; C. Peter Wagner, *Apostles and Prophets: the Foundation of the Church*, Ventura CA: Regal Books, 2000.

[26] A three-day prophecy school in Kumasi featured prophet Jim Smith, an Anglican from England (*Crusading Guide*, 26 June–2 July 01, 5).

[27] For Vagalas Kanco of Vineyard Chapel, see Asamoah-Gyadu, *Renewal*, 247–57 and 261–2. Another famous prophet is Emmanuel Kwaku Apraku of King Jesus Evangelistic

Salifu Amoako takes his name from Evangelist Francis Amoako, sometimes credited with beginning this prophetic tendency in Ghana. Since
1994 he has been operating at the Orion Cinema at Nkrumah Circle, and
is gradually establishing his prophetic ministry—at first loosely conceived—into a church, Alive Chapel International. His following is
much poorer than other churches, consisting largely of women (and it is
obvious that marriage is their largest existential problem), and although
the sermon is mostly preached in English, the rest of the service is in Twi.
His basic message is roughly the same as others we have studied: Christianity is about wealth—'If you serve God for two years and remain the
same, you are not serving real God, but a devil God.' (20 Jan. 00) Here it
was plain from the context that the expected changes were financial.
'Many mighty businessmen with hardly food to eat are sitting here
tonight. You are coming out tonight!' (23 Jan. 01) The congregation are
made to shout 'My days of shame, reproaches, sickness, poverty are
over. My days of prosperity, success, health are here.' (17 Sept. 00) Each
must say to his neighbour 'You are the next rich man in Ghana. You are
going to the other side where there is prosperity, honour.' (20 Jan. 01)
'Grab your neighbour and say "I refuse to fail. I will never fail in life."'
(23 Jan. 01) They then tell their neighbours 'I am the next millionaire in
Ghana.' (1 Oct. 00) Again they can be confident of this because of their
special destiny: 'I believe what God says I am. Devil, you won't cheat me
out of it. What God says I am, I am. Where God says I go, I go. Where
God says I reach, I reach.' (19 Nov. 00) There is much motivational
preaching in this: 'Tonight the way you think about yourself is going to
change' (20 Jan. 00); 'People who insult you today, God will tell them to
salute you tomorrow.' (24 Dec. 00) Perhaps because of a less affluent clientele, Salifu has to place more emphasis on the present situation of lack
or hardship: 'God must bring you to zero so he can bring you to hero'
(28 Oct. 00) and 'Demons attack only those with a future.' (22 Jan. 00)
   Since the basic message is the same, the biblical texts are also roughly
the same as we saw above. The Bible has in fact only limited material

Ministry at Madina, who raises the dead with holy oil, lemons and his handkerchief
exhibiting the photograph of Jesus. One German he cured of AIDS has bought him a
Mercedes. He is a regular on 'Channel R' and 'Peace FM'. At his crusades witches con-
fess (*Top Model*, 1–8 Aug. 00, 1–6; *Top Story*, 62, undated, 4 and 63, and 25 Sept.–
1 Oct. 00, 3–4; *Newsmaker*, 28 Aug.–4 Sept. 00, 3. Another Most Senior Prophet, Philip
Acquah of the Church of Bethesda at Anyaa, Accra, is reported to have instructed the
youth to write all their problems on pieces of paper, which were collected to be burnt—
the ritual symbolising the burning away of their problems. It was reported that 'fire from
heaven' descended to light the paper before the Prophet could do so (*Top Story*, 29 Jan.–
4 Feb. 01, 4).

relating specifically to demons—it was mainly after the Babylonian exile (586–539 BC) that Israel was exposed to thinking in terms of evil spirits. There are a few Old Testament passages which illuminate the idea of generational curses, an important concept enabling both deliverance camps and prophets to explain blockages. In the synoptic gospels Jesus is sometimes presented as an exorcist, and there are a few such texts in the Epistles, e.g. Ephesians 6.12 and II Corinthians 4.4. Of more use are the narratives of the call of the prophets, which are used to give status to these modern prophets, understood as seers or diviners of hidden realities. This is evident at Isaac Anto's International Christian Miracle Centre (ICMC) where a banner over the platform proclaims: 'Surely God will do nothing without revealing it to his prophets?' (Amos 3.7) The biblical prophets are thus seen not as champions of social justice (as they tend to be in Latin American or South African liberation theology) but as traditional African religious professionals: diviners of spiritual causality who, moreover, are endowed like Elijah or Elisha with the special gifts to control it.[28]

The services at Alive Chapel include the basic elements mentioned above—praise and worship, the offering, a long sermon. The praise and worship are exuberant and unrestrained. The choir of about forty, largely women, who vary their costumes almost weekly, is probably the best in any of the churches we are considering; they (along with the instrumentalists, groups and soloists) are largely responsible for ensuring the almost frenzied mass participation. The music draws members of the congregation to dance unrestrainedly below the stage (Salilfu can call on them to remove shoes and anoint their feet, and command 'prophetic dancing'), and it is not uncommon for others to show their appreciation by mounting the stage to put banknotes down the collars of singers. However, there are differences here. The sermon is not the climax of the service—in contrast to most others, but similar to Winners'. It is followed by the ministration of the prophet, and then comes a lengthy period when he is remunerated. The prophet frequently changes his mode of ministering, which may involve moving around singling people out for treatment, remaining on the stage and calling up groups of people, 'slaying in the spirit' entire sections of the cinema, dowsing rows of people in oil, leading the congregation in rituals—everything is done with the maximum of frenzy and participation, and normally accompanied by the band to an accelerating

[28] One text admirably combines these motifs: 'Believe his prophets and you shall prosper' (II Chron 20.20). Pauline Walley, *Receive and Maintain your Deliverance on Legal Grounds*, London: PWCC, 1996, 61–91, argues that many Old Testament figures lost their standing because of 'demonic contamination', thus reinterpreting swathes of OT literature through the prism of the demonic.

tempo. Frenzy is positively encouraged: 'Before you take your seat, jump, clap, shout, scream', Salifu urges. (24 Dec. 00) Before ministering he may shout 'Get ready!' up to twenty times, or 'You shall receive power!' up to five times. (20 Jan. 01) Some in the congregation have whistles, as at a football match, and even while he speaks he is continually interrupted with shouts of 'Powerful! Powerful!' There is great physicality about this—at one evening service he was actually hoisted on the shoulders of the throng on the stage—and a real danger of people in a state of frenzy (exuberance rather than possession) doing themselves and others harm; the prophet is always surrounded by security guards who protect him.

Spirits, witches and ancestral curses are discerned at every turn. Enemies are detected everywhere, and need to be countered. The prophet will even pronounce death on them; referring to the death of Uzziah (Is 6.1), Salifu exclaimed 'Somebody is going to die tonight... Any person trying to do you down will die tonight. Some people around you are not proper. These people will die tonight... If you refuse to kill them, they will kill you.' (22 Jan. 01) Moral issues hardly ever arise; evils are caused by spiritual forces that require diagnosis and defeat by an anointed man of God. This means that the entire ministry is predicated on the gifts of Salifu; because of his special 'anointing' he is able to diagnose problems, cancel curses and effect blessing. He shouts, 'Take it!', 'I release it on you!' or 'Receive it!', and all respond 'I receive it!' Again we meet the paradox that although the only thing necessary is the Bible ('If you knew the Bible, the sky would be your limit', 28 Jan. 01), it is only through the revelation to someone like Salilfu that we can understand the Bible properly (so many have not prospered because 'they didn't take instruction from the man of God').[29] Although Salifu has a large team of assistants, he himself is indispensable; when he travels overseas, as he does increasingly and for weeks or months at a time, the numbers at home noticeably decline. It is *his* gifts that people come for.

As is the case at Winners', Salifu indulges in several rituals. He uses both oil and water. He has special services at which people bring passports or, if they do not have one, passport photos of themselves, which he anoints for visas. (His congregation obviously includes those who would have the most difficulty in persuading a Western embassy they have a skill that might be needed in the West or a genuine intention to return to

---

[29] The same identification is made by Duncan-Williams preaching at Salifu's Alive Chapel: 'Your level of power is determined by your knowledge or understanding of the scriptures.... I came along with some of my books and tapes, both audio and video. Invest your money in the Word of God.' (2 Oct. 1998)

Ghana.) On 28 January 2001 Salifu asked about thirty people what they wanted to own. Replies included a company, a photo studio, a 15-wheeler truck, a block of apartments, a fishing vessel, an import-export company, a restaurant—one even said an airport. Then all anointed their hands and laid hands on their desire 'in the realm of the spirit'. They had to claim it in prayer, and tell witches and wizards to return what they had stolen; 'I'm taking it back, before I leave today!' Then the prophet declared the year to be one of 'building houses'. All had to take out a key, 'a token and symbol of this new house'—and no ordinary residence but 'a five- to seven-bedroom house, with a "boy's house"'. Each then anointed his or her key with oil, and on the count of three, turned the key as if in a lock 'to symbolise taking possession'. Then all took off their shoes and anointed their feet, and were told to go and walk on what they wanted— 'car, business, land, because God would honour his word' (the reference here was to Joshua 14.9, which talks of possessing the land one's feet have trod). Then all had to change their seats in the auditorium, to symbolise that 'all conditions had changed'.[30]

Again, and to a degree not equalled in the other churches we are considering, the element of remunerating the prophet for his gifts is undisguised. Here thirty or forty mount the stage to give testimonies every Sunday—not directly, but relayed through a pastor. Immediately all who testify place money in a basket. The fundraising can sometimes be performed under real pressure, almost blackmail—and sometimes with substantial results, as when one woman deposited 500,000 cedis (in gratitude for a £7,000 car she had acquired in London).

Salifu is the author of various books but only attendance at his church can give some idea of the Christianity he represents.[31] Consider this

---

[30] One Sunday when Salifu was away (17 Sept. 2000), the assistant pastor had all women open handbags and hold them out in front; men were to put their hands in their pockets. Then he declared: 'I release finances'. Later all had to hold up their right shoe, so 'it may take you where your breakthrough is.'

[31] Salifu has written four books: *From Ignorance to Knowledge* (1997), *Your Angel will Come* (1999), *Vision and Provision* (2000), *Power to Make Wealth* (2001)—all published by the author's Alive Publications. The first is a standard faith gospel text; the word (knowledge) will bring success, plenty, power (argued from Job, Abraham, Joseph, Daniel, Joshua, David and Elijah). The second is a recapitulation of biblical teaching about angels. The third is motivational, its theme well expressed as follows: 'You cannot fail. You are a winner. As a child of God you are destined for victory and a stranger to failure. Your victory was determined some two thousand years ago. See your vision and wait for its fulfilment. It may tarry, but in the end you will have cause to praise God and rejoice over every situation. Remember that you are fighting a winning battle.' (p. 52) We will return to the fourth below in Chapter 6. None of these books gives any suggestion of the degree of his preoccupation at services with spiritual agency, or the sheer exhilaration engendered.

session of 24 December 2000. After his sermon, Salifu called up a woman who had to be helped on to the platform and was obviously very ill. He had a revelation that she was to die within three days. He saw that she had snake and a lizard in her stomach; the snake was drinking her blood, and the lizard was eating her intestines. This was caused (spiritually) by a rival with whom she had recently fought over a man ('Is this true?' 'Yes, it is'). The prophet pronounced this fate reversed, and called for someone with a camera to take a photo of the woman because in five days, after her recovery, she would be unrecognisable. He then called out a pregnant woman who had been married for four years but with no sign of a child, and had been HIV positive. The prophet had previously treated her, reversing this condition (he claimed that tests showed she was now negative) and had prophesied a son for her (hence her present pregnancy). He then called up a man for whom he predicted great riches through a printing business. Next he pointed to a woman in the congregation (four or five vied with each other to be the one he was singling out) and told her that at that very moment a car was coming for her from Germany. At this point he put oil on the lectern and called out all those who wanted to 'sow seed' for foreign currency; about eighty went up, throwing bundles of 20,000, 30,000 and 50,000 cedis on to the stage. As they came to touch the lectern, some seemed as though they could not let go, others recoiled as though they had touched an electric cable (one young man performed a backward somersault—one might question its spontaneity but not its dramatic effect). Then Salifu repeated the process for those who wanted to 'sow seed' for a car (about eighty went up). While they were all touching the lectern, Salifu was shouting 'Fire! Fire! Holy Ghost! Receive it!' Then he repeated the exercise for those who wanted a financial breakthrough (about 300 went up). By now the stage near the lectern was covered with banknotes.

Then he called for a testimony from a plumpish man—one of twins—over whom Salifu had prophesied some time before ('when he was as thin as I am') that a white man would take him up. A gold dealer had come, and the brother was abroad already (it was difficult to follow all the testimony due to the shouting and applause). At this point Salifu led the congregation in singing 'God you are wonderful'. He then called on ten to come forward and pledge one million cedis each; in fact twelve responded, so he called for another three (he ended up with sixteen). A Nigerian pastor on the stage with him, Abraham Chigbundu (see below, pp. 100–1), prayed over them: 'Your story will change into glory... I release it to you, your finances, business, marriage... You won't regret, you will prosper beyond your imagining.'

A footballer was called up, and as Elijah's mantle fell on Elisha, so the footballer was promised that he would receive the mantle of Samuel Osei Kuffour of Bayern Munich, one of Ghana's current stars.[32] The footballer began running on the spot, then round the stage, and finally he fell amid all the notes, thrashing around as though in a fit, kicking up banknotes like leaves before gusts of wind—a spectacular display. The next to be called was a pastor about to go to Switzerland to preach a crusade that Salifu himself could not fit in. The pastor lay down, was anointed and given the power to cure cancer.

Now Salifu called for the offering, telling the congregation to stretch their notes out (they were forbidden to crumple them in their fist to prevent others seeing the value), and he then told them to put the other hand in pocket or bag and bring out another note of the same value (thus, in theory, doubling the offering at one stroke). He chanted to the money 'Bye-bye. Come back.' About 200 tithers went into the aisle to pass forward their tithes (the congestion allows no other method), and all brought out their handkerchiefs and oil. Salifu prayed for 'the oil of influence, the oil of performance', and said 'I release this anointing in you in the name of Jesus... After anointing, your cup will run over, you will prepare a table before your enemies.' Then he 'soaked the handkerchiefs in the blood of Jesus'. Chigbundu called forth evidence 'to be seen in children, cars, visas', and commanded all curses to be 'returned to sender'.

All this was done with humour, deft personal touches, and wonderful dramatic effect. The fundraising was conducted without any reticence or embarrassment, and that part of the service alone lasted for the final two-and-a-half hours.[33]

Consider another service, on 28 October 2000. After a sermon on 'Loose him and let him go' (Jn 11.2, a key text for deliverance Christianity), Salifu led the praying: for doorways to be opened (relating to finance, family welfare, obtaining a husband etc); against a premature death; against sickness ('by the end of this prayer that sickness must go'). He called up a girl who wanted to commit suicide, who he said was possessed by the 'spirit of death'; all the pastors huddled round her, and she was exorcised with the aid of physical pummelling. He detected a water spirit in one woman (and instructed all in the congregation to clench their right fist in the shape of a gun; all then repeatedly shot at this spirit,

---

[32] This was how it appeared, although amid the clamour it was impossible to follow what was being said with certainty.

[33] In February 2001 the *Chronicle* took Salifu to task for 'extorting money' by preaching on Is 45. 1–3 ('I will give you the treasures of darkness, riches stored in secret places') and commanding women to bring their handbags to the stage for anointing so that they would be blessed with hidden treasure the next day (8–12 Feb. 01, 6).

making a deafening noise). Another woman was said to be possessed by 120 spirits, and all stretched out hands to pray and deliver her. Another was declared to be married to the River Pra; another was married to the marine spirit 'Queen of the Coast'; another had a snake spirit in her; another had a black cobra spirit. At this stage three women were rolling and writhing on the stage, with pastors and minders restraining them. The playing of music increased this frenzy. Salifu had his handkerchief (his symbolic mantle) in his hand, touching people with it, while many in the congregation waved their own handkerchiefs.

Then a man involved in witchcraft (only women had been singled out up to this point) was said to have eight wives pregnant in the spirit realm, who included crocodile spirits and the spirits of rats (which were cast out). Then Salifu picked out a girl in the front rows and declared that the rats had gone into her; she immediately appeared possessed, and we were all urged to pray hard so that these rats should not enter us. The man was then told that his penis was a snake, which would bite any woman with whom he had sex; it had to be treated, and while he lay on the stage his trousers were loosened and oil was poured on his penis. One really forlorn pregnant woman who admitted she had no husband was told she had been impregnated by a spirit taking the form of a man; she had three snakes in her belly, not a baby at all. It was destined that she would die within a year during an operation to remove the snakes, but the prophet annulled this fate.

One woman was told that she had a snake inside her; the pastors gathered round, with hands on her stomach; my translator expected to see the snake drop from her there and then (it did not). Another had a stone inside her rather than a baby, again caused by having sex with a spirit. Another was summoned and told that at night she became a cat and would cut the throats of others. Another was told she was having twins, which her family wanted to 'sell in the spirit world'. Salifu assured her that all would be well (at this stage he uttered a warning: 'Don't play with prophecy'). Another woman was told she would die in twenty-eight days; she would be asleep with her husband and he would wake up and touch her and find her dead. The husband was called up, to be told that devils were plotting to make him have an accident; he was not to worry, for in the first week of November a couple of the plotters would die.

A man was brought up with a heavily bandaged leg, which had been cut 'in the spiritual realm' by adversaries because of a dispute over land. It would not need amputating because Salifu cast out the spirit there and then. Another man in the congregation was singled out because, although he had been in Germany before, spirits had ensured that this time he would be refused a visa twenty times. Salifu negated this. A girl was called out to be told that Salifu saw a spirit of madness coming over her; her mother, who was a witch, was causing this. He called others out and then invited those who wanted to make an offering of over 50,000 cedis, then those offering 20,000, then 10,000. They went and threw their money on the stage.

As drama this was magnificent, and it lasted all day. At any one time there were about forty people on the stage writhing, flailing, whirling; oil was being dispensed lavishly (with evident effects on clothes), Salifu's minders were kept busy protecting women, especially those pregnant, from harming themselves, or others rushing and overwhelming the prophet. He began to treat some cases, and then left to return later. At any time he was liable to turn and single out someone in the congregation and tell her what her problem was. While the central drama was unfolding on the stage, other pastors and security men and ushers were moving down the aisles catching and pulling out women whom spirits were affecting (no men were so affected). All the congregation were totally participating (as in shooting the spirits), and there were continuous gasps as Salifu revealed the full extent of what was going on in the spirit realm.

At one session in Alive Chapel, on 21 October 2000, conducted by an assistant when Salifu was away, a woman had dreamed that a snake was entering her vagina. This snake was a spirit which prevented any man from marrying her. The prophet cast the snake spirit out. Another woman had dreamed of water; the prophet understood this as the spirit of the sea which had married her in a spiritual marriage, thus also preventing her from marrying in the human realm, and he cast out this spirit so that she could marry normally. He broke the curse on a woman whose husband, he asserted, was trying to divorce her. Another woman (it had been revealed to him) was also possessed by a snake spirit; he summoned her to the stage, which she approached slithering on her stomach. Then he called up a paralysed man in the front row and prayed over him—when there seemed to be no response, he reassured those carrying him that when the man awoke he would be cured. He said he was curing a woman of witchcraft, and immediately an old woman at the back felt hot, and came to the stage; it seemed that she had killed her own son, and two of her other children were at that time in Korle Bu Hospital ('Yes', she admitted). He said that both would recover.

Then he called barren women to the stage (about thirty went up). They lay (or fell) down and he threw oil all over them. When they stood up, he put more oil on them, tapping some on the stomach. Then he called up people with cancer and boils. He told them to receive their healing: 'Go!' One woman had had a dream of someone sucking her breast. The prophet said that this was cancer, so he cast out the spirit. During all this, the congregation sometimes joined in with outstretched arms, shouting 'Blood [of Jesus]', or 'Fire [of the Holy Ghost]'. While this was happening, four women who had had hysterectomies were lying on the middle of the stage. At this point a girl from a group of three or four backing singers tried to leave the auditorium; he noticed her leaving, and called her back because he had seen a coffin following her, with 'Nadi' written on it. 'Do you know Nadi?' he asked, and she replied that it was her name. The prophet then told her that she was going to die before 25 December—her family were trying to kill her out of jealousy, because she had a big future with a happy marriage. He reversed the curse. Another woman was called up who he said was going to have a car accident; she worked in a bar and was going to lose her job. The prophet told her that her mother was responsible for all her problems but would die before 5 November; they were not to mourn the mother because she was responsible for those ills. Then a girl with a baby, both affected with AIDS, was called up. The prophet claimed he saw a vulture over her head and told her that two men, one selling things at the roadside, had had sex with her, which she tearfully admitted. The prophet prayed for her (it was unclear whether he reversed this curse or not). At this point he got round to the women with hysterectomies lying on the stage; he tapped their stomachs with his microphone, sprinkled them with oil and shouted 'Restore!'

After this everyone in the congregation was invited to hold both hands outstretched, because he saw in a vision heavens opening and money flowing down (at this point there was loud shouting, encouraged by the music's increasing tempo). The prophet proceeded to call up those with 30,000 ccdis to sow; about ten went up. He touched them with oil, and one woman was informed that her husband was in gaol in Europe, but would be out within twenty days. Then those with 20,000 cedis to sow were called up (another ten); they too were given special treatment. One of these women was told to bring $100. When asked if she had such an amount, she replied 'No, not here nor at home.' He told her to change money to dollars and to bring $100 to the senior pastor on Monday because God was going to change it into a car; she would become rich. He then called up those with 10,000 cedis (about 150 people), 5,000 (200), 2,000 (200), and 1,000 (almost all remaining) to sow their seed, and as they all filed past he touched each one, calling 'Signs and wonders!', 'Miracle!', 'Power!' or 'Take your miracle! Take it!' As the donors of 1,000 cedis filed past he interrupted the proceedings to say that if any were just putting a hand in the basket and not depositing money, that hand would wither. He then called for a second offering. Finally all held up water they had brought. He blessed and prayed over it, and they poured it on their heads, drank it or took it home to drink to bring prosperity and fight demons.

Salifu hosted a convention in January 2001, at which one of the main speakers was Abraham Chigbundu of Mark of Christ Ministries in Benin City, Nigeria. As we have seen, Salifu incessantly refers to witches and wizards, but Chigbundu took this dimension further, and argued that 'behind every bondage, trouble, confusion is witchcraft.' Witchcraft operates through ancestral curses or even things we say inadvertently (for example, in an argument a husband may say 'I should never have married you', and even if he forgets that he ever said that, it is a witchcraft deposit which can ensure that the marriage never succeeds). Again, someone may be named after an ancestor who 'didn't perform his destiny', and as a result 'is going to lead a life of under-achievement'. Going to *mallams* (Islamic specialists), even to dubious 'Men of God', performing rituals in graveyards, exchanging business cards with dubious people, throwing anything into water (which may serve as an entry point for a river spirit), or giving 'native doctors' old coins may mean you have 'sold your finances'. Giving money to a beggar may be a point of contact ('not everyone in the street is a human being' but someone may be 'a spirit in disguise').

Sex may be a point of contact. 'If AIDS can be transferred through sex, what about a spirit?' The moment of orgasm is 'zero point in spirit' or the point of least resistance. Certainly 'not everyone in a skirt and blouse [in the street] is a human being.' He told the story of a man who picked up a girl in the street, only to wake the next morning and see 'a very big white rat wearing a skirt and blouse'. Such encounters are often the reason for impotence and infertility. This applies also to oral sex ('If you do it, you bring a curse on yourself. No, you must do all in accord with the provisions of scripture'), and to masturbation ('There's a spirit behind masturbation'). Dreams too may be points of contact: dreams of climbing mountains, riding an old bicycle on sandy ground (which indicates a 'spirit of stagnation'), climbing stairs or going back to primary school all indicate spiritual hindrances. Erotic dreams do the same in various ways.[34]

Then Chigbundu set about destroying every witchcraft deposit causing blockages: 'I destroy you, witchcraft spirits, all deposits of witchcraft, by the blood of Jesus.' He did this through a ritual: all had to breathe deeply ('In, out—in, out', he intoned). 'By air or liquid—by mouth, ears, every opening of my body, you must go. Move out of my life. Come out!' 'It's leaving you, that spirit ruining your finances, marriage... Let it go,

---

[34] For Chigbundu on dreams, see his *I Believe*, 69–82; 133–6. It is worth noting that dreams, given the prominence accorded them in some studies of AICs, are not a major theme in the churches studied in this book.

through your legs.' 'That spiritual husband, I command you, loose her. That invisible wedding ring on your finger, burn it now.' Women were vomiting on the floor ('Don't worry, we will clean the floors'), and pastors were going round attending to them, and women followed with rags, buckets and toilet paper. That spirit 'responsible for stagnancy, backwardness, disappointment, non-achievement in my life, I destroy you now... The years which witchcraft has wasted, I command them to be restored tonight. Whatever they stole from you, be restored sevenfold. The spirit of greatness, I release it! I reclaim the spirit of greatness tonight. Receive it!' In reply all shouted 'I receive it!' Chigbundu is a powerful speaker, with gripping anecdotes and earthy humour, and it was obvious from the congregation's reaction that he had touched a nerve.

Consider Owusu Bempa, founder of Accra's End Time Power Ministry International, at Salifu's convention, 31 January 2001.[35] After a rather defensive sermon on the importance of prophetic gifts for Ghana, the prophet called a young man to the stage and explained that he had seen a ring of family members plotting his downfall; he even named an uncle in Cape Coast as ringleader of the family plotters. The plot was that he would become insane and then, after three years of madness, die at the age of thirty-nine, in three years time. The prophet broke the curse on the young man, and then called a young woman to the stage. He saw in the spirit that her grandfather had had some dealing with a traditional religious figure, and that she would therefore have difficulties bearing children. After two miscarriages, she had two living children, but the prophet revealed that one of these would die at the end of that month, of convulsions, on her way to the hospital. He commanded the woman to fast the following Monday, along with him, and their combined fast would break the curse, and prophesied that she would soon marry; because of her problems she had had trouble finding a husband. Bempa then revealed that 100 people in the audience would give 100,000 cedis for a financial breakthrough (he later broadened the benefit for the women coming forward to finding a husband). Twenty-one people responded spontaneously, but he tried to bring the number up to 100, which involved considerable pressure. One woman was told that she would die of a stroke if she did not come forward—which she did. Another woman had her name revealed as 'Beatrice', which induced her to come out. He finally had to be satisfied with about sixty.

---

[35] Bempa is also from Kumasi, and likewise of limited education. His church has increased to 3,000 in four years. He is referred to as a 'supersaturated man of God', 'super-anointed prophet of God', and 'megaprophet' in *Gospel News*, Dec. 00, 8, and Jan. 01, 4.

Other prophetic churches

A prophet very similar to Salifu is Isaac Anto, of the International Christian Miracle Centre (founded June 1999), which has a Saturday morning Metro TV programme, 'Let the Prophet Speak', which is half-sermon and half-ministration. The form of the ministration section of the programme never varies; the prophet singles out in turn three or four individuals in the congregation, usually women. He tells them what he sees happening in their lives spiritually, often proving his credentials by announcing their name or home village—facts which he implies he could not possibly know unless he received revelation. He normally 'breaks' all spiritual influence, with much oil and frenzy, and helped by several muscular attendants. On 18 November 2000 a woman was called out whose brother in Canada was going to die; Anto broke the curse by anointing her. Then came a woman called Rosina whose family had sold her to Satan, ensuring that she could never marry; again Anto broke the curse. Rosina's brother Willy and her daughter were to die before Christmas, and be broke that curse too. Then he called out a woman who he revealed was sick with HIV; he poured oil over her, declared her diseased blood replaced, and drove the curse of AIDS away.

The next Saturday (*25 Nov. 00*) Anto singled out a man to tell him that 'the struggle in your life is over'; by the following February a rich man abroad would take him overseas where he would flourish. The prophet saw a black dog following a woman who was becoming sicker by the day; a family member, jealous of her good destiny, was responsible for her ills, preventing her from marrying (the family member said from inside the woman, 'I am responsible for this woman's illness'). The prophet cast her out, while the woman possessed by the spirit entered convulsious. On 12 December the prophet called out a young woman, and told her he saw her brother being pursued by a goat; this was death, sent by people fighting him over money. He reversed the curse. Then came a woman whom a spirit had married; the prophet saw her spiritual ring. He cast out this spirit, enabling her to marry. He called out a man whom he saw followed by a black dog, set on him by enemies. The man was trying to go to America, but if he went he would go mad on arrival. The prophet promised him he would have a visa within a week and broke the curse.

On 30 December Anto called out a woman whose daughter was pregnant and ill; family witches were planning to kill both her and her baby (the prophet saw one reaching into her womb to bring out the baby). He assured the woman that God was intervening to protect her. Then a woman came whose daughter the prophet saw being bitten by a snake; family witches were plotting to make the daughter blind. The one responsible was a woman, now dead, who had sent a spirit against both mother and daughter, and because the mother was so often in church she was hard to attack, so the spirit concentrated on the daughter. The prophet broke all these curses. On 6 January the prophet called out a woman whom family witches and her best friend were plotting to cripple for life. He broke every curse. He then called a second woman who had a shrine in her house; the spirit of this shrine had married her four daughters, and would prevent all four from marrying; he broke this curse. Then he called out a man whom three family members had plotted against and brought back from Germany eight years before; he had become discouraged and taken to drink, but the prophet assured him that God would take all his problems away, and even gave him some money to start a business; by 2001 he would drive his own car and own a house.

On 10 March the prophet called up a woman whom he saw having an accident, planned by her family, and a man whom spiritual forces were preventing marrying; he broke both curses. He called up a woman who he claimed was involved in a land dispute in her village; one of the litigants, whom he named, had gone to a mallam to work magic on her; he broke this arrangement. On 17 March he called up a woman whose son and whose sister's two sons were to die at Easter; the prophet broke all the family curses. On 24 March he called up a man whose breakthrough was prevented by a woman—he would never marry or make money—but God intended him to be a big man, and the prophet removed all hindrances. Then he called a teacher whom he saw writing on a blackboard when others rushed in to tell that her son was being burnt in a fire; he pronounced, 'I break all the plans of the enemy.'

On 7 April he called up a woman married to a spirit, sent by the woman, ostensibly her friend, who was renting her house. He broke that 'marriage'. Another woman as a baby had been cursed by a family member so that she would die at forty, and her fortieth birthday was that month. The prophet broke the curse. Then it was the turn of a girl with a stomach problem caused by her mother-in-law, who had never accepted the marriage and had prevented any children; he broke the barrenness. On 28 April he called out two hairdressers whose prosperity was impeded by two old women and a man who had spiritual control over their premises. The prophet cast out the spirit of poverty. Then a woman came whose dead mother was plotting against her and her children; this influence was broken. And so on. With Anto the idea of evils being inflicted by family members is particularly evident.

Another well-known prophet is the young and personable Nigerian, Prophet Abubakar Bako of the Logos Rhema Foundation. His ministry is basically the same as Salifu's, and he is equally liable to be sidetracked by a revelation about someone in the congregation. Being from Nigeria, he speaks in English all the time, and perhaps for that reason his followers seem slightly more educated and affluent than Salifu's. In his services the choir is less prominent. Abubakar is also less physical with those he calls up—there is no group of heavies to restrain the frenzied, nor are there bodies lying all over the platform by the end. He gives more importance to cosmic phenomena like thunder, hail, storms and animals; for example, on seeing an alligator in someone's stomach, 'That alligator will be killed by the thundering of God', and 'that monkey-like spirit, I declare your hands cut off now.' (2 Dec. 00)[36] He too can have dramatic rituals, like having five people blow the shofar or ram's horn ('to affect your finances tonight'). While the horn is being blown, the congregation hold their offering aloft and chant: 'I'm released, I have total victory, triumph and freedom in the name of Jesus.' It is of particular note that someone so preoccupied with spiritual forces preaches from a handheld pocket-book computer, into which the Bible has been programmed.

This preoccupation with spiritual agency is evident well beyond the specifically prophetic sector. Consider this preacher at Korankye Ankrah's RHCI (he was the pastor of the London branch) on 25 March 2001. Speaking of spiritual warfare, he insisted that it was the spiritual forces behind people that had to be fought. If you attack your boss who has sat on your promotion for five years, it is like lopping off a branch when you should take an axe to the root of the tree. 'Your real enemy is not your [future] in-laws refusing to accept you, but the spirit who doesn't want you to get married.' In grappling with the spirit, the person through whom it is working may get hurt. He gave an example from his own life. When he was in a village doing his year's national service after university, a young girl worked for him as a maid. He used to fall ill regularly, and had to come to Accra for treatment, thereby using up much of his money. One day lying ill in bed he saw the shadow of the girl coming towards him, and he realised that the girl was a demonic agent, but he decided to attack not the girl herself but the spirit of infirmity, the root cause. He fasted, and prayed using biblical texts like 'Whoever touches you touches the apple of my eye, says the Lord.' Two days after he prayed, children came running to tell him that the girl in question had collapsed at school. Experiencing what felt like an arrow in her stomach, she had rolled from her

---

[36] In many ways he seems idiosyncratic. His prayer bulletin for December 2000 urges: 'Instruct the sun, moon and the constellations in their courses to rise up and fight against anything that prevents people from coming to Christ.' He is also particularly conscious of Africa: 'Pray that God's anger will be kindled against all leaders in Africa who are ruling by the inspiration of demonic water spirits and that the judgement of God will be released against all who will not repent.'

desk, down the stairs right out into the compound. The pastor had run to her, and 'in my foolishness' prayed for her. It was too soon, for she recovered to continue her attacks on him. The lesson was that if members of your family, even your mother, are responsible for your ills and are hurt by your counter-attack, don't pray for them; 'Let them die, let them die, let them die! Sometimes God chooses to throw both the horse and the rider into the sea.'

He also said that in the previous week he had visited a woman in hospital who had been hospitalised three times already that year, and knew that the cause was the mother of a rival for her husband; this woman was set on killing her so that the daughter could marry the husband. The pastor, on hearing the story, had prayed: 'No weapon formed against me shall succeed... You shall not die, you shall live, and declare the works of the Lord. Lady, I came to tell you that this marriage will not be broken.' He continued, 'I said "Return to sender", and as I speak to you today she is discharged.' The preacher did not make it explicit, but 'return to sender' usually means to visit on the originator the fate intended for the victim, in this case death.

Consider a normal weekday deliverance session at the Jesus Connection Prayer Centre. This begins at about 9 a.m. with music and dancing, much of it provided by Jesus Connection Vibes, a trio of well-accoutred young women who are making a name for themselves in Ghana's Gospel scene. By about 10.30 the area was packed and the crowd of about 3,000 were spilling over into the road outside which had been blocked off and seats arranged under awnings served with closed-circuit TV. Starting at about 11, about twenty-five gave testimonies, mostly about deliverance from spiritual forces or witchcraft, and sometimes from women claiming to have been witches. The prophet, dressed casually with open-necked shirt, arrived about 11.40 and from then until closing at 2 he directed the proceedings. For most of this time he spoke, quietly enough, although about four times in the course of his sermon he introduced a song (taken up by the Jesus Connection Vibes) which would then be accompanied by the congregation, and which brought them out to the front dancing, just as in the introductory session. His address was a variation on the theme we have met so often before: you are downtrodden now, but you have a glorious destiny, which the prophet can ensure for you by removing all blockages. It included another common theme—that the blockages are, more often than not, caused by family members. The address was based on Luke 7.2–17, the healing of the centurion's servant, and the raising of the son of the widow of Nain. (The centurion's story easily lent itself to fundraising; the centurion received his miracle because he had built a synagogue for the Jews (Lk 7.5) and JCPC badly needs a substantial building.) After the address came the deliverance. On this particular day the prophet concentrated first on blockages caused by the owners of the houses we rent, who may have left some 'medicine' there to block our destiny. The congregation then prayed with fervour, and 'shot' (with their right hands formed into the shape of guns) the demons responsible. During this prayer some women became possessed and were carried to the front where they writhed and struggled and had to be forcibly restrained, with their knees tied together for modesty.

After this the praying shifted to blockages placed in mattresses by demons. While these demons were being shot, about fifteen women were carried to the front, and the entire platform was a mass of seething bodies, restrained by the deliverance team (sometimes three or four to one flailing woman). One of the spirits in one woman said she had been possessing the woman for a long time and had stolen much from her, including a visa, refusal of which the demon had ensured; the spirit admitted that she was no longer able to resist the prophet's ministrations, and would now leave her. Another demon had blocked a woman's chance of marriage. When these women, some now calm while others still kicked and struggled, had been carried off for further prayer, the congregation prayed against those spirits who bring diseases through dreams.

JCPC (established as a church in August 2001) is just as centred on spiritual forces as Salifu's Alive Chapel, although in the former case the demonic world is more often confronted in general, rather than in the specific cases which are Salifu's speciality. The congregation also seems to be drawn from the less well educated, and to be 95% female. Again no attempt is made to downplay the collecting of money.[37]

One last church deserves to be mentioned here. Prophet T. B. Joshua's Synagogue Church of All Nations, with its headquarters in Lagos, established a branch in Accra in 1998, and in December 2000 moved to a huge disused industrial building in Agbogbloshie in the centre of the city. Brother Peter Kayode, the Accra representative of Prophet Joshua, replicates the Lagos services for the 1,000 who attend the Sunday and Wednesday services (women form the great majority, although those seeking cures include a higher percentage of men). Petitioners are interrogated beforehand, and sit together to be called up in lines of about twelve. All

---

[37] See headline in *Spectator* (16–22 Sept. 00, 1): 'Pastors, Doctors at War' over JCPC Prophet Fred Kwasi Ansah's claim to have delivered a woman of a four-year-long pregnancy. For testimonies of witchcraft (especially within families) see *Jesus Connection*, Dec. 99–Feb. 00, 28; and April–June 00, 15; and Oct.–Dec. 00, 4–5, 15, 16, 32. A speciality of JCPC is to bless a soft drink before it is consumed, which then effects the required cure. See also Fred Kwesi Ansah, *Divine Revelations in the End-Time—the Way Forward*, Accra: the author, 2002.

stand holding in front of them placards proclaiming the (usually) three or four problems they need solved, how long they have suffered, their name, age and region. (Here we see again how a procedure has come to be determined by the media; the placards ensure that viewers of the inev-itable video can see at a glance the problems suffered and the cures sought.) Brother Peter, like Prophet Joshua in Lagos, rarely touches the clients but prays over them all; he stretches out his hand from a distance and moves it in a way that purports to guide selected ones, as if by a spiri-tual force, backwards, forwards, in circles or to the ground. The problems are various—AIDS, visas, financial breakthroughs, husbands, children—and if in Accra the spiritual origin of the problems is not highlighted, this is the obvious understanding underlying them; about ten per cent of those prayed for would end up vomiting out the spirit responsible. If the Syna-gogue Church is no longer characteristic in that diagnosis is completed before the service, it is wholly characteristic of the new wave in that everything depends on the special gifts of the Man of God. If the Syna-gogue is remarkable in that no oil is used, it has developed its own rituals. Building on the story of the pool of Bethesda (Jn 5), both the Lagos and Accra synagogues have a pool where taps run with water that has been blessed and is considered to be the blood of Jesus. Although the water/ blood does not feature in the service itself, all bring plastic bottles to take away a supply to last till the next service.[38]

Moral agency

This 'prophetic Christianity' is described here at some length since it is seldom given the prominence it demands. Many observers of Pentecostal-ism allow that one may occasionally discover references to, say, witch-craft, but indicate that these are insignificant, even negligible, and that the phenomenon is best analysed in other terms altogether. But there is a whole swathe of Ghana's new Christianity where this element is

[38] The Zambian President Frederick Chiluba spent a weekend at the Synagogue in Lagos (*Graphic*, 14 Nov. 00, 5; *Independent*, 16 Nov. 00, 7; *God's Voice in the Synagogue*, vol. 1 no. 2, pp. 7–8). If the press in Ghana seems rather uncritical of the Synagogue, particu-larly claims about curing AIDS (see e.g. *Mirror*, 4 Nov. 00, 3 and 28 April 01, 1; *Cru-sading Guide* 8–14 Feb. 01, 5), compare Karl Maier, *This House has Fallen: Nigeria in Crisis* (London: Allen Lane, 2000), where he deals at length with both Winners' and the Synagogue. He sees them catering for Nigeria's elite and losers, respectively. 'These modern-day pastors and so-called prophets practise faith healing and sometimes magic to prey upon the gullibility of their wealthier adherents and the desperation of the poor.' (p. 252) In his very sympathetic treatment of Nigeria this is almost the only instance of Maier's sympathy deserting him.

constitutive, and the examples enumerated here under 'prophetic Christianity' therefore cannot be brushed aside.

This prophetic sector is the one which has exploded in recent years. More and more religious figures describe themselves as 'prophets'. The tabloid media play up their exploits and powers, like their ability to reveal the colour of women's underclothes. 'Powerful Pastor tells colour of panties during prayers', blazons *Love and Joy* on its front page.[39] And these are the churches which attract; in terms of numbers Salifu has totally eclipsed his better-established rival next door, Matthew Addae-Mensah of Gospel Light International, an advocate of deliverance. And Salifu attracts more to a normal weekday or Saturday session than Duncan-Williams attracted to his 2000 annual convention.

We shall see below that charismatic Christianity has undergone a shift enhancing the personal status of the pastor—a trend that is most marked in these prophetic churches. These great 'men of God' and their personal gifts or 'anointing' achieve all that is required. They have become famous figures, who draw crowds to consult them. It is obvious that people flock to them for their gifts, not to form communities with other believers; of the crowds who flock to a prophetic ministry most will not know others there—the links are all vertically towards the prophet, rather than horizontally between followers. Many of those attending Salifu's services still identify themselves as Methodists, or Presbyterians or members of the Church of Pentecost. What will happen as he forms his own church remains to be seen; presumably, many will leave their former denomination and associate with him.

In this Christianity spiritual forces are at work everywhere, and have brought about the petitioner's predicament. We mentioned in sketching Ghana's pre-Christian religion the importance of the notion of destiny (*nkrabea*). Again, although human responsibility is not ignored, this fate allotted by God is a kind of predestination,[40] and it is against that background that these prophets can be seen as manipulators of people's destinies. However, it would be too simple to think of this as no more than traditional religion with a Christian overlay. Traditional religion had its own context—of community, kinship duties, obligations—a context which in a city like Accra has been largely dissolved. Nevertheless, it is obvious that this kind of Christianity, whether in its prayer camp or prophetic form, preserves many of the preoccupations, concerns and orientations of the traditional believer transposed into the modern setting.[41] The pre-

---

[39] *Love and Joy*, vol. 18. n.d.
[40] Pobee, *Religion*, 38–43.
[41] 'The needs presented at the prayer centres ... are not any different from those presented at the shrines by traditional worshippers in the early 1900s. The needs have not changed,

occupation with spiritual agents also explains some of the salient features of these churches, not least the almost total lack of interest in moral or ethical issues. Although, when asked, all prophets would declare themselves against sin, that word is seldom heard, and it is difficult for the concept to find a place. It is spiritual forces that largely determine states and actions, and it is the role of the man of God, through his miraculous gifts, to reverse unpropitious situations. Salifu's books allude to moral issues,[42] but even these passing references have no place in his services, because problems are considered to arise from curses or forces of which the sufferer may well be entirely unaware, and are solved by the magico-spiritual gifts of the prophet.[43]

The position argued here is thus very different from that adopted by Larbi, who writes: 'When Pentecostals talk of "salvation", they are talking primarily in terms of the atonement, forgiveness of sin, and reconciliation with God.' He maintains that for those who attend prayer camps 'the concept of salvation is fully stretched to cover the present existential needs of supplicants as well as issues dealing with original sin and the atonement.'[44] In other words, sin and salvation remain important, but salvation is extended to this-worldly realities. By contrast, the present author's experience with one large sector of Accra's Pentecostalism, the new prophetic churches, is that salvation is understood almost exclusively in terms of this-worldly realities, and notions of sin hardly arise. Larbi refers to Mbiti's claim that in African Christianity sin is not important, but rejects it. Mbiti wrote as follows: 'Even if the question of sin features a great deal in missionary or historical churches, it is highly doubtful that African Christians understand its centrality in the New Testament teaching about the atonement and redemption. A great deal of what is said about being "saved from sin" is simply a parrot-type indoctrination from the bringers of the Christian message. Converts appreciate

---

only the shrines have changed. The new shrine is the prayer centre, whose leader plays the role of the traditional fetish priest.' (Sampong, *Growth*, 121)

[42] In *Power to Make Wealth* he alludes to living uprightly and avoiding sin (74, 79, 82–3), but the statements are marginal and hardly related to the main theme. In Chigbundu's *I Believe* there is no moral element.

[43] A Pentecostal church that gives significant stress to moral issues is Deeper Life (more properly, Deeper Christian Life Ministry), the Nigerian transnational church of W. F. Kumuyi. Though not unaffected by the faith gospel of prosperity (see its monthly magazine *Life*, Nov. 2002), it manages to combine this not only with millennialism but also with its traditional emphases of holiness, discipline, self-denial and separation. Statistics for Deeper Life are hard to obtain; although in Ghana it draws several thousands to its Christmas and Easter retreats, it is not prominent in Accra, and seems to be totally eclipsed by the churches that are the focus of this study.

[44] *Pentecostalism*, 407–11.

more deliverance from the physical evils than anything else that would be in the nature of spiritual or moral depravity.'[45] Experience of Accra's prophetic churches largely confirms Mbiti's observation. Sin is hardly ever mentioned.[46] This reinforces my reluctance to use 'Evangelical' as a team embracing all these new churches. So many of them place little stress on conversion or on 'cruciformity'; indeed, such elements have no place there.

We noted that in pre-Christian religion the question of responsibility was ambiguous and unresolved. In Ghana it is not uncommon for those accused of crimes before the courts to attribute their deeds to evil spirits.[47] The same motif appears in the tabloid press in confessions and letters to agony aunts. Apostle Ahinful, in a column entitled 'Sexual Offences of Pastors', asks: 'Who exactly are to blame—pastors themselves, women, or Satan?' He concludes: 'My arithmetical estimates are that 10% of the blame should go to the pastors who have inborn habitual lust, and 40% to Eve-like tempting women, and 50% to Satan.' He explains that pastors are particularly prone to Satan's attacks in order to stop them 'converting and saving souls drawn from Satan's territory'.[48] Such thinking appears to be widespread. At Salifu's conference Chigbundu actually stated that Solomon was 'not responsible' for his problems with women; they were a result of his father David's sin with Bathsheba. This also seems the logic behind much of the talk about his congregation's problems. The only religious leader known to this writer who has directly questioned this preoccupation with demonic forces is the head of the country's Ahmadiyya Muslims, who insists that Ghanaians take responsibility for their own actions: 'It is most disturbing and terribly injurious to the moral health of the nation to be constantly bombarded with an image of the devil which seems to have control and power over people.'[49]

Traditional witchcraft also explains the repeated emphasis on family members who are deemed to be causing spiritually the woes of church members. This is present in all these churches, but particularly prominent in Anto's ICMC. Few of these pastors have a problem about 'reversing the curse', when it involves killing those deemed responsible. Besides the prophets mentioned above, Addae-Mensah claims to have killed people

[45] *Pentecostalism*, 408.

[46] See Meyer: 'The awareness of personal sin—already missed by the missionaries—still hardly seems to be present.' ('"If you are a Devil"', 114)

[47] See for example, *Spectator*, 16–22 Sept. 00, 4 and 9–15 June 01, 1; *P&P*, 12–18 Oct. 00, 7 and 26 July–1 Aug. 01, 3; *Newsmaker*, 11–17 Sept. 00, 3; *Graphic*, 25 Aug. 01, 3; and 'My Dwarfs instructed me to kill him.' (*Love and Life*, 15–21 Oct. 00, 3)

[48] *Mirror*, 2 Sept. 00, 16.

[49] *Graphic*, 16 Sept. 02, 1.

who were attacking him spiritually.[50] Duncan-Williams has killed businessmen through his anointing.[51] James Saah of ACI seems to approve of his mentor Benson Idahosa killing two members of a 'juju man's' family, including a child, in a power struggle.[52] According to Hughes, Kwabena Damuah the founder of Afrikania, was killed by the prayers of Christians: 'God answered their prayer. This man died woefully by paralysis.'[53] So also Oyedepo[54] and the Rev. Nick Garshong, a frequent writer in Ghana's tabloids.[55] I have heard only Ahinful deplore this tendency: 'Any prophecy that brings discomfort to a person or chaos in a person's family is of the devil.'[56]

As we have seen, remunerating the religious figure for services provided can loom large in this sector of Christianity, which emphasises the similarity with traditional religious practitioners who also make heavy demands.[57] It must be said that the image of pastors as crooks, charlatans,

[50] Matthew Addae-Mensah, *Walking in the Power of God*, Belleville: Guardian Books, 2000, 145 and 147.

[51] Sermon, 'The Mystery of the Oil' at Alive Chapel, 1998.

[52] Saah, *Finger*, 28.

[53] Hughes, *God's Hands*, 56.

[54] Oyedepo, *Prophetic Wings*, 163.

[55] 'A certain unbeliever used spells, curses and fetish powers to snatch a husband from the legal wife. The terms in the spell from the fetish priest was that the man should divorce permanently the legal wife, which should terminate in the death of the legal wife... When [the legal wife] reported the case [to me], we stood on the biblical basis in marriage and intercession and deliverance. The spell and curses on the legal wife was broken and reversed back to the rival, which killed the rival under pregnancy and revitalised the marriage with the legal wife, to the amazement of all concerned. They are now enjoying flourishing marriage.' (*Love and Joy*, vol. 17, 7; and vol. 2, no. 19, 6)

[56] Kwamena Ahinful, 'Controversy', *Mirror*, 4 Nov. 00, 16. Ahinful's weekly (later fortnightly) column is a strange mixture. With his impeccable English (of which he is very proud) and vast erudition, he comments on national affairs, focusing on their spiritual causes. He can be very critical. 'Something disgusting is happening in some of our penteco-charismatic churches', but it is due to the 'occult powers' of pastors (17 Feb. 01, 16). He never doubts that all the accounts of vomiting or passing solid objects are factual, but the phenomena are caused by demons (that is why some shout 'In the name of Jaahss', because 'the name of Jesus would frighten away their conjuring spirits' (9 June 01, 16). He finds demonic powers in cosmetics (14 Oct. 00, 16—for another sophisticated columnist arguing the same case, see 'Sikaman Palava', *Spectator*, 7 Oct. 00, 8) and see 9 Sept. 00, 16. Ahinful also had 'prophetic visions' for President Kufuor, and criticises the new president for not taking them seriously (12 May 01, 16).

[57] Some examples give an idea of current rates: a politician was charged 6 million cedis for a smock sewn with talismans that would ensure re-election (*Ghanaian*, vol. 1, no. 1, 6); four sheep and two bottles of schnapps and 100,000 cedis were required to pacify gods after an affair with a niece (*Chronicle*, 1–2 May 01, 4); 'a spotlessly white sheep, 12 metres of calico and a bundle of white twine' to prevent a husband from straying (*Love and Life*, 16–22 Jan. 01, 3); 'four kegs of local gin, two bags of maize, two kegs of palm oil,

exploiters, which is common currency in Ghana's media, is closely linked to this prophetic sector.

It is obvious that for a large sector of Ghana's new Christianity, the traditional preoccupation with witches persists. As Meyer has argued, through equating witchcraft (*adzeto*) with Satan (*Abosam*), 'witchcraft belief becomes part of Christian ideas… it is a structural element of their Christian faith.'[58] It is just as obvious that many scholarly treatments of Ghana's or Africa's Christianity give witchcraft only the most cursory mention. Yet this element deserves far more attention than it receives. In a characteristically insightful article on Pentecostalism and politics in Ghana, Meyer has asked: 'How can one write about politics and sorcery in Africa without evoking an image of the continent as hopelessly backward, fundamentally different and exotic? This question kept haunting me during my struggle to write this essay and I am still not sure what my answer is. But for me, not writing about the relationship at all was out of the question.'[59] This book does not claim, any more than Meyer, to have solved this question. But to avoid the real issues arising here would be to present a defective picture. It is because some are prepared to avoid them that Africa's new Christianity is sometimes misrepresented.[60]

This chapter has considered one form of charismatic Christianity in Ghana. We now turn to a very different form.

---

a number of fowls and an amount of 600,000 cedis' to forestall calamity (*Mirror*, 23 Sept. 00, 1); 500,000 cedis to cure severe abdominal pains (*People and Places*, 26 July–1 Aug. 01, 3). A Christian pastor demanded 700,000 cedis to exorcise a strange force preventing a fisherman making a good catch at sea. (*P&P*, 28 Sept.–4 Oct. 00, 3) Another pastor charged 300,000 cedis to bring a husband back. (*Top Story*, 18–24 June 01, 6)

[58] Birgit Meyer, '"If you are a Devil"', 119. This is what Etounga-Manguelle has in mind when he writes of African Christianity more widely: 'Contrary to what some might believe, the Christian religion, far from putting an end to witchcraft in Africa, has legitimised it.' ('Does Africa?', 73)

[59] Birgit Meyer, 'The Power of Money: Politics, Occult Forces, and Pentecostalism in Ghana', *African Studies Review*, 41 (1998), 32.

[60] The Catholic Theological Week, 20–22 Nov. 2000, dealt with the charismatic explosion, taking as its theme 'The Proliferation of Churches'. These sessions were remarkable for the poor attendance, revealing almost zero interest in the topic among Catholics, and the fact that the three speakers, all from the University of Ghana, Legon, gave almost no importance to the worldview underlying so many of these churches.

5

MENSA OTABIL AND CULTURAL ADJUSTMENT

Origins and development

Mensa Otabil was born about 1960 in Sekondi, and moved to Tema near Accra in 1966. Family circumstances forced him to drop out of secondary school after 'O' levels (or after three years of secondary school). He began life as an Anglican, moved through various charismatic milieux, and began his International Central Gospel Church (ICGC) in 1984. In the early years he tended to be exclusivist, calling for the true born-agains to come out of not only the mainline churches but even the established Pentecostal churches.

The nature of Otabil's Christianity in the 1980s and early 1990s is easily discerned in three books published in 1992. *Enjoying the Blessings of Abraham* reveals him as a fairly standard faith preacher (he readily admits that one of the early influences on him was Kenneth Hagin). *Four Laws of Productivity* shows that he always had a concern for effort and productivity as well. He finds his four laws in God's first command to men: 'Be fruitful and multiply, and replenish the earth and subdue it.' (Gen 1.28) However, the third book *Beyond the Rivers of Ethiopia: a Biblical Revelation on God's Purpose for the Black Race* reveals him as something rather different in Ghana. This book finds Blacks in many crucial parts of the Bible, and is written to instill pride in them, since he thinks they are still inclined to regard themselves as inferior to Whites.[1] The present author

---

[1] This Black biblical theology is not common in Ghana. Hughes, *God's Hands*, has a very different agenda, being directed against Afrikania and others who advocate 'African culture' without Christianity. Hughes too is no externalist, seeing Africa's problems as arising mainly from realities within Africa (36), but for reasons very different from what we will see are Otabil's. Hughes writes: 'There is now the general realisation that the root cause of our woes in Africa lies deeper than mere economic, social or political factors, but rather with flagrant abandonment of the Judeo-Christian God.' (49) Sampson Baning, *Pan African Renaissance and the Hidden Prophecy*, Accra: Black Lineage Reality Research

has discussed these books elsewhere in some detail, and they will not be dwelt upon here, but all three are reminders that charismatic Christianity is something alive and constantly developing; Otabil is no exception.[2]

His church has grown considerably. His main church in Accra has perhaps 7,000 people attending every Sunday, and there are about 100 ICGC churches in Ghana and five overseas (two in the United States, and one each in England, the Netherlands and South Africa). These constitute a fairly loose association. All ICGC pastors would see themselves as inspired by Otabil, and would probably model their operation on his. Pastors of branches near Accra have occasional meetings addressed by Otabil, and all have an annual retreat, but there is no attempt to oversee day-to-day operations. On his trips overseas Otabil is far more likely to speak at other churches than ICGC ones. Otabil sees himself primarily as the pastor of his own headquarters congregation, rather than overseer of anything like an entire denomination. He thus exerts over his churches perhaps the loosest control of all these founders: less than Duncan-Williams (whose headquarters regularly transfers pastors) and certainly less than Heward-Mills does over his. Otabil's church is not immune from the trends we have been documenting in Ghana. The headquarters church (although not Otabil himself) runs a 'Solution Centre' every Thursday—a deliverance ministry in all but name. Similarly, the head of the ICGC at Madina, effectively a suburb of Accra, practises as a prophet. However, despite these elements (it would hardly be able to flourish without them) the whole church is really identified with Otabil's preaching or message. In Accra this is spread beyond his church through 'Living Word' on TV3 and Radio Gold, and through 'Believers' Voice of Hope' on Joy FM.[3]

Centre, 2001, is more idiosyncratic, using archeology to establish that the Nephilim (Gen 6.4) reached Ghana.

[2] Gifford, *AC*, 80–4. Larbi deals with Otabil, *Pentecostalism*, 335–63. It is remarkable, given the literary output of so many other Ghanaian charismatic pastors, that for a decade Otabil concentrated deliberately on the spoken word, and wrote no more books until his *Buy the Future: learning to Negotiate for a Better Future than your Present*, Lanham, MD: Pneumalife, 2002, a motivational treatment of the tale of Jacob and Esau.

[3] Beyond Accra, his TV programmes are screened on commercial TV in Kumasi, and his radio programmes are broadcast on Luv FM, Otec FM, Kapital FM, all in Kumasi; on Sky Power FM in Takoradi; and on Sky FM in Sunyani. In 2000 'Living Word' began screening on Kenyan TV, and negotiations are in train for other countries. Series broadcast or screened include: Developing the Winning Attitude (10 programmes); Living the Abundant Life (6); Principles for Effective Living (16); Finances (4); Leadership Principles of Jesus (16); How to Accomplish your Desire (8); Africa must be Free (8); Principles of Prosperity (8); Positive Attitudes for a Happy Life (16); Transformation (8); Marriage 101 (10); Turning Failure into Success (12); Walking the Faith Walk (8); Christ in You the Hope of Glory (8); Walking in the Footsteps of Blessing (12).

No viewing and listening figures exist, but some ICGC promotional brochures claimed that in 2001 as many as 25,000 watched 'Living Word' each Sunday evening on TV3.

Otabil freely admits that his appeal is restricted. Although branch ICGCs operate in local languages, he conducts everything in English in his headquarters congregation, and inevitably that means 'the schooled population'; the unschooled, he insists, must look elsewhere. He explains: 'Some Christians believe Otabil is too "book long" [a nice Ghanaian phrase for "learned"], so they won't come here... Some want prophecy [obviously in the form discussed in our previous chapter] to touch their lives; I am not called to them and I will not make any attempt to reach them. Their orientation will not attract them to me, but they will be attracted to another church, because remember all of us are working for one master' (this admission that 'the church' must take different forms for different people is perhaps another departure from his exclusivist early days). Similarly those looking for 'power' must go elsewhere. He knows that some say of him: 'Where is he coming from? Is he a psychologist, a philosopher or what? He should preach the Bible.' Otabil responds: 'I am happy with that, because once people say that, I know I am not called to them. The people I am called to...want practical information from the Word of God that is usable in their lives for personal development and personal improvement.'[4] As the main speaker at the launching of Agyin Asare's Gospel Outreach (31 Mar. 2001) he made the same point; praising Agyin Asare for his healing gift and for his commitment to evangelisation, but admitting that he himself was called to neither. He has a *message*—a message for the *élite*.[5]

Otabil's stature increased steadily throughout the 1990s. Since the mid-1990s the church's NGO Central Aid has been assisting good causes—for a cardio-thoracic unit, the physically handicapped, breast cancer, the blind, and in 1998 even *Trokosi* women (see page 41)—and the church itself stages a much-publicised concert every Christmas Eve to raise funds for these causes.[6] Central Aid has also throughout the 1990s given scholarships worth over 200 million cedis to 500 outstanding but needy

---

[4] Sermon tape 'The ICGC Vision'.

[5] His media programmes are introduced with the jingles 'Bringing Leadership and Vision to our Generation' and 'Raising Leaders, Shaping Vision and Influencing Society through Christ'.

[6] The *Graphic* (20 Dec. 00, 14) preview of this concert revealingly states: 'Talk about ICGC doing things differently! The medium is music all right, but it is not the loud type that throws people into emotional frenzy...' Billed to perform were 'the Winneba Youth Choir, the National Symphony Orchestra, *the ICGC's own reputed Philharmonic Orchestra*'. Targeting the élite in this way brought in 50 million cedis. (*Graphic*, 1 March 01, 16)

students, many of them Muslims.[7] But two things made him emerge as a national figure. In 1998 he established Ghana's first private university, Central University College (quite a step for someone who had begun by denouncing mainline churches for their involvement in education and health rather than the one thing necessary)[8], but above all his preaching on radio and, from late in 1999, on TV has made him a household name in Accra.

Throughout the 1990s too, Otabil came to be seen increasingly as a political figure—and indeed, while many of the other charismatic leaders were seen as tacit or explicit supporters of the Rawlings regime—as an opposition figure. He certainly spoke out on national issues, but he rejected this 'opposition' label, claiming (for reasons that will become obvious below) that those who applied it to him had not understood him at all. However, in June 2000 he delivered the sermon at the annual memorial service the Bar Association holds for the judges murdered under the PNDC in 1982, which in the eyes of the Rawlings regime identified him as an enemy.[9] In October 2000 he gave the eighth William Ofori-Atta Memorial Lectures, named after one of the original 'Big Six' credited with effecting Ghana's independence, who himself became 'born-again' when imprisoned by Nkrumah. Sponsored by the National Association of Evangelicals of Ghana, the lectures aim to address 'national issues from a Christian perspective'. Otabil chose as his theme 'The Quest for a New Ghana'. The ideas expressed in the lectures were no different from those in his sermons, which we discuss below. However, two points should be noted. First, in one lecture he quoted de Tocqueville, David Landes (*The Wealth and Poverty of Nations*) and Thomas Kuhn (*The Structure of Scientific Revolutions*), and this distanced him considerably from most of

---

[7] *Graphic*, 1 March 01, 16.

[8] CUC grew out of his church's Bible college, and has two schools, the School of Theology and Mission, and the School of Business Management and Administration (the latter offering degree programmes in secretaryship, accounting, marketing management, human resource management, banking and finance, agribusiness. CUC claims distinctiveness in its stress on IT, French-language proficiency, and worker-friendly programmes. This last-named consist of three concurrent streams—morning, evening and weekends. CUC hopes to open schools of science, medicine and engineering, although how feasible this is without access to enormous funds from overseas remains to be seen. So far its two schools are kept operating through student fees (3 million cedis per student per semester), so its intake is limited to those who can afford such steep fees.

[9] The sermon stressed purpose and conscience. An excerpt: 'The nation's moral anchoring in its own self-proclaimed motto of "Freedom and Justice" has been so undermined that its original dream to deliver quality life to her citizens after the attainment of independence appear shipwrecked and abandoned.' Sermon published in *Chronicle*, 3–6 July 00, 4; & 7–9 July 00, 11.

Ghana's charismatic pastors. Second, he was widely misunderstood; according to the *Chronicle*, he had 'called on Ghanaians to vote for a change in the nation's status quo', by which they meant voting against Rawlings and the NDC, but this did not at all reflect Otabil's position.[10] The attitude of the Rawlings regime to Otabil was revealed after the 2001 transition when an erstwhile head of the Serious Fraud Office explained that he had been forced to cancel an anti-corruption conference because he had invited Otabil to address it.[11] Indeed, just before the transition Otabil was strongly attacked in the state-owned *Graphic* in an article considered by some to have been written by a Rawlings functionary.[12]

Message

Otabil, then, *is* his message. Before we consider the message itself, something must be said of the style which is inseparable from it, and equally distinctive. Otabil speaks in good simple English with remarkable fluency, and his messages are clearly structured. There is no background of organ music or drums to increase the emotional tempo. The seeming simplicity conceals painstaking preparation, as became obvious in 2002 when he began to back his sermon with a power-point presentation on a huge screen suspended above him. He begins from biblical texts, and throughout cites others as it suits him, but even in a series like the one he gave on Abraham, no attempt is made to claim that his message is the only meaning derivable from the texts. Unlike Agyin Asare particularly, he can give whole sermons only drawing lightly on the Bible. Occasionally he invites responses and calls on hearers to tell their neighbour

---

[10] *Chronicle*, 4 Jan. 01, 4. Other comment: *News*, 23 Oct. 00, 1; *Graphic*, 18 Oct. 00, 9, and 19 Oct. 00, 1. Earlier lecturers include Kwame Bediako and the Catholic Bishop Charles Palmer-Buckle on 'Bribery and Corruption: Challenges for Ghana in the 21st Century'.

[11] *Chronicle*, 5–6 Feb. 01, 6.

[12] 'Pastor Mensa Otabil has now become more of a political campaigner than a pastor of the flock of Jesus… Most of his political outbursts display a lot of ignorance of the very word and principles of God he professes to teach in the way they relate to nation-building.' The article criticises him for choosing to operate in the city instead of the rural areas, like Jesus; for founding an expensive university with fees of 1.2 million cedis per semester (in fact they were 3 million at this time), well beyond the means of his church members; for encouraging them to '[blame] the government for all their woes' instead of working hard; for the 'bad policy decisions and the dictatorial leadership style' that have driven away all his colleagues; and for constructing a 'magnificent fantasy temple' while neglecting his deprived neighbours. All this raises the question of 'gross mismanagement of church resources' (Baafuor Kissiedu, 'Dr Otabil in Contemporary Politics', *Graphic*, 27 Dec. 00, 9). A rejoinder, not by Otabil, appeared in 30 Jan. 01, 9.

something, but this is not marked—there are no standard charismatic formulae like 'If anyone is here with me, shout "Amen!"'

An essential ingredient is the person himself. Otabil is very tall, and wears striking and obviously expensive *agbadas*, standard formal wear in much of West Africa (he admits to owning a Western suit, which he had to buy when his luggage was lost on a trip overseas, but it is doubtful if he has ever been seen in it). The platform is cleared of everything that might distract; there is no choir or group of ministers sitting behind him. He alone is the focus. This is no folksy chat, so he does not come down and walk among the congregation, or address individuals by name. He remains near the lectern on the platform, and the higher level underlines his authority. Authority, dignity and total self-possession are part of the message, as is a certain reserve—he discloses little about himself or his personal life. Self-deprecating anecdotes are one of his regular rhetorical techniques, but they are remarkable for how little they actually reveal. His sermon is normally the climax of the service, although there is sometimes an altar call inviting sinners to give themselves to Christ.

Otabil is considered to have a broader horizon than most of Ghana's charismatic preachers. His readiness to address national issues is what the general public associates with him, but this perception is partly influenced by the media. To save funds, a film crew makes four half-hour programmes from two hour-long sermons on a single Sunday morning. Thus Otabil's monthly TV output is filmed on a single Sunday each month. This leaves him free to intersperse other messages or even series on Sundays that are not filmed, in which he can treat more specifically church-related subjects such as sin (10 Dec. 00; 31 Mar. 02), the meaning of communion and the person of Jesus. The television audience tends to see the social concern and the political awareness, but that is not his exclusive emphasis.

In many ways his Christianity is of a piece with what we have considered above. Certainly he belongs solidly within Ghana's charismatic Christianity—for most he would be one of the three or four figures who personify the entire phenomenon. We can briefly mention the similarities. A service is likely to begin with the invitation to tell one's neighbour: 'Even if you try you cannot fail, because the unfailing God is on your side. You're a winner!' (14 Sept. 00) A sermon may be entitled 'More than conquerors'. (18 Mar. 01) He gave a whole series on Abraham in 2001, entitled 'Walking in the Footsteps of Blessing' in which many familiar motifs recurred. Echoes of the faith gospel were evident throughout this series (especially 6 May 01), and indeed Copeland's and Hagin's magazines are sold at the church door. He preaches the need to tithe (1 April 01), and offering time can be introduced (though by subordinates) with familiar motifs of divine fundraising. (24 Sept. 00, 5 Nov. 00)

He can be as motivational as any of them—'Turn to your neighbour and say: "You are a child of destiny. It's coming"' (12 Nov. 00), or 'Say to your neighbour "I am unburyable".' (18 Mar. 01) He places great emphasis on one's 'vision'; TV advertisements for his programme present him saying: 'No matter what prison you are in, no prison can imprison your power of imagination.' Preaching on Abraham, he takes the text 'Look from the place where you are' (Gen 13. 14): 'I like that phrase: not "*at* the place where you are"... You can start a journey from any destination. Everywhere is a good place to begin movement to the next destination.' (18 Mar. 01) A few weeks later, still on Abraham, he said that 'God took Abraham outside' (Gen 15.5) was 'one of my favourite parts of the Bible', and explained: 'In a tent your vision is limited. God says change your location. The problem of most of us is the location and position of our minds.' (6 May 01) Many Ghanaians simply describe him as a motivational preacher (and indeed he won an award in 1998 for 'Best Motivational Speaker').[13]

Yet there are marked differences. In many ways Otabil constitutes a one-man refutation of much that has been written above—with no oil, no 'anointing', no healing, no enemies, no witches, no demons (certainly none with rights over the Christian), no prophetic gifts, no promises for 'today', little stress on the miraculous, no cries of 'Receive it!' Let us examine some of these differences in more depth.[14]

We mentioned that it is almost axiomatic for Ghanaian charismatic preachers to proclaim the faith-gospel motif: 'Don't believe your senses; believe the Word of God.' Otabil will have none of that; far from urging his listeners to ignore their situation, he rubs their noses in it. It is a standard charismatic motif to assert 'It is well', but Otabil insists that this not the case at all—rather, 'it is appalling.' Here is Otabil in full cry on the African situation: 'We are conceived in dilapidated rooms, born in filthy, unhygienic hospitals, covered in dirty rags, feed on contaminated milk,

---

[13] His church bookshop stocks much motivational literature from the world of business, including well-known titles by such as Peter Drucker.

[14] Admittedly there are what I must call 'inconsistencies' in his theology. Sometimes (as in his series about Abraham) he comes close to the classic faith gospel. I have heard him say that one must not be influenced by observable reality: 'If you are born in a country like this and you live only by what you see, your heart will fail you.' You must speak reality into existence (7 Apr. 02; 14 Apr. 02). In this same series 'Turning Failure into Success' he implies that once you have found Jesus, all automatically becomes well (5 Sept. 02). I have also heard him announce that a woman anointed at a convention miraculously received $ 5,000 (18 Aug. 02). These exceptions do not invalidate the picture outlined in the body of this chapter.

roam practically naked in smelly neighbourhood back alleys, strive with countless siblings, mice and cockroaches for sleeping place on the cold floor, go to school to learn ignorance from poverty-flogged teachers, share our lunch of unripe mangoes with other infant comrades in suffering, wait for Christmas to eat a piece of chicken leg and sample a bottle of Fanta, argue and fight with a drunken father, drop out of school, sleep in the junkyard while learning a trade in vulcanising, make the groundnut seller pregnant and reincarnate your suffering all over again in the life of your child. On and on this cycle of misery turns.'[15]

As for prosperity, Otabil remarks: 'Some people call us charismatics prosperity preachers. I am happy [with that]; I am not a poverty preacher, but a prosperity preacher.' In the same sermon he claims: 'We believe that God provides abundance for all and we believe that the Christian life is a good life, it is not a punishing life.'[16] And preaching on the Beatitudes, he insists: 'The Christian life is a life of victory, power, triumph over sickness and disease, fulfilment, happiness.' (8 July 01) Many even among his own pastors take him at his word and call him a prosperity preacher, but I think that is misleading because that label normally indicates a faith gospel perspective, and it is the standard mechanics of the 'name it and claim it' preachers that he has transcended. This was particularly clear in his series 'Principles for Effective Living'. To those who ask 'God give me money' he says: 'God will not give you money; take it from me. Where would God get it? But God can give you wisdom and with that you can go to his earth, and you can [make] that thing.' He imagines this dialogue with God. '"Please give me a car." "When did you hear that Nissan has a branch here [in heaven]?" "God give me a house." "When did you hear that I'm in the stone-making business?"' No, says Otabil. The proper prayer should be '"Give me wisdom", *that* he manufactures in abundance. Your God won't give you wealth; he gave you *power to create* wealth.' (30 July 00)

Nor does Otabil foster any preoccupation with ubiquitous spiritual forces. His references to dreams are in the following vein: 'If you had a dream that your mother-in-law was holding a cutlass and following you, when you wake up from your dream, what will be your reaction? Just be honest with yourself; what will be your reaction? Do you know that in some other places [in the world] the person will call the mother-in-law and tell her "What a funny dream I had" and everyone will laugh and that will be the end of it.' But here, says Otabil, 'You start praying "Jesus,

---

[15] 'Is Africa Cursed?' (29 June 99), the second of three 'Heritage Lectures': 'Creating Hope for African People', delivered at Accra Teachers Hall, 28–30 June 1999.

[16] Tape 'The ICGC Vision'. In his Beatitudes series he deals with 'Blessed are the Poor in spirit', which he interprets as an exhortation to humility. (8 July 01)

Jesus, the blood of Jesus!" Then you go to your mother-in-law, and tell her "I know what you have been doing in the spirit, but I have caught you. I don't fear you." The result? "That's the end of the marriage." Similarly, a President will dream of a minister of state holding a chicken, get up in the morning and say "You are holding a chicken against me", and dismiss the minister.' Otabil concludes: 'You know, there is something wrong about our interpretation of life and realities.'

It is revealing to consider his occasional reference to witches. More than once the present writer has heard him say something like 'Maybe there are witches; maybe there are even some here today to hear me preach. In that case, welcome! You are most welcome!' This is typical; he does not confront the issue directly, but deflects it with some humour, quietly moving on to another plane where witches simply have no place. He may not directly address the issue of the existence of witches, yet he is totally dismissive of the power and significance attributed to witches in so many charismatic churches: 'You want to be a success, with families, houses, job, education finances, wealth... You don't become a failure through witches, wizards or juju; you become a failure because of choices made by you or on your behalf. We must take full responsibility for how our lives turn out.' (*6 Aug. 00*) Arguing that God is his shield (Gen 15. 1), he says: 'That's why I don't spend time [worrying about witches]. I haven't got time for that. When you know your shield, none of that matters. When you know your shield, you don't go about accusing family members... I'm not going to spend my time saying "She's one!" "She's one!" "She's one!" [All that] is under my control.' (*4 Mar. 01*)[17]

He also does not attribute agency to demons. In fact, his few references to Satan are rather to the classical tempter of the West (*7 Jan. 01*), and not to the commander of ubiquitous unseen forces. Human responsibility replaces demonic control. 'Everyone is where he is because he has chosen to be there. Human beings are not victims of circumstances; human beings are products of choices. You don't become who you are because circumstances made you so. You are where you are because of choices

---

[17] The same approach evident on *4 Mar. 01*, *25 Mar. 01*, *1 April 01*: 'You are a result of choices you have been making. You see, in our part of the world, Ghana, Africa, we tend to blame unseen forces which fly by day and by night, winged, some unwinged, bodiless entities; they have been accused of all our failings. And sometimes even in the church world we take that line. Much as there is a devil and agents of the devil, the devil is not a Ghanaian and does not reside in Africa... If I were the devil, I wouldn't live in a poor continent; I'd go where the rich people are. So we can't let him be responsible for all our failings, although he is behind evil in the world, but we have responsibilities. Things don't just happen; they are made to happen, either by you or by others.' (*21 Aug. 00*) It is obvious that by 'the choices made by others' he means only choices like parents sending you to school or the government plundering the economy, not witchcraft.

that you made yourself or choices that were made on your behalf.'[18] Thus there are many areas where deliverance is simply inappropriate. 'We have to attack ignorance and illiteracy as though [they were] the devil himself... You are sitting there saying "Jesus is Lord, Alleluia!"'... Don't hide behind binding [ignorance] and casting it out in Jesus' name. No, Sir, it will not be cast out. You can't cast out ignorance in the name of Jesus. You cast out ignorance through education!' (*13 Aug. 00*)

We have referred to the annual conferences of other charismatic churches, especially Duncan-Williams' ACI and its faith gospel, and Salifu with his prophetic ministration. We should consider the contrast presented by Otabil's 1999 conference, with its theme 'Lift up your Head, Africa'. Setting the tone, Otabil called his opening address 'The People Don't Care'. It was based on Jeremiah 5.30–31: 'The prophets prophesy falsely and priests rule by their own power, and my people love to have it so.' It was a savage attack on the people of Ghana for putting up with their situation (so much for ignoring circumstances, as is advocated by most faith preachers). Jeremiah says that something terrible and horrible is happening, and the crime is that the people love to have it so. 'In Africa we say "No problem". The economy may be going haywire, "No problem". Everything may be going wrong, "No problem, we don't care." And the people who do not care about their own welfare cannot change their condition.' 'Do you really care about what is happening in your country and on your continent? Do you care when you see an African child reduced to a human skeleton begging for food with flies all over him? Do you care when you see pictures of Africans in Rwanda lying down dead from starvation? Do you care or do you say, "It is all right"?' Things will change for Africa only when the 'ordinary citizens of Africa say, "Enough is enough: I'm tired. I need something better than this." Until we have people who demand better than what they are receiving, this continent has no future.' Two days earlier someone with whom he had been talking had asked: 'What is wrong with us? Are we under a curse?' 'You know what is wrong: we don't care, you don't care, and many people don't care. That is why you don't take anything seriously in this country.'

He continued (and here we see how he came to be seen as an opposition figure): 'One should not expect anything from Africa's rulers. At a conference all the Presidents will say all the nice things. They always say nice things, they talk about peace and promote civil war—and the people just smile.' He attacked his listeners for putting up with what authorities mete out to them.[19] He referred to the practice of controlling crowds at

---

[18] Tape 'Talents, Work and Profit'.
[19] At the following year's conference, on the theme 'Renewing Hope for our Generation', he began with a sermon entitled 'Run with Endurance'. In this at one stage he drew attention

Accra's airport with canes (as is also done at the border with Togo). 'You cannot do that to an American. Is he a better human being? No, but he thinks he deserves better treatment than being whipped at the airport... Is there any difference between the American child and the Ghanaian child? As human beings there is no difference. But *they* live in economies which promote opportunities, so the American child... goes to school, he can learn. We go to school, we come back as illiterate as we were before we went to school. Some of you sitting here cannot write one sentence intelligently!'

'Let's not joke with our destiny, our future... The world has left us; they don't care about us any longer. Nobody cares about Africa ... [In Rwanda] the Americans said, "We won't intervene; if you are foolish enough to kill each other, go ahead." Nobody is going to solve our problems for us, nobody is going to care about us. *We* have to start caring about ourselves. That's why I have a serious problem with our politicians. Somehow I feel that they like to keep the people ignorant, so they can rule over them. It's easy to rule over ignorant people. That's how the white man was able to rule over all of us. Ignorance is a disease... Our chiefs sold our brothers and sisters to America, to the Caribbean; it's not the white man who did it... In the slave trade [the whites] were only at the coast, they never went to the interior. And who were doing the catching? Black people. The trading? The selling? Black people. When we talk about the true story of the slave trade, the black man is more to blame than the white man. But we don't talk about it [because of African American visitors]... We bring them here and tell them lies for tourism, just because we want their little dollars. We tell them lies and give them a sense of emotional relief. The truth if it be told is that African chiefs arrested their sons and daughters, chained them, and paraded them to Elmina castle to be sold. African chiefs are still doing it today; these days they are not called chiefs. They are called Presidents and Prime Ministers, and they are still doing it!'[20]

---

to the fact that in France petrol prices had increased by 2%, and the French had barricaded roads and ports; in Ghana, by contrast, the cedi had depreciated by 150% in four months—he seemed to be asking why Ghanaians were not protesting. He went on to say that the situation in Africa was so bad that he gets tired. He had to preach, because 'it's the only weapon I've got. I don't have a gun. If I did it would be a different story. I think I would have gone to the [recent] OAU summit and said a few things.' (11 Sept. 00) This is the only occasion known to this writer when the NDC informers who kept his church under surveillance might have had something specific to report to headquarters.

[20] Again: 'Corrupt politicians, following in the traditions established by the earlier African collaborators, continue to sell our continent's future to the highest bidder and stash their immoral wealth in European banks. This is the new slave trade. It does not chain us on

For African American visitors, he continued, 'We dance. It's all right, once in a while we need to dance, but I think we are dancing too much. What we need to do is start getting angry with ourselves, and we need to start making progress. Until we accept responsibility, we cannot change our condition.'[21]

He mentions Kofi Annan: 'If he had stayed in Ghana, he wouldn't be any UN Secretary General. He would probably have had his assets seized or something like that and he would just be begging for a pension at the pension office or at the labour office looking for some miserable money at the end of the month.' Otabil laments the future available to the youth in Ghana, because of the woeful education system. 'If you ever have the opportunity to read people's [secondary school] exam sheets you will weep for Ghana. That's our future!' 'We complain about the slave trade, that the youth of Africa were shipped to the Americas and to Europe and we say that if they had stayed it would be better. The youth are now staying, nobody is shipping them anywhere, and we are destroying them right here!' He lambasts Africa's dictators (and is fully aware that some of them are 'spirit-filled, born-again, tongue-talking dictators'). 'Dictators rule all over Africa, and all of them have people who should have spoken the truth to them but never told them. If that is how we are going to run our nation, there is no hope for us.' He insists that the church must be this pro-phetic voice. He ends: 'Listen to me! I did not come here to tell you that I will lay hands on you and all your problems will be solved. There is a time to lay hands on people, and there is a time to make them think, and today is that time.'

It is this readiness to confront the African situation, as an integral part of what Christianity must be concerned with, and to confront it at this supra-personal or national level that makes Otabil distinctive among Ghana's new charismatic leaders. Some think that this approach takes him close to mainline Christianity, but that is only half of the truth. Otabil's real uniqueness is that he goes far beyond the mere socio-economic or socio-political to address the issue of culture as a factor in Ghana's plight. In this he is very different from the mainline churches. They are very

---

ships across the Atlantic, but it chains us to poverty, illiteracy and diseases at home.' (Second Ofori-Atta lecture, 18 Oct. 00)

[21] The different perspective on slavery is an example of a fundamental difference between African charismatic Christianity and the African American or Caribbean type: 'When the Africans in the Diaspora recount the horrors of slavery they are talking about a system in which Africans were entirely victims... However, what took place here on our continent was made possible because our leaders allowed it and enthusiastically participated in it for the benefits it brought them.' (Second Ofori-Atta lecture, 18 Oct. 00)

conscious of the accusation that they denigrated all African culture in the last century and therefore would never criticise African culture today.

Culture

Otabil introduced his first Ofori-Atta lecture with the words: 'I wish to propose that our inability to modify our culture is one of the fundamental causes of our under-development.' He notes, following Landes, that culture is a 'no-go' area for development economists. Since 'criticisms of culture cut close to the ego, injure identity and self-esteem... benevolent improvers have learned to steer clear.' Otabil asks: 'Is it any wonder that the well-intentioned packages of our donor communities barely scratch the surface of our under-development?'[22] Just because others refuse to enter the field Otabil is not daunted. It is culture that Otabil has come to make a prime focus of his theology.

In 2000 he broadcast over ten weeks a series on 'Pulling down Strongholds' (based on II Cor 10.3–6) in which he addressed the factors which, in his understanding, are holding Africa back. The strongholds he focused on were in the minds of Ghanaians. He listed the following: an inferiority complex, tribalism, cultural stagnation, idolatry and fetishism, the village mentality, ideas of leadership and apathy. He was aware that these are sensitive subjects. He appeared almost apprehensive in approaching some of the issues (in fact, his fears were groundless since he was continually interrupted with applause). 'The real problem nobody wants to touch because it is too sensitive. When we talk about poverty, the enemy really is not poverty, it is the people who produce poverty... Poverty doesn't sit somewhere to say "All right, I have left Bangladesh and my next plan is to go to that West African country... OK, Ghana. I will see you next month", and then when poverty comes all of us become poor. No! No! No! No! There is nothing like that. All the conditions were created, man-made strongholds. They are not natural. If they are man-made, the solution is ... eradicating the things in the people that produce the problem.'

The strongholds are 'our assumptions, our desires, our understanding and our values; all these are part of what is generally labelled as our culture. There, I have landed [Ghanaian English for 'I have come straight out and said it'].' Otabil is aware of all the complexities in the question of culture, but defines it simply as 'the totality of everything you have learnt and practise'. It is not inborn: 'Culture is not in your genes. It is made out of what you have been taught. But the tragedy is, were we taught right?' 'Habits [and] behaviour can be learned. Behaviour can change. That is

[22] Landes, *Wealth*, 516–17.

the power of the gospel...Christ says when you come to him he can take the old nature and replace it with a new nature.' 'May I suggest to you, my friends, that one of the major reasons why Africa is where it is today is because of old, antiquated, unusable, unworkable traditions.' Therefore, 'You can talk about structural adjustment. It doesn't really change anything. The real adjustment [needed] is cultural understanding adjustment.'[23] He notes the fine values in African tradition (respect for the aged is one he often singles out), but 'Paul tells us to pull down the negative ones, and I can tell you there are many of them in our culture.'

The first stronghold he discusses (each stronghold was given two programmes) is 'inferiority complex. It is a major stronghold for all African people, the inferiority of our blackness.' 'Somehow we believe that our answer is in Europe. It is foundational to almost all the problems we have. That's why we never discover our own greatness.' 'We believe everything the white man says. We cannot accept an election result unless verified by observers from overseas.'[24]

The second 'stronghold' is tribalism. It affects everything. 'We are fighting about little traditions which have no clues to solving our problems now. You are proud. "I am a Ga," you say. Who told you? The other thing about tribalism is that nobody knows who he is. Now you say you are a Ga, but go back five generations and you see your great-great-grandfather came from Burkina.' 'You have been told your ancestors were proud warriors. Yes, they were killing people and killing elephants. Well, my friend, we don't kill people now. We are now on email, we are now on the internet, we are [trying to solve] more complex problems than killing enemies.' Tribalism gives rise to different standards: 'We are so tribal, if one of our tribesmen does wrong we don't see it. If one of us does something it must be right. How can a nation and a people think of developing with that mentality?' He laments the 'us' versus 'them' mentality: 'We are mismanaging our country because of tribalism. We are pushing people with potential out because they don't belong to our group.' Even the IMF funds are distributed by tribe. All this must stop, and it must begin in the church. 'The church must be the most detribalised community in our nation, where people don't care where you come from; they care only that you are washed by the blood of Jesus.'

---

[23] He discusses similar ideas under 'Mental Structural Adjustment' as a prerequisite of any 'African Renaissance' in his second Ofori Atta lecture, 18 Oct. 00.

[24] Self-reliance is inculcated in his 'Becoming a Leader' series: 'We are a "trouble-free" people. If the battle gets tough, we lie down. [Clinton visited Accra to a rapturous reception.] We call [such a welcome] Ghanaian hospitality. No, it's African beggar spirit, saying: "We can't do it, you do it for us." We are beggars. We have developed a spirit of beggars.' (29 Aug. 02)

The third stronghold is 'cultural stagnation'. 'Let's not live our lives locked into the past. Let's release our lives to embrace new technology, new opportunities, and that is why our culture also must be positive-looking instead of backward-looking.' With some humour he illustrated his case with the way of preparing fufu, a Ghanaian staple food made from yams, plantain or cassava. It takes hours of physical exertion to pound, so someone invented a machine to prepare fufu, but 'it didn't catch on because we said culturally it was not sweet. Although fufu is tasteless, we said the machine one is not sweet, the manpower one very sweet.' Thus labour-intensive traditions persist. 'How can we advance... when culturally we hinder new technological development?' Otabil has instituted his own personal rebellion, and on principle refuses to eat fufu.

The fourth stronghold is idolatry and fetishism (building on Jos 24. 14–16). 'Idolatry and fetishism is the major problem in our part of the world... Because of fetishism, development has been hindered.' He marvelled at the marks and talismans adorning all bodies. 'In Ghana we don't believe in hard work and merit; we believe in jujuing our way to power... People, instead of working hard and gaining access to greatness, want to use spiritual influence. It gets more ridiculous by the day. A man wants his wife to love him. Instead of being nice, being romantic, talking nicely to his wife—"Sweetheart, how are you?"—and just spending time with his wife, no, he wouldn't do that; he goes to the juju man to give him a certain potion to put under the wife's pillow so that the wife will love him. So human effort is not encouraged. Women who want their men to love them, instead of changing their character, change their fetish!' He continues: 'It gets more and more ridiculous', referring to Ghana's attempt to qualify for the football World Cup. A player has been told that whoever scores the first goal in a match will be crippled; so, when given an easy penalty, he deliberately shoots wide. Otabil laments: 'How can we develop?'[25] 'Effort is what produces results, not concoctions and mysterious applications.' Fetishism is based on fear: 'We cannot build our nation on fear; it has to be based on knowledge of what is right and beneficial for us.'

His fifth stronghold is what he labelled 'village mentality', the narrow, backward-looking attitudes that define Africa—even for CNN whose

---

[25] The incident referred to occurred in fact not in a World Cup qualifying match, but in the December 1997 Africa's club championship final between Accra's Hearts of Oak and Hafia of Guinea. Hearts' 'native doctor' had predicted that the scorer of the first goal would die—hence the reluctance to score. The Guineans eventually won 1–0. An article covering 'Witchcraft in Football' concludes with something significant for a study of Ghana's new Christianity—Pentecostal pastors have replaced 'native doctors'. Thus the old worldview persists, now carried forward by charismatic Christianity. (*African Soccer*, Aug.–Sept. 2001, 14–21)

'Inside Africa' programme is introduced with the words 'Africa, a continent rich in culture and diversity, with its future rooted in its past'. When they talk about Asia, says Otabil, they don't talk about their rich past, 'they talk about a continent on the verge of breakthrough.' 'Our world has been defined in the old, and we can't break from that image. Read the "African Writers" series, and almost everything is about the past of Africa. When are we going to write our science fictions, when are we going to project our imagination to conceive of a new world, a new environment, a new people and a new culture?' Every nation used to dress in loose cloth, have chiefs, complicated land tenure; but others have moved on. It is the same 'village mentality' that leads family members to litigate over some dilapidated family house, rather than get on and build their own new ones, or to hang on to some gold family heirloom while they cannot pay children's school fees. 'All societies began from the village; villages are not African. Everywhere people have lived in villages, but have grown into more cosmopolitan outlooks of life.'

The sixth stronghold 'that has kept us underdeveloped for all these years is the stronghold of wrong, negative leadership. When you look across Africa it looks as if we have a copyright on dictatorship, as if it has been patented for African society, or natural for us to produce bad leaders.' But bad leadership is evident not only in the political sphere, 'it is within every sphere of our lives, including the home' and school. Using Matthew 20. 20–21 Otabil argues that good leadership is about service. However, African leadership is concerned not with performance or responsibility but with status, power, even titles. 'Chiefdom is the basis of most of the leadership in Africa.' (Voicing his apprehension, he remarked: 'I don't want to say "chieftaincy", because people will say I am attacking a noble institution, so I say "chiefdom"—at least I am protecting myself.') 'The moment we get into leadership we think we are chiefs.' There are several defects in this understanding. Position is held for life. Leadership is restricted to a certain line 'whether you have the qualities or not'. Conversely, others who might have the requisite qualities are excluded. No opposition can be entertained: 'All those not in agreement with chiefs are called rebels, … an enemy who must be expelled.' In chiefdom there are praise singers 'because the chief is a representative of the ancestors and so is always right.' So go to any African country, and you will hear songs about the president like: 'We were sitting in darkness before he came.' Thus people come to believe their destiny is determined by the favour of their chief; 'if he lifts you up, you come up, if he puts you down, you are down.' It is for this reason that hypocrisy and sycophancy are so rife in Africa.[26]

---

[26] In an interview on Joy FM he criticised the institution of chieftaincy, expressing the hope it would just fade away, or be replaced with one ceremonial 'King of Ghana': 'We have to

The final stronghold in this series is apathy (here Otabil made some of the points listed above in summarising his sermon 'The People Don't Care'). Apathy is encouraged by the ubiquity of suffering and squalor—foul gutters, people urinating publicly (something that Otabil regards with special disgust[27]), women carrying enormous loads. 'If we want to pull down this stronghold, we must consciously and deliberately reject what is unacceptable. We must learn to be angry.' 'The second cause of apathy is insensitivity of leaders. It doesn't matter how much you protest in our part of the world; people in leadership positions don't care... We learn it from childhood. When the leader is wrong, it is the child who apologises. Everybody knows that the leader was wrong, but they will say: "It is all right; it is part of our culture; you go and apologise." When in a marriage the husband is wrong, it is the wife who apologises.' The third reason for apathy is religious fatalism. 'We define things religiously... We feel and believe that the forces against us are so powerful that we can't do anything about it. There are people who are poor who believe that is how God made them... There is nothing you can do by yourself to change the situation; religious fatalism produces apathy.'

If these strongholds ('These are the things that have crippled our continent') are to be pulled down, 'old assumptions must be confronted, honestly, respectfully and boldly ... We must take responsibility to design a new map for our journey. We must distance ourselves from practices that

---

get used to the fact that we are not being ruled by chiefs but by elected officials who have been elected by the people to govern them.' (see *Daily Guide*, 17 April 01, 8) What he saw as the deficiencies of chieftaincy were discussed in his first Ofori-Atta lecture (17 Oct. 00).

It is this 'cultural' understanding of leadership generally rather than Rawlings or the NDC in particular that Otabil characteristically criticised, although he could be fairly specific at times: 'One of the reasons why Africa is where it is today is because of the immoral leadership we have had for a very long time. Leadership that has elevated corruption of virtue, corruption of character, corruption of choices, corruption of decisions, which has resulted in mismanagement of our national resources.' (speech at CUC matriculation, 13 Jan. 2001, in *Pathfinder*, 1 (2000), 10) Also: 'The political leader is busy calculating his ten per cent interest on spurious contracts which will increase our national debt but add no value to the life of the citizens. His ears are plugged with dollar notes and pounds sterling.' (Second Heritage Lecture, 29 June 99)

[27] 'If we get to that level [of urinating and defecating in public] we are in serious trouble. We can't talk about investors when that's how we are living. Anyone who sees human beings doing that, they will think these people either just arrived from a tree, or they came from a hole... Who would want to invest in a country where people have no control? Who? Who? If me, I wouldn't, because the way they treat their country is the way they will treat my investment. They have no value for honour, beauty, dignity, self-respect, and a people who has no value for that, you cannot trust with wealth in their hands. They will abuse it and destroy it. We need to clean up our lives, clean up our nation!' (27 Aug. 00)

are unhelpful to the journey we have embarked on.' In his concluding sermons he drew lessons from incidents in the account of Joshua's entering the promised land. 'We must be willing to face anger and criticism from people who are comfortable to stay where they are.' 'Between us and economic development… and technological advancement are the seven strongholds I have talked about.' We must understand these issues and have courage, 'because when you are the problem yourself it takes courage to say, "I am the problem".' Effort must be concerted, and we must not be played with politically: 'Politicians carelessly fuel our underdevelopment.' And (from Joshua 6.5) 'We must shout against the stronghold till it crumbles…If it is bad leadership, shout against it until it falls, if it is injustice, poverty, tribalism, shout against it until it falls. When we keep quiet over that which is wrong we empower that which is wrong… Africa must start shouting till dictatorship falls, till tribalism falls, till the wrong leadership falls. We must shout and shout till all our walls of Jericho are down… Africa cannot continue in this present state any longer. We have to have zero tolerance for our underdevelopment because our underdevelopment is man-made and not God-made; it is man-made, self-inflicted and self-imposed… We are not poor by accident, we are poor by choice. We are not illiterate by accident, but by choice.' He stresses (from Deuteronomy 20.19–20) that Ghanaians must be discriminating, and preserve all that is noble from African traditions.

Finally he addresses the inevitable question: 'Somebody will say, "You are a preacher. Why are you talking about these things?"' He defends himself from the Lord's Prayer (Mt 6.9–13) that God's will be done 'on earth as it is in heaven'. The situation in Africa is not heaven on earth, but hell on earth, and an affront to God who made us in his image and likeness. (Gen 1.27)

This series succinctly gives the flavour of the Christianity that Otabil stands for and deepens our perspective on the range of Ghanaian charismatic Christianity as a whole. Not every Otabil sermon or every series of sermons is like this, but this perspective or awareness colours his treatment even of religious topics like sin and communion. This is the tenor of what is broadcast every week on several different outlets, and is the message with which he is identified. We return to this in the following chapters where economic and political issues are raised. However, it is already clear that calling Otabil 'anti-Rawlings' or 'anti-NDC' was a serious misunderstanding. His critique is far more profound than that. In brief, his point is that an individual's plight is inevitably related to the national situation. And Ghana's plight, he claims, is not caused by demons, witches or ancestral curses; nor are its fundamental causes slavery, colonialism, neo-colonialism and the IMF. It will not be rectified by tithing, anointing with oil, impartation from an anointed man of God, or by God's miraculous intervention. It is caused at least partly by deep-seated values and practices, and will be rectified only when Africans themselves address them.

In the struggle to address them, education is his crusade. 'We have to be aggressive for our people... We have to attack ignorance and illiteracy as though [they were] the devil himself.' And in another sermon: 'If there is any one thing I can achieve in your life as your pastor, I want you to hate your ignorance with a passion. Illiteracy has no relevance, semi-literacy is a liability, ignorance is your enemy. If you are ignorant you become a disaster to yourself and a menace to society.' 'A nation with 70% illiteracy has no future... Get education, get knowledge, improve yourself, develop your talent, develop your skill, go to school, take corre-spondence classes, start!' All must aim high. 'The power to do it is in your head; there is nothing you cannot learn; nothing.'[28]

He goes further and links education to mastery of the English lan-guage. 'My desire is that every member of this church should gain a mas-tery of the English language...Don't sit down there and say "It is not my language". It may not be your language but it is the language of the busi-ness world, and if you don't master it you will be sidelined.' Fante, Otabil's own language, has about 8,000 words; the English language has over 2,000,000, including the 'words that have to do with medicine, law, computer technology... If all you know is your language you limit your-self, because the world is talking about gigabytes and megabytes and hard disks and viruses and macros. New words, new technology is mak-ing us obsolete by the minute.'[29]

Ghanaians must look to the future, and accept change. 'The problem with Ghana and I suppose most African nations is that we allow our his-tory and our past to influence our present and design our future. Much of what we call our culture is actually the lifestyle of people who lived about 300 years ago and their way of understanding the world they lived in. It's not *our* culture; it's *their* culture, *their* way of life. The way some people thought 300 years ago is not the way I should think in the year 2000. Their principles can often be salvaged, but not their practices.' Later: 'The past that we have called our culture most of the time prevents us from change, and no society can develop without change.' Otabil refuses

---

[28] 'Talent, Work and Profit'.

[29] Ibid. Again: 'Fante is a good language, it holds our social beliefs, cultural practices, it binds us together as a people in our tribes, but if we are going to make progress in the next century, in addition to speaking Fante, we have to speak English, because it is the most widely spoken language in the world.' I have heard him on other occasions give different numbers for words in Fante and English.

to accept things as African because they were done in the past, like eating with hands, or sweeping with brooms made of palm branches: 'That's not African; it's antique, antiquated... Change is necessary for every society to move from one plateau to a higher level, and we as a people have plateau-ed for too long. The reason is that we are afraid of change.'[30] Look at postcards from abroad—'skyscrapers and things'—but 'a post-card of Africa is giraffe, elephant, naked girl, hut. Don't tell me that I am supposed to stay there so that you can call that my culture! No! And Africa is far behind the rest of the world and falling further behind.'

His passion for modernisation is given urgency by this feeling of falling behind. 'For us especially, Africans, the gap we have to cover is too wide. [A recent CNN report] really shocked me; that at this rate of development in Africa, Ghana or sub-Saharan Africa it's going to take us 250 years to be where America is today. That's for your information. If we keep going at this pace, and just rejoice—O Culture! Culture! Culture!— it's going to take us 250 years to be where America is today... [Meanwhile], guess what? The people we are trying to catch up to, they are moving at just the speed of light. In the next ten years it should be about 300 years, in another ten years it could be about 400, 500 years behind. While all this is going on we are joking and are engaging our minds in arguments, debates, discussions which bring no development to anybody, and yet we focus our minds there and kill for that.' This reference to killing is to annual disputes in Accra between the Ga traditional rulers and Christians over the former's ban on drumming in church in preparation for the annual *Homowo* festival. In mid-2001 this again led to violent clashes. Otabil refuses to go on TV to debate such trivia. 'When the rest of the world is talking about information technology, we are talking about beating or not beating drums.... That's wickedness.'[31]

A different voice

Much of this preaching was genuinely original. It was also bold, not because Otabil was confronting a repressive NDC government, but because in many places he was saying the unsayable. At times he has even had his own congregation gasping. I once heard him remark, stressing the urgency of modernisation, that others were building ships and trains 'while we were in our little huts commanding golden stools from the sky.'

---

[30] 'Traditionally, many African people see modernisation as the exclusive preserve of the white man and therefore resist progress as a way of maintaining "cultural purity".' (First Ofori Atta lecture, 17 Oct. 00)
[31] 'Talent, Work and Profit'.

This almost dismissive reference (incidentally, not in a broadcast series, when perhaps he is more careful) to the foundation Asante myth brought a sharp intake of breath from many.[32] However, although he was obviously touching a nerve in mentioning these issues, he was interrupted several times by applause. We noted that in Ghana the majority opinion on Africa's plight seems overwhelmingly internalist rather than externalist; so too in his church, his position is not seriously questioned, and his broadcasts are met with wide approval.

Otabil is a skilful speaker. Although he does not normally raise his voice, when he launches into Africa's situation he burns with passion, rage, anger, and exasperation—like an Old Testament prophet in full cry. He did not directly attack the NDC, but in passing could allude to the actions of government officials in a tone of voice indicating complete incredulity or total contempt. He treads a fine line. As we have indicated, he can berate his congregation—'What was the last book you read? What? What? ... When was the last time you seriously read anything? I'm asking *you! you! you!*' (13 Aug. 00). But no one keeps coming back to church just to be berated; he also encourages, uses humour and anecdotes—he too, no less than the others, is an entertainer. He can show considerable sensitivity; for example, on the issues of witchcraft and juju referred to above, although they are obviously key obstacles for him, his treatment was characterised by humour and wonder rather than contempt and derision. He looks to the future, but is not dismissive of the past: 'We must honour our ancestors' contribution and find ways to celebrate their memories, but the greatest memorial we can give them is to go beyond survival and attain greatness in our time.'[33] He can criticise Africa profoundly, but at the same time he is fiercely proud of Africa—hence the attire.

The pride, self-confidence, if not arrogance, is also part of the performance, part of the persona he needs to project as a successful, assured, self-confident individual, the embodiment of Black pride, an African who is the equal of anyone. I have seen him at a conference in Zambia ask his audience of several thousands: 'You think I am proud? No, I'm a very

---

[32] He was instilling urgency, describing the women's relay at an international athletics meeting that he had been watching on TV. The USA were pulling ahead at every leg, and were well in the lead, even before the baton was passed to Marion Jones, the fastest woman in the world. This, says Otabil, is an image of Africa in relation to the rest of the world The race is going on, we are far behind. 'Already far ahead and going further... the people we are running with couldn't care less about us.' (11 Sept. 00)

[33] First Ofori-Atta lecture, 17 Oct. 00. He continued: 'We may have to discard some of their views and practices, without disowning them as our noble forebears. We must ascend new mountains and cross uncharted rivers in order to preserve a heritage of worth for the generations after us.'

humble man—a very *confident* humble man.' And again, to loud applause, 'Proud? No, I'm just an African being the way God intended us to be.'[34]

In the first chapter we outlined the change in the debate about the economies of Africa, noting that it has entered the realm of political culture. We are unable to say how familiar Otabil is with academic debates, or whether he has been influenced by them—probably not. He has not been interpreted here in the light of any voices in that debate; he has his own view of Ghana's political culture, as we have seen. Nevertheless, he is clear in his own mind that this dimension is significant: 'Many of the societal ills ravaging our national life, such as corruption, nepotism, dictatorship and cronyism, have their origins rooted in old traditional values which are not well adapted to our present political and economic realities.'[35] From that understanding he theologises about the plight of Ghanaians. This is a genuine theology of liberation, but ironically not in the sense in which he has often been acclaimed as a liberation theologian. His 'black consciousness', as manifested in his *Beyond the Rivers of*

[34] He can be humorously self-deprecating; for example, referring to a biblical text, he says: 'Don't say Otabil wrote it. No, I haven't written a Bible—not yet.' (24 Sept. 00) However, even some of his own pastors think that the arrogance is not all feigned. He has concluded a message: 'As members of this church you have no right to be a failure... The stuff I am giving you in this church you will not get anywhere [else]. I am not saying this to brag, I know who I am and I don't need to boast. I stopped boasting a long time ago. I just say the facts. You can't get this anywhere, not anywhere in this country, not anywhere in this continent and all over the world it's only a few places that you can get messages structured in this way for your consumption. I spend hours to prepare to minister to you. I spend days, weeks, months, and sometimes years thinking, volumes of information, research, books, to preach a message of 45 minutes. Don't waste that effort... I bring knowledge that will shape your mind, shape your future and focus you.' With this sometimes comes an oblique disparagement of others. 'I could come here and preach Daniel in the Lions' den, Noah in the ark, Samson and Delilah, and create jokes about it, and not give you any point... when I finish I would shake my body a little and I will say the anointing is upon me, and I will say "Bring your olive oil", and I will pour it on you and push you to the ground and you would be blessed. I could do that, it's an easy way, but I choose to prepare, to focus to where you really need help.'

[35] First Ofori-Atta Lecture, 17 Oct. 00. Other cultural features he questions include the money (*3 Dec. 00*) and time spent on funerals: 'No wonder we are in the third world!' (*9 May 01*); untidiness—'We are dying every day because of a little insect called the mosquito which can be eradicated simply by neat hygienic practices. Simple. But there is a stronghold that keeps us from being neat' (Stronghold series); formal procedures of operating: 'Any culture that sets value on slow, cumbersome deliberations and protocols in decision-making will find itself constantly out-run and out-paced in the new global economy' (First Ofori-Atta Lecture, 17 Oct. 00); family relations: 'Most Africans are not good parents. We inherited a culture that undervalued children, and undervalued marriage.' (*22 July 01*—in a most imaginative treatment of 'Blessed are those who mourn' [Mt 5.4] which he turned into an exhortation to value things) He also refers to 'husbands who are culturally undeveloped' (video 'Opening New Pages for your Life'). He attacks the notion of 'African time' (12 Nov. 00), the reluctance to fix appointments and the stress on titles: 'Titles are a hindrance to performance.' (*18 Feb. 01*)

Ethiopia, has been labelled an 'Evangelical-Pentecostal Liberation theology'.[36] But Otabil has moved beyond that. His passion is still to raise the self-image of the Black peoples (we saw him treat 'inferiority complex' as the first 'stronghold' that has to be destroyed) but the way to free Ghanaians is now envisaged differently. In 1992 he was talking about 'the oppressor', but this is less the case now. This is not to say that he has repudiated his earlier stance. While not dismissing colonialism, the debt burden, or unfair trade flows as contributing to Africa's plight, he has certainly transcended his earlier position in the dimension he has added, in the new weighting he gives to the different factors, in the different angle from which solutions must be sought.[37] There is genuine novelty here. In certain respects Otabil is probably the most interesting Christian voice currently being heard in Africa.

Over the years, through persistence and application, he has established himself as the star in the charismatic firmament of Ghana, and possibly of Africa. It was significant that already in 1994 at a Pan African Christian Leadership Assembly (PACLA) conference in Nairobi the two speakers at the plenary session on the opening night were Archbishop Desmond Tutu, then at the height of his fame after South Africa's first democratic elections, and Mensa Otabil. Accra's mushrooming if often short-lived Christian newspapers need a story of Otabil on the front page to establish themselves. Others need him for their special occasions, like book launches.[38] Agyin Asare made him the key speaker in launching his Agyin Asare Gospel Crusade. The organisers of the visiting 'Winning Ways' needed him on board before they could prepare.[39]

---

[36] Thus Ogbu Kalu; see Larbi, *Pentecostalism*, 335, 349–53.

[37] Well caught in the conclusion of his second Heritage Lecture: 'We are not only bound by the shackles of the white man's slavery and colonialism, but more so by the limited and narrow confines of our ancestors' world. Their world did not conceive of nationalisation [nation-building?], globalisation, cyberspace and space travel. We, their descendants, are part of a world going through change on a magnitude and scale that the world has not experienced before. It is a change which renders a lot of their assumptions and views redundant. This world challenges us to change many of our cherished and accepted ways.' (29 June 99)

[38] Ebenezer Markwei invited Otabil to launch his book (*Graphic*, 21 June 01, 14; *Chronicle*, 19 June 01, 4), and Eastwood Anaba likewise with *Oil of Influence* (*Graphic*, 21 July 00, 14); so too Duncan-Williams with *Destined to Make an Impact* (*Graphic*, 8 April 02, 3). Otabil spoke at the opening of the Africa Institute of Journalism and Communication school (*Graphic*, 2 Feb. 01, 16); opening an interdenominational fellowship at Tema (*Graphic*, 18 April 01, 13); the Salt and Light workshop on 'Being the Best that God wants you to Be' (27–28 Oct. 00—message reprinted in *Chronicle*, 1–3 Dec. 00, 10); the culmination of the celebrations marking the opening of Korankye Ankrah's RHCI, 12 Nov. 00.

[39] 'Then somebody whispered that Ashimolowo is being hosted by Otabil. That settled the matter.' (*Graphic*, 28 Feb. 01, 9)

A good illustration of his stature is offered by the 'Winning Ways' crusade. We have covered this in some detail, arguing not only that it is paradigmatic of Africa's new Christianity, but also that such crusades are one of the vehicles by which it is promoted. We explained that for the three international speakers, acknowledged giants of this Christianity, the two themes were success and (if it be considered a separate theme) the way to success, namely giving and 'the anointing'. In the course of one of his presentations, Myles Munroe had argued: 'Your purpose cannot be defeated.' This point, received with great acclaim, was that your life has meaning, indeed was given meaning before the creation of the world, and that this purpose will be attained despite any current apparently negative circumstances. Otabil, given a speaking slot on the final morning, began by heaping praise on the three visitors for all they had done, but then set out to explain what 'Myles had really meant' in case some had misunderstood him. 'I feel there are things we should put in perspective. Pastor Munroe made a very profound statement... Sin cannot cancel purpose. Sin cannot cancel purpose, but sin will prevent you from fulfilling your purpose.' 'God has a purpose, but that does not work itself out automatically, and certainly if you are living in sin you will abort your purpose.' Then Otabil, for some the byword for motivational preaching and for others a philosopher of social improvement, delivered a very old-time tirade against sin.[40] He stressed the need for self-discipline in life. 'The Christian life is a life of discipline.' 'You don't have a purpose. It is God who has a purpose. It's not yours. It is God's intention, and God requires that I live in a certain way to catch the purpose.' There are some conditions to fulfill, and one of them is that 'Your Christian character must match your purpose.'

Munroe in one of his sermons had indulged in a rhetorical flourish that 'All these pastors [here] have committed adultery.' After letting the shock sink in, he explained, using Matthew 5.28, that looking at a woman constitutes adultery. Obviously stung, Otabil in his message countered: 'I don't commit adultery.' ('Ever since I was called, I have not defiled myself; I am not going to run the risk while preaching of having some woman shout out from the back: "What about you?"') He harangued the pastors present about their need to lead spotless lives. 'Pastors, don't destroy your purpose with reckless living.' It is the same for Christians who are not pastors: 'He will take everything from you [the effect of sin]. You will end up with nothing.' He concluded (after a call to put the faith gospel into perspective too): 'Sin will abort your purpose, I tell you. Put

---

[40] Compare the large segment of this Christianity where, I argued, the issue of sin seldom arises (pp. 109–10 above).

your principles into perspective. This thing is not mechanical. If you don't get that right you will self-destruct.' Without mentioning Murdock by name, he argued that nothing is automatic or mechanical—it is the logic of Murdock's position that 'principles' like the principle of sowing and reaping work at all times and for everyone. In the context of that convention, this added a whole new dimension. Had Otabil not spoken, the 'Winning Ways' convention would have promoted success for both the individual and the nation, achieved through giving, and (if Agyin Asare, the other local speaker, had not introduced the idea of evangelisation) nothing else.

This preoccupation with the wider picture leads some to leave Otabil's church; it is possible to find people leaving 'because his message does not bless me'—there is no anointing for visas or husbands here. He is aware of this, and faced it directly at the beginning of his 'Strongholds' series. 'Normally when you talk about the problems of Africa, people will say, "Well, but you're talking about the big problems. I don't want to hear about Africa's problems. I want to hear about my own problems." What you fail to understand is that your own problems are the reflection of the bigger problems.' His socio-political awareness also leads some within the charismatic sector to murmur that Otabil has fallen from his evangelical correctness and become a social commentator or development consultant. A similar criticism of reductionism was directed against Latin America's liberation theologians, that they were essentially politicians, promoting a social programme under the guise of a theology. Otabil could doubtless defend himself on this issue. His basic insight seems to stem from Genesis 1.26–27—'Created in the image and likeness of God' which he quotes incessantly. As he looks around Ghana he sees most Ghanaians brutalised by poverty and ignorance, far from the dignity intended by God. He has committed himself to restoring this image and likeness through his church.[41]

But his influence is far wider than the charismatic family. His TV and radio programmes have probably made him better known than any of

---

[41] After the final Ofori-Atta lecture, he was asked: 'What is the role of the church in all this?' He replied: 'To represent God. What would God do when confronted with this poverty, this ignorance? God would say, "Let my people go. Teach them wisdom." That should be the church's role.' (19 Oct. 00) Also indicative were remarks at the end of his series 'Principles of Effective Living': 'Some one will say, "But Pastor, you didn't talk too much about *the anointing*, about *the power*. All that you talk about is knowledge, knowledge, knowledge." That's the problem with us. We think of knowledge as an enemy. God himself has revealed himself in us in knowledge. His Word is knowledge imparted to us... Man lives by the Word of God. Our job as a church is primarily to give knowledge. The number one job is not to provide bread, but to give knowledge so people can make bread.' (27 Aug. 00)

Ghana's mainline churchmen. He has become a national figure. In June 2001, after the transition from the NDC to the NPP, the Centre for Democratic Development held an International Conference on National Reconciliation to discuss ways of reconciling the nation after the divisive Rawlings years. It was significant that Otabil provided the Christian presentation.[42] It was significant that the Catholic President Kufuor, to mark the first anniversary of his election, attended a thanksgiving service at Otabil's church.[43] A few weeks later Otabil preached to parliamentarians of both parties.[44]

Even those attacking Ghana's new pastors tend to make an exception of Otabil. An editorial in the *Chronicle*, which has devoted pages to vilifying Duncan-Williams (and suggesting or implying all sorts of things about other charismatic pastors), called him the 'nation's most respected and outstanding teacher of the word of God', and continued: 'Pastor Mensa Otabil has stirred millions of Ghanaians with his awesome messages that cut through the waffle and strike the consciousness. Even to unbelievers, his persuasive sermons have a way of challenging their unbelief and impacting them positively. And in a nation loaded with all manner of prophets and necromancers coming to us as Christian evangelists and miracle workers, it is soothing that there are preachers like Anamua Mensa Otabil who connects completely with the people.'[45] On Radio Univers' 8 May 2000 'Media Review', panellists discussing a story implicating a pastor in an armed robbery agreed that something had to be done about Ghana's explosion of new churches. The programme's Muslim controller remarked to murmurs of agreement: 'When you listen to Otabil you are so happy but when you listen to some of [the pastors on] our radio stations you get so mad.' Otabil's national standing was suggested on another programme of the same 'Media Review' (*24 Oct. 00*) when after a survey of news so depressing that the panellists almost despaired of Ghana, the same Alhaji was led to ask in desperation: 'Would [even] Otabil be able to change things?'

We have devoted a chapter to Otabil because one of the aims of this book is to illustrate the diversity within charismatic Christianity. Obviously Otabil represents a very different strand from that discussed in the

---

[42] CDD, *National Reconciliation, International Perspectives*, Accra: CDD, 2001.

[43] At the service it was revealed that Kufuor came to Otabil for prayers a few days before the 2000 elections. (*Chronicle*, 10 Jan. 02, 1; see also *Graphic*, 7 Jan. 02, 1)

[44] *Chronicle*, 21 Jan. 02, 1—under the banner headline 'Otabil's Chilling Message to MPs'.

[45] *Chronicle*, 24–25 Nov. 00, p. 5. Another editorial praises him 25–27 Aug. 00, 5, and a news item refers to him as 'the respected pastor' (*Chronicle*, 9–10 Jan. 01, 8) and another 'Rabbi to the Nation' (21 Jan. 02, 1). It is readily admitted that the virulently anti-NDC *Chronicle* would naturally warm to Otabil.

previous chapter. General discussion of 'Ghana's charismatic Christianity' as some single reality does not do justice to either strand. Another aim was to enter the debate about the socio-political role of these churches. Observers often presume that charismatic churches affect the political sphere only indirectly, unlike the liberal mainline churches with their theologies of engagement. Here, however, is a charismatic Christianity that consciously makes Africa's condition a central concern, and addresses it not through any imported liberation theology but on a cultural level. This theology has emerged from the charismatic and not the mainline sector. If it is not yet extensively preached, it seems none the less to be received with wide acclaim in Ghana. We will meet Otabil again in the following chapters when we specifically address the economic and political effects of charismatic Christianity.

6

ECONOMIC ROLE

We have established that there is a wide diversity within these churches. And we have insisted throughout that there have been marked changes over time, which make generalisation even more difficult. This chapter addresses in general terms some issues arising from the economic challenges facing Ghana in an age of modernisation and globalisation.

Motivation

As we have repeatedly seen, all these new churches act in some measure as motivators—some to such a degree that they are commonly defined by this function alone. In all of them the stress is to get on, to succeed, to be important, to possess things, to take control. Moreover, these things are your right and inheritance, which you should expect and can demand. The emphasis is on self-esteem, ambition, confidence. Sometimes a racial element enters into this: you can succeed like the Whites. Being Black does not mean subservience and poverty—this is reinforced from the scriptures.

Any encouragement to self-belief must undoubtedly have positive effects. To take a simple example from an area of crucial importance for Ghanaians, someone who believes her visa has already been granted 'spiritually' may go to her interview at the Western embassy with head high, relaxed and confident, and thus perform better than someone apprehensive and diffident. Likewise, one who believes victory is his right may show enormous persistence and determination, and thus overcome difficulties that would defeat others. Obviously a sufficient number must succeed for the movement not to be discredited, although we have noted that, despite the stress on testimonies in this Christianity, strict verification of 'biblical' promises is not a priority.

All this remains true, no matter how solid the basis for this confidence actually is. If one is convinced that spiritual forces are holding one back, a conviction that those spiritual forces have been defeated might release

the wells of energy so crucial for success.[1] Nevertheless, although someone with self-belief will tend to achieve more than one without, Ghana's
circumstances are very different from those of the United States in the
1950s and '60s when Norman Vincent Peale was so popular and perhaps
so effective. In Ghana no amount of personal determination and ambition
does much to touch the neo-patrimonial structures that serve Ghanaians
so badly. We noted that many (not least in Ghana) are now convinced
that it was primarily those structures that had Ghana going backwards for
much of the past four decades, and despite the rhetoric these structures
were not much improved during the Rawlings era. We return to this in the
next chapter.

In the matter of personal transformation, the focus is usually on creating a 'new work ethic', and it has been argued that these new churches,
especially in Latin America, do exactly that.[2] We will examine this issue
in Ghana.

On this score one only has to talk to charismatics to recognise the
bewildering variety. In the case of Otabil it is clear that work is an essential part of his religious vision. In 2000 he broadcast over sixteen weeks a
series of sermons from Genesis 1 entitled 'Principles for Effective Living',
and from these principles he elaborated a whole theory of work. He
argued that God revealed himself as a creating God, a 'God who works, a
working God, not a lazy God. The principle of work is the most important
principle by which man also manifests what is inside him. A person's
attitude to work will determine how good their lives will be.' From the
principle that 'God is a spirit yet produces material things', he argued that
the way a Christian proves he is spiritual is by producing material things.
'The proof of "the anointing" is not shaking, jumping or falling, but
the products that can be verified here on earth and attributed to you...
Spirituality without productivity leads to superstition. It just becomes
something to dull your senses with, or something to feel good by, but it
produces nothing.'[3] God transformed chaos into order and introduced

---

[1] This may not be so new. Peter Brown claims that 'revealing the bankruptcy of men's invisible enemies, the demons' was the main reason for the success of Christianity in late Antiquity (*The World of Late Antiquity*, London: Thames and Hudson, 1971, 55).

[2] Most notably Bernice Martin, 'New Mutations of the Protestant Ethic among Latin American Pentecostals', *Religion*, 25 (1995), 101–17; also Bernice Martin, 'From Pre- to
Postmodernity in Latin America: the Case of Pentecostalism' in Paul Heelas (with David
Martin and Paul Morris), ed., *Religion, Modernity and Postmodernity*, Oxford: Blackwell,
1998, 102–46.

[3] He continued: 'That is why, in spite of Africa's spirituality, we are still poor, and yet probably we are the most spiritual people... It is when your spirituality helps you to discover
creative principles by which you can now remove your life from ordinariness, to become a
master of conditions that influence your existence, then you can say: "I am anointed and
this is the proof."' ('Principles', tapes 3 & 4)

light into darkness—'I believe in prayer, but God did not pray over the problem; he introduced light into the problem.' The word 'light' enabled Otabil to return to his fixation on education, without which he insists no person or nation will succeed in today's world. From the principle that God has already put the seeds in the plants he created, Otabil expounded the need to take what God has already provided and produce from that.

Let us consider in a little more detail a series of four sermons (eight broadcasts) he preached on precisely this topic, 'Talent, Work and Profit'. The first text he used was Matthew 25.14–29, the parable of the talents. Otabil insisted everyone has been given something: 'It may not be money, it may be brain, skills in your mind, talents in your feet, ability in your hands, but whatever it is, it is useful.' The parable tells of two different approaches to the gift received. The men given five and two talents, 'received, went, traded, gained'. In the same way everyone must 'do something with it. Develop your skill, go to school, go to a vocational school, learn something… Don't keep what you have in its raw state, polish it, develop it.' Everyone must add value to her gift. Even if you sew or sell stew, do it differently, better, so you can charge more. He used the example of Kentucky Fried Chicken's Colonel Sanders; Sanders was a pensioner, but realised that one of his mother's old recipes could be turned into a goldmine. 'I keep telling you over and over again, especially women, don't waste your brains, you were not made for the kitchen; have greater abilities. Yes, cook all right, but that is not the only thing you can do. And if you never marry, don't destroy yourself [don't let it ruin your life]. You may not have a husband, but you have brains, talents, abilities. Use them. Trade with them, exchange better terms and conditions for yourself, because of the talents you have developed. Don't leave your talent in the natural state… Every year make it your aim to learn a new skill, learn something different, know something different, understand something better, improve on your performance. Every year you must go up higher.'

He compared this approach with the very different attitude of the servant given one talent, who would not risk losing it and dug a hole: 'That is wickedness.' Otabil made much of the fact that this 'wicked and lazy' servant would lose even the little that he had. 'It is not a matter of *praying* for change; you must *work* towards change. Undeveloped resources will be lost. The more you develop resources, the more you receive.' The rich get richer, and the poor get poorer; this is the plight of Africa in a globalised world. Otabil urged all his hearers to be the best in whatever they did, and never to admit failure. 'Don't limit yourself because the West African Examinations Council says you are a failure. No.

Your life is not based on the verdict of an Exams Council. Your life is based on your own initiative.'[4]

The second text he used in this series was II Kings 4.1–7, the story of Elisha and the widow reduced to penury. From the little oil she had remaining, Elisha miraculously filled every container she could provide. As remarked above, the miracle cycles of Elijah and Elisha are staples in this charismatic Christianity (and this particular story is normally used to inculcate the need to give to the man of God). Here the narrative is reworked very differently. Otabil developed eight points from the words of the prophet. First, 'What do you have in your house?' Everybody has something that can be used; the key to your victory is within you. Secondly, 'Borrow Vessels'; vessels stand for knowledge. What knowledge you don't have you must get from every available source. Third, 'Don't limit the vessels'; be hungry for more, never say you have everything, keep learning and keep discovering, for there is no end to what you can do. Fourth, 'Go inside your room'; your greatest victory will be won privately. Live frugally so you can invest your initial earnings. Study your Bible, pray, develop your spiritual strength (not least to resist the juju others will direct against anyone successful[5])—become 'God-dependent and self-reliant'. Fifth, 'Shut the door'; allow no interference or disturbance to distort your focus. Let neither critics nor praise-singers deflect you from your purpose. Prepare to be seen as abnormal ('In Africa we have to be abnormal'). Sixth, 'Pour your treasure into the vessels you have borrowed'; new knowledge, technology and ideas must change what you already have; they must change your life. Seventh, 'Set aside the full vessels'; do not rest content at any level of achievement and be prepared to move on. Life must be full of new challenges (especially for Africa which, he claims here, is 250 years, behind the rest of the world). Eighth, 'Sell your oil'; sell your produce, never yourself. Do not lose your profits in foolish contracts.

Here there are several points relevant to the question of constructing a new work ethic. First, in this whole series there is not a single mention of faith; indeed Otabil leaves no room for doubt that the faith gospel and deliverance are not what he has in mind. 'When the woman came to the prophet he did not say: "Kneel down and let me pray for you." He did not

---

[4] Another series on the same text (Mt 25. 14–18) reinforced this thinking. Writing the numbers '5', '2' '1' on a board, Otabil moved the decimal point backwards and forwards; one might start with 5, but by one's own attitudes one could make it 5000.00 or 0.5; 'We do not determine what we are given at the beginning... Life can give you poverty—*you* can turn it into prosperity. Life can give you opportunity—*you* can turn it into destruction.' ('The Value of the Dot', *25 Aug. 02*)

[5] As remarked in the previous chapter, 'juju' is not normally a concern of Otabil's.

say: "Let me cast out some devils from you." He did not say: "You need deliverance." The prophet said: "What do you have in your house?"'— or, in other words, what are the personal resources at your disposal? Again, 'You don't become top by saying "I am the top, I am the top" [as the faith gospel teaches]. No. You don't get to the top by just praying or by studying your Bible, you get to the top by being an expert in the area of knowledge you have chosen.' Also, there is no mention of the anointing, of his own prophetic gifts which will bring about the success of the listener. His role, though not negligible, is of another order: 'If you hear me today and become a failure in life, don't blame me. I have told you what you must hear; the rest is left to you to motivate yourself.' There is no chanting 'Receive it!', answered with cries of 'I receive it!' There is nothing about the legal right of the Christian to wealth and success, or about obstructive witches and spiritual forces; no promises of miraculous 'breakthroughs' or that anything will happen 'today'; nor will any success be achieved through giving. The most remarkable thing is that from a narrative specifically about the miraculous, the miraculous has been completely excised; everything is the responsibility of the individual, particularly the individual's determination to be educated and trained, to acquire skills, to show initiative. The understanding rehearsed here might well be seen as a modern-day work ethic, with the obvious difference that Weber considered the new economic order to be an unconscious side-effect of a new religious understanding; there is nothing unconscious here, for Otabil has deliberately made it a key focus.

The miraculous

However, it is just as obvious in Accra that, in this matter as in others, Otabil is not representative. In what probably amounts to a majority of these churches there is a very different understanding of the place of work in the life of a Christian. Getting on is still the goal, but the means are conceived very differently. We have noted how the miraculous almost defines this Christianity. We have avoided ascribing an 'essence' to charismatic Christianity, but if one had to be identified, it would be 'the miraculous'. Much of the success and achievement that is the Christian's birthright is to be achieved miraculously. This idea is everywhere met with: 'Only a miracle can save', 'Only the hand of God can take us through', 'It's only a miracle that can change you'.

Indeed, the coming change in our fortunes should be so miraculous that it can be attributed only to God; it should be, as in John 9.3, so inexplicable that 'God's glory be manifest.' (as at Jesus Alive, 17 Sept. 00) Agyin Asare expresses it thus: 'God wants your financial crisis to come to a place where every banking principle and rule of economics would have woefully failed, so that when the miracle comes, you will know that it has come by the doing of the Lord.'[6] He insists that God will take a nobody and make him a somebody, 'so people see it and say: "This is the hand of the Lord".' (26 Aug. 00) And Adamson Aromaegbe at World Miracle Church International said: 'You prosper so much and you know it is not you... that favour marks you and separates you from the crowd.' (27 Oct. 00) Similarly Winners': 'God's plan is to make you [such a] success that through you he can draw the attention of the world to himself.' (1 Oct. 00) And later 'God wants you to be successful so that men may be envious and drawn to your God.'[7]

So your success should be miraculous. More often than not, as we have seen, you take possession of your miracle by faith or by giving to God or to his representative—normally the presiding pastor. More recently it is said that the miracle will come about through the power of the pastor, or his anointing, often through what Korankye Ankrah calls his special 'anointing to prosper'. (6 Nov. 00) This understanding of their special gifts as accomplishing the required miracle lies behind the stock phrase with which many pastors' prayers are concluded: 'In Jesus' name, I call it done.' (e.g. Agyin Asare, *23 Dec. 00*) As we have seen, this prophetic gift is often now manifested through a ritual. In Korankye Ankrah's words, 'How take [poverty] away? By oil. You need the anointing.' (*12 May 01*)[8]

We have seen that the faith gospel puts great emphasis on not being influenced by what you see or feel around you—ignore your situation, preachers insist, and simply believe what the Bible says. Chris Oyakhilome of Christ Embassy is typical: '[If you say] "I'm broke", you are looking at the wrong things, for [the scriptures say] "My God supplies all things".' (*31 March 01*) The same idea lies behind the distinction between talking intellectually and talking spiritually, or between reality and truth or fact and truth. In this way the idea arises that Christians do not operate according to the rules of worldly economics. At Winners' the head pastor urged the congregation (3 Sept. 00) to open up to a 'heavenly calendar. It's time to run a spiritual timetable. Some say the Ghana cedi is collapsing. If you are running a spiritual calendar, it doesn't matter. Even if the cedi [comes to be worth] 10,000 to the dollar, even if you have to carry sackfulls of it, it doesn't affect you. Why? Because where it comes from [namely, God] it never runs out. Stop wondering "What is happening to

---

[6] Agyin Asare, *Miracle Time II*, 95.

[7] So also Otabil, preaching on Abraham, 1 April 01; that entire series fits uncomfortably with his major emphases outlined in the last chapter.

[8] On another occasion Korankye Ankrah asserts that we achieve our success 'through the name, the blood, the oil'. (23 June 01)

my business?" Nothing bad is happening to your business. The one who brought you [thus far] is extremely faithful.' Businesses might be collapsing everywhere, but not a Christian's 'because I am fulfilling my destiny. God is the chairman of my business.'[9]

This conviction that where God reigns ordinary economic theory does not apply is widely encountered. Witness the front page of the middle-range *Spectator*, under the headline 'Pastor Prophesies Economic Boom'. Evangelist Obeng, preaching at his Mount Zion Prayer Centre at Abeka La Paz, Accra, 'revealed that God has told him about the deliverance of Ghana from economic bondage and that everything will be alright in the country... [Soon] every Ghanaian can afford to buy any commodity he wants to... Pastor Obeng emphasised that the triumph over the country's economic difficulties is not going to be performed by the strength and might of any politician, pastor or Ghanaian, but by the spirit of the almighty and sovereign God. He urged all Ghanaians, particularly the leaders and top politicians, to pray and fast constantly for the glory of God to manifest itself.'[10]

For much of Ghana's charismatic sector, ordinary economic factors are unimportant in comparison with spiritual forces. Another story from the *Spectator*, headlined 'Kyebi is ruled by Demons', begins: 'It has been revealed by an anointed man of God that Kyebi, the ancient capital of the Akyem Abuakwa State, is controlled, dominated and ruled by demonic powers, principalities and powers of darkness.' These demons are so powerful that, in the words of the Rev. Yao Paul, 'anybody who rises or progresses in his profession of God-given talent is brought down as soon as he is about to reach or reaches the apex of his career.' Not only is this the case for individuals; it also affects the whole region: 'Kyebi has more gold embedded in its soil than Obuasi [the seat of Ghana's economic giant, Ashanti Goldfields]. It has other rich and invaluable minerals, which can make Kyebi one of the richest and [most] prosperous towns in the world. But what is happening is that [the demons] have covered them up. They have sat on them. They don't want the town to progress.' This situation arose because former rulers of the area entered into agreement with these demons, in order to increase their power, and when those rulers died the demons simply ran out of control. Yao Paul prescribed the solution: special days must be set aside by the authorities for intensive and joint

---

[9] So always Oyedepo, Winners' founder: 'It has nothing to do with the government in power in your country. The government of heaven, of which you are a citizen, is still intact and in power... Jesus is still the King of Kings and Lord of Lords. So you are not controlled by the policies of your nation, you are controlled by the covenant of God with His chosen people.' (*The Hidden Covenant of Blessings*, Lagos: Dominion Publishing, 1995, 64)

[10] *Spectator*, 16 June 01, 1; the implied reference to Zechariah 4.6 is typical.

special deliverance services by a number of powerful anointed men of God.[11] So for both individuals and the region economic considerations really do not arise; the problem is spiritual, as is the solution. Demons have caused the poverty; exorcising them will bring prosperity.

Apostle Ahinful, in a column asking 'Can Charismatic Gifts help Society?' answers affirmatively on several scores. The last gift he considers is the gift of miracles, which can be utilised by the state. 'If indeed God's miracle power is used to make the blind see, the cripple walk etc., I don't see why crude oil cannot be made to flow in an area by miracle-working pastors invited together by the state, and secretly given such an assignment. With God all things are possible.'[12] Thus, again, the national economy will be turned around not by economic planning or competence, but by miracles.

This idea that for his chosen people God will do everything necessary is the sense of some of their key scriptural texts. The classic text advocating doing nothing but just sitting back and letting God act is Exodus 14.14: 'The Lord shall fight for you; you need only to be still.'[13] Other texts making the same point are frequently heard. II Chronicles 20 is frequently cited. In II Chronicles 20 the combined armies of Moab, Ammon and Mount Seir advance against Judah. At the urging of a prophet the army of Judah simply praises God. God sets the armies of Moab, Ammon and Mount Seir to destroy each other, so that the army of Judah just has to gather the booty, which is so great that it takes three days to take away. So God does it, we just praise God, watch—and prosper. In Ashimolowo's words: 'When God decides to fight you just become a bystander.' (*27 Jan. 01*)[14]

This seems to be the normal way in which one of their key scriptural mantras is understood. 'It is not by might, nor by power, but by my Spirit says the Lord' (Zech 4.6—also sung as a hymn) is usually taken to mean 'Not by education, nor by training, nor capital, nor budgeting, nor planning, nor enterprise' and so on. Another frequently quoted text, 'The race

---

[11] *Spectator*, 21 July 01, 12.

[12] *Mirror*, 1 Sept. 01, 16.

[13] I have heard this text used only at RHCI (although I have seen 'Ex 14.14' painted on at least three tro-tros and one truck, emblazoned across a private house in Adorkor, and there is an 'Exodus 14.14 Real Estate' company in the Accra suburb of Pig Farm). Heward-Mills quotes it in *Principles*, 33–34.

[14] I have not heard the point made as explicitly as in July 1991 in Nairobi when a white American preached on II Chronicles 14 and 16. In the first passage King Asa relies totally on God and is successful; in the second he relies on himself and is defeated. The preacher explicitly drew the conclusion that in future he would not contaminate his faith by preparation or planning. For II Chron 14, see Victor Osei, *Breaking through Barriers and Limitations II*, Kumasi: the author, 2000.

is not to the swift nor the battle to the strong' (Eccles 9.11), is usually intended to imply that it is the one without the skills and know-how who will reach the top. Similarly, another text (often quoted in conjunction with the two just cited), 'Promotion is not from the East or the West... but from God' (Ps 75.6), seems to be understood to mean that advancement comes not from skill or effort or application or excellence, but miraculously.[15] Another text carrying the same sense is Psalm 33. 16–19: 'No king is saved by the size of his army...' Thus Agyin Asare argues: 'Not by qualifications, abilities, capabilities, but God... because "promotion is not from the East or West, but from God."' (26 Aug. 00) Heward-Mills proclaims: 'Many here can't speak English well... I tell you now that all limitation because of lack of education is removed right now'— repeated four times. (5 Sept. 00) Similarly Duncan-Williams: 'Certain things you are not qualified for; you are now qualified for'—through his anointing (*11 March 01*). Also, at Winners': 'It is possible for divine favour to put in your hand what you are not qualified for. You are not qualified, but *justified* for it... What they said you were not qualified for, today I (decree) you *justified* for it.' (18 Feb. 01)

Of course, for those without education or English or qualifications of any sort, such proclamations could result in heroic effort, but on some occasions human effort is explicitly discounted. At a Gilbert Deya crusade (7 Sept. 00), it was announced that Jesus was 'the giver, the healer, the deliverer; you won't have to work for your miracle.' On the programme for the graduation of the 34th Winners' Bible School, Deuteronomy 6.10–13 was printed in full. Here God promises to give the Israelites a land of cities they did not found, houses they did not build, wells they did not dig, and vineyards and olive groves they did not plant; in a phrase that sums up Winners' theology perfectly, they were to reap what they did not sow (Lk 19.21).[16] These were precisely the words used by Eastwood Anaba preaching at ACI: 'You are not here to labour, but to prosper. Reap where you did not sow.' (*6 May 01*) This expresses the underlying

---

[15] These texts are standard (as is the reference 'Dt 28.1–2' ['Obey and be Blessed'] painted on taxis). Eastwood Anaba has his own motif, that of 'crossed hands', referring to Jacob's crossing his hands to give the blessing destined for the older Manasseh to the younger Ephraim; this 'swapping of preference' can be ours. (Eastwood Anaba, *Birthrights, Blessings and Crumbs: Attitude determines the Portion*, Bolgatanga: Desert Leaf Publications, 2001, 30–1, 66) The same ideas were in his sermon 'The Mystery of Crossed Hands' delivered at ACI, *6 May 01*. Anaba's book well illustrates the point argued later in this chapter; the author mentions hard work (49–50), but the book's argument is that our coming wealth, status and influence are essentially a blessing, a gift freely bestowed on us (esp. 72–85).

[16] This intake of students was identified by the motto 'My Struggles are Over'; February 2000's intake by 'Sweatless Overtakers', and June 2001's by 'Unlimited Achievers'.

anthropology of so many churches: a true Christian is already at the top, and all that is required to succeed or possess is to clear the demonic blockage presently hindering what belongs to that person by right.

A variation on this is that our wealth will come not from anything we do, but through others raised up by God for this purpose, others whom we may not even know. This is the meaning of the 'uncommon favour' that Mike Murdock invoked on all his listeners at the 'Winning Ways' convention. You pay tithes, give to God, and as a result others, perhaps totally unknown to you, come into your life and bless you. Murdock makes it explicit: 'When God wants to bless you, he puts somebody close to you who cares about your life and needs.'[17] Myles Munroe expressed this same idea in his explanation that when Jesus entered the world the wise men came bearing gifts. Munroe even had all the congregation shouting 'Your camels are coming!'[18] Heward-Mills, in a sermon on Isaiah 60. 10–22, 'The Wealth of the Nations for you', had the same theme of God's miraculous provision through others. (5 Sept. 00)

The testimonies contain the same message. A woman testifying at Duncan-Williams's 2000 convention had given 95,000 cedis on 28 November and the next day was given 9 million. Why did she receive 9 million cedis? Purely because she had given the 95,000. Of course the woman may work very hard, but hard work is irrelevant for the logic of the testimony. The congregation were told: 'If it can happen to her, it can happen to you. Say "I will not be denied; Next time it will be me."' A visiting speaker at a Heward-Mills convention, Edwin Alvarez of Paraguay, told (*30 Oct. 00*) of how a woman entered a car showroom and sat in a vehicle she liked. When asked 'Are you going to buy it?', she replied: 'Not now; my father is going to buy it for me.' She left her address and departed. Three days later the shop owner called: 'Madam, come over. Your father has deposited $62,000 for a Toyota Land Cruiser with all extras.' She said, 'My father is dead.' 'Is it your husband?' 'No.' She went to the bank, and was told: 'A man came here. Not a tall man. He gave money and disappeared.' He was never seen again. Alvarez concluded by shouting 'My Father!' five times, implying that this is the way God's paternal provision functions. Alvarez went on to say that he himself had been able to buy a $45,000 parking lot for the church because a stranger was directed by

---

[17] *31 Reaon*, 240.
[18] 'Don't live by what you see [your surrounding circumstances]. Live by what you saw [your vision]. You are coming out from where you are. Your success is coming! [shouted three times] I feel something moving. Receive it! You're not crazy. It's real. Lift your hands and call your camels to you. If they are in Asia, America, Japan, wherever they are, they'll find you… they'll find you.' (7 March 01) So too Gordon Kisseih: 'Even if you don't go outside [i.e. abroad], people outside will bless you.' (25 Feb. 01)

God to give him the money.[19] Such is the standard logic of the typical testimony.

The place of work

All these Christians, if asked, would undoubtedly insist that they believe in the virtue of hard work. Mike Murdock is such a believer. On pages 162–3 of his book *31 Reaon People do not Receive their Financial Harve$t* he says as much. However, this constitutes 38 lines in a book of 250 pages. The logic of the rest of the book is that hard work is quite immaterial. It is 'sowing into God's kingdom' that brings your financial harvest. In his words, 'One day of favour [is] worth a thousand days of labor.'[20]

Salifu's *Power to Make Wealth* pronounces the same message. He is clear: 'Child of God, your Father in heaven wants you to have all the wealth you could possibly get'[21]—something that needs to be addressed by those who insist that prosperity for these Christians means mere sufficiency. Chapter 6 of this book deals with 'Hindrances to Wealth'. These are ignorance (referring not to lack of training but to a Christian's ignorance of the 'privileges and power' at her disposal), spiritual hindrances (evil spirits, ancestral curses, disobedience), lack of giving, and an 'inability to think creatively and to pursue business ventures' (this final point is stated in only three sentences). Chapter 9 deals with 'The Way to Divine Wealth'. The ways are: abiding in the Word, faith, giving to God's work (six pages), giving to the poor (one page), hard work (two pages). Thus Salifu does advocate hard work, but it is not given prominence in comparison to other factors. More fundamentally, though, work simply does not fit into the logic of his basic argument that 'Wealth is our inheritance... God will not withhold our inheritance from us...Inheritance is received through faith and not earned.'[22] It should be remembered that here we are analysing a book ghosted by someone other than the named author, and with a wider readership in mind. At Salifu's services this writer never heard work mentioned, and members of his congregation never raised the idea with the present author; it does not easily arise in a

---

[19] Another example: at offertory time Senyo Bulla of ACI told how he had paid a pledge he had promised; the very next day he received an 'instant financial miracle.' (6 May 01)

[20] Murdock, *31 Reaon*, 240. See stories on pp. 86, 124, 170–1, 244–6, 247–8, stories (like give a suit and be given suits) which he told at Ghana's 'Winning Ways' convention.

[21] Elisha Salifu Amoako, *Power to Make Wealth*, Accra: Alive Publications, 2001, 65.

[22] Ibid., 43–5. In Salifu's *From Ignorance to Knowledge*, Accra: the author, 1997, 19–22, he argues similarly that there are only three legitimate ways to wealth: work, inheritance and the supernatural workings of God, and it is the third that commands most of his attention.

context where it is assumed that every demonic blockage will be removed then and there through his gifts.

Consider also Dr B. Matthew's *How to Become Rich*, where the author makes it clear that by 'rich' he means 'billions of currency of any country'[23]—again, not mere sufficiency. The way is through laws—which do include diligence, planning and acquiring know-how (although, unsurprisingly, the first law is giving, especially the tithe).[24] But apart from those laws, the argument of the book is what might be expected. All is yours anyway: 'All things are His and all that are His are ours—understand this and be free... You and your Father the sole owner of all these things are one... You too have no lack if you are in oneness with him.'[25] So in practice not much work is required at all: 'Getting rich does not require too much hard work but mere understanding of the working principles.' In fact, believe and claim it: 'Everything is yours—therefore claim all... It is only belief that brings wealth and money in very big ways to those who so believe.'[26]

Again, consider Eastwood Anaba's *Oil of Influence*, which is significant for its attempt to re-express the whole charismatic experience through the prism of anointing. Again, the logic of his position is best caught in these words: 'The natural man must toil with all his might before he gets his material needs. These material things are however given by God to the believer as gifts. He applies different principles such as sowing seeds of money (giving) and he is blessed. The spiritual man works but does not have to toil before he is blessed. The *dashen* anointing [one of Anaba's categories of anointing] guarantees this.' Later he deals with Abraham's sacrifice of a ram instead of Isaac: 'Your blessing [like the ram] is also caught by the horns. It is there for you. It cannot get away. It cannot fight against the will of God. You don't have to struggle to capture a ram tied by the horns. You do not have to struggle for your blessing. Abraham went and took the ram. You are to go and take your blessing. There is no struggle here.'[27]

Another good example is Spencer Duncan's *Releasing your Miracles*. One chapter is on 'Principles of Human Initiative'. The word 'initiative' might lead the reader to expect that we humans have a crucial preliminary

---

[23] B. Matthew, *How to Become Rich: Conquer Poverty for Yourself*, Accra: the author, 2000(?), 5.

[24] Ibid., 6–8.

[25] Ibid., 14–17.

[26] Ibid., 17–18. I might mention that I bought this book in the bookshop of the Catholic Parish of Christ the King, which indicates that this thinking is not restricted to charismatic circles.

[27] *Oil*, 62 and 66; the bracketed word 'giving' is in the original.

role to play. But our contribution to receiving the miracle is not work but merely faith and obedience. 'Obey him totally and your life will be a life full of miracles… Our Lord Jesus still calls us today to remove the stone of doubt and unbelief and he will bring our dead business or marriage back to life.'[28]

Apostle Kwamena Ahinful argues similarly in a column on 'Spiritual Way for Business Prosperity'. He begins by explaining that he is taking readers into the 'spiritual realm' where they can find the true *spiritual basis* of business prosperity. 'I shall of course cite the Bible as my source of reference, for after all, far from being a "book of poverty" the Bible is a *"book of prosperity"* throbbing with prosperity teachings from the Old Testament… to the New Testament.' Success or failure in any business is 'to a large extent influenced by some spiritual factors or forces'. He explains: 'It doesn't matter whether a businessman has excellent expertise, the top-most academic qualification, or a special training or abundant technological or financial wherewithal, his business can collapse or suffer badly if it has no divine backing, and if the spiritual forces arrayed against it are malign or evil.' On the other hand, 'If his business operates on divine principles or with divine support, it is bound to prosper, even if he has very little expertise or knowledge or capital, for the Lord is God of increase and abundance.' (Jn 10. 10b) However, Ahinful does concede that 'High expertise plus divine support gives the biggest prosperity.' He then proceeds to expound 'the Biblical truths and laws on prosperity'. The first is 'the law of *vacuum creation*—that is the deliberate creation of emptiness through the giving out of part of one's resources, in order to receive more' (in other words, through the tithes and offerings we have so often encountered). The only other two principles he mentions are the law of forgiveness and 'faith prayers'.[29]

Heward-Mills, in *Unbeatable Prosperity* (dedicated 'To the Millionaires Club of LCI', which again suggests that mere 'sufficiency' is not the aim), argues that prosperity is provided by divine provision. There seem to be 'four laws of divine provision': first, the tithe; second, the offering; third, seeking the kingdom (spiritually by prayer, or physically by 'using your money to construct chapels and other buildings for the glory of God'); and fourth, by 'financing evangelism, missions and ministers'. (In the last-named the individual man of God takes precedence over the others: 'Any time you minister personally to a man of God you invoke the laws of divine provision.' (in bold, p. 35) It seems that poverty

---

[28] *Releasing*, 25–7.
[29] *Mirror*, 18 Aug. 01, 16. Elsewhere Ahinful, in explaining why 'some fasting brings no results', gives as an important reason 'the non-observance of the law of *giving*'. (*Mirror*, 31 March 01, 16)

is a curse—the result of the 'global curse' from Adam, and (particularly in Africa's case) of the 'sectional curse' from Noah.[30] He does refer three or four times to working hard (e.g. pp. 14 and 17), but the argument of the book is something entirely different.

Even when work is mentioned, other factors are more significant. James Saah, when speaking about economic empowerment, as we noted, did allude to the need to work, but he made it explicit that giving was the most important factor.[31] Agyin Asare's dogmatics, in the section on 'Bible Prosperity' has a subheading 'Work Hard', but likewise it is one factor among many, by no means the most important, and it sits rather uncomfortably with the logic of his basic position.[32] The deep logic of Dele Bamgboye's 'Covenant Day of Prosperity' is the same: 'It is not the amount of sweat in your work that brings the blessings; it is the covenant blessing that comes upon your work that shows you are a blessed man... It is the blessing of God that makes you rich and that of the devil that makes you poor.' (11 June 00) The same logic underpins his sermon 'Prosperity is my Heritage': 'God is ushering you into a very strange realm of prosperity, sorrow-free kingdom prosperity. You are entering into a five-fold release of heaven's blessings in this one month. It will go beyond your handiwork to God's handiwork. It will go beyond your sweat to God's sweat. It will not be according to your own labour, it will be according to his riches in glory.' (1 June 00) Consider, too, Korankye Ankrah: 'If God multiplies and increases our seed, why are some believers poor? I will give you five reasons: curse, lack of knowledge, neglect of spiritual laws, disobedience to God, slothfulness.'[33] Obviously he is in favour of hard work, or at least finds sloth reprehensible, but at his church this writer never heard work mentioned, but heard him speak at length on each of the other four reasons.

---

[30] Dag Heward-Mills, *Unbeatable Prosperity*, Accra: Parchment House, 2000. The section on curses from Noah (pp. 41–7), though not perfectly clear, seems to go close to explaining the economic state of Africa through the Hamitic curse: 'Some of the differences we see in the world are due to the fact that curses are operational in certain regions.' (43)

[31] See also James Kweku Saah, *The Finger of God: Let Heaven Answer*, Accra: Design Solutions, 1999, for the same balance; the deep logic of the whole book (see esp. 15, 88) is that work is not as crucial as giving. Quame observes of ACI: 'Though [ACI] would claim that it expects its women to exercise diligence of effort to ensure prosperity, the emphasis is not on physical effort but on spiritual means to attain that end. To prosper, the woman needs the anointing of the Holy Spirit to cause her to break through. She will also need to set certain spiritual structures in place (e.g. seed faith) to bring about prosperity, healing, visas, cars, mansions, etc.' (*Christian*, 130)

[32] Agyin Asare, *Rooted*, 407.

[33] Sam Korankye Ankrah, 'Pentecostalism and Finances', *Pentecostal Voice*, April–June 2000, 17 (see all 16–20).

This is an appropriate point to refer to Michael K. Ntumy's book, *Financial Breakthrough: Discovering God's Secrets to Prosperity*. This book is of some importance, because Ntumy is not only the president of the Ghana Pentecostal Council but chairman of the Church of Pentecost, the country's biggest Protestant church and one of the classical Pentecostal denominations. We have not dwelt at any length in these pages on the extent to which the established Pentecostal denominations have retained an ethos distinct from that of the new charismatic churches. Ntumy's book, however, provides some evidence to suggest that the older are very much influenced by the new. It propounds the prosperity teaching of Murdock—indeed, it is dedicated to Murdock who funded its publication and has helped Ntumy to attend conferences in the United States. Ntumy finds six causes of 'poverty bondage', one of which is failure to work.[34] In his 'Ten steps to deliverance from financial bondage', number four is hard work (the fifth is 'begin to tithe').[35] So work is there, yet in his personal testimony it is clearly not work but 'abnormal favour' that has made him prosperous.[36] Also, in his section on how to multiply finances, only two things are mentioned: 'sowing' and investing.[37] And in the final summary work does not feature at all.[38] This book, no less than the others we have considered, reveals that it is ultimately tithing and giving that count; work may be added (as well as saving and investing), but the argument does not require this.

We have laboured this crucial point. One can indeed hear work mentioned in these churches, but that sometimes obscures the essential religious logic. It is not claimed here that in this Christianity wealth is to be acquired purely by miraculous means; it is more complex than that. Agyin Asare gave two sermons on 31 December 2000; as we noted the first sermon stressed the importance of giving if we are to 'take possession'; the second was dedicated to 'Contending for your Possessions', which involved effort. So he does tell church members that their advancement will come through work—but not as frequently or as insistently as he suggests to them that wealth and victory are already theirs by right, and will materialise through a totally different dynamic.

On 11–13 May 2001 a three-day 'Winners' Business Conference' was held, with the theme 'Conquering in the Business World', coupled with a

---

[34] Michael K. Ntumy, *Financial Breakthrough: Discovering God's Secrets to Prosperity*, no publisher, no date, 42–4.

[35] Ibid., 54–63.

[36] Ibid., 75–8. It is implied here that this prosperity teaching was not in the Church of Pentecost in his early years.

[37] Ibid., 82–5. Investing is a more complex matter than Ntumy suggests, since cedis banked forty years ago would now be almost worthless.

[38] Ibid., 102.

'Business Covenant Day' with the theme 'Breaking the Curses of Business Failure'. Success in business is said to come through a combination of what the pastor called the 'spiritual/professional/impartational'. He built on three biblical texts: 'The Lord has taken away your punishment; he has turned back your enemy' (Zeph 3.15), the parable of the tares and wheat (Mt 13), and 'God turning the curse' (Gal 3.13). In the light of these texts he proclaimed: 'I say to every businessman: No curses will work against you this year.' He established his credentials in this area by describing his history of breaking curses against business success. A man had been very ill in Nigeria, and spent the equivalent of 60 million cedis at Enugu hospital. He attended all sorts of clinics, but to no avail. One day, when passing this pastor's church, the man had gone in, and given his life to Christ; as he left the platform after giving his life to Christ, he staggered and when asked why, replied that his burden had been lifted. He wanted to go to the toilet, but as he approached the one in the church the light bulb blew. A security man lent him a torch, but again as he was about to enter the torch bulb blew. So he went home to go to the toilet. His wife had the toilet door broken down two hours later, and he was found lying in a pool of blood on the floor, along with three tortoises that he had delivered. A business rival had cursed him, and was going to make him pregnant with a tortoise every November for seven years; these were the first three. Later the business rival wanted to know the name of the pastor who had thwarted his plans, but the delivered man would not tell him. However, God revealed to the pastor that the rival was again trying to harm the new Christian (this was not perfectly clear—it may have been the pastor that he was trying to harm) and allowed the pastor to reverse the curse; the business rival was dead within twenty-four hours. Even though in Nigeria funerals are delayed to allow time for mourners to gather, they could not delay in this case because the body began to putrefy immediately (like Herod's in the Acts of the Apostles, the pastor said). The pastor concluded: 'Everyone putting a curse on you, I command their body to rot.'

Thus there is a complex dynamic here. Winners' was inaugurating a fellowship of businessmen, whose meetings were expected to foster the entrepreneurial instincts of its members. Yet at the same time business success was predicated on the spiritual powers of the pastor. Which of these strands was the more effective might well depend on the disposition of the individual participant.[39] For a considerable number of Ghana's

---

[39] Throughout his development Oyedepo, Winners' founder, has never stressed work. In his *Covenant Wealth* (1992) he writes of prosperity: 'Remember, it is a supernatural act of God. It is not something to labour for.' (78) And 'You never get rich through sweat, at least not in the kingdom... We are commanded not to be idle, but your strength is

charismatic churches, faith, giving, deliverance and the pastor's gifts are much more important than hard work in achieving victorious prosperity. These are the most characteristic ways to progress—something only infrequently noted by Western observers of Africa's new Christianity. Work is not stressed at all in many of these churches, and indeed it goes against the religious vision. Of course, even if work is not explicitly mentioned, and is against the religious vision, enhanced work habits might still be an unintended result. After all, Weber's Puritans thought they were confirming their salvation, but they unintentionally invented modern capitalism. Those who dismissed works as a means of salvation and trusted only in faith nevertheless brought about unprecedented productivity. So it may be that Ghana's new Christians, through their emphasis on faith, are similarly transforming Ghana's economic situation, but this cannot simply be presumed. The case would have to be argued, particularly since the *prima facie* evidence seems to point the other way—the years that have seen the growth of these churches have also almost certainly witnessed a decline in Ghana's *per capita* GDP.

Ghanaian doubts

Ghana's new churches may be transforming work habits, but it is not self-evident. Many Ghanaians have real doubts, and there is a general perception that much of this new Christianity is doing little in this regard. It is common to be told before conferences like Duncan-Williams's that you should take the week off work to attend the all-important teachings. The numbers regularly attending deliverance sessions and 'all nights' have caused alarm, which was articulated in an editorial of the *Daily Guide* entitled 'Ghana's Booming Industry'. It noted that over the previous ten years there had been enormous growth in one area, namely Christianity, 'which many have described as a booming industry' rather than as a source of 'spiritual upliftment for the people of this country... Today in

---

inadequate to guarantee you riches; so don't sweat over it, the sinners are the ones sweating over it.' (81) In *Releasing the Supernatural* (1993): 'Everything depends on the Lord's mercy which is only enjoyed by them who are at rest in the Lord... Rest implies that you have ceased from doing it yourself, you have ceased from your own efforts.' (127–8, where he cites Ex 14.14; and see 133) In *Breaking Financial Hardship* (1995): 'If we join the world in the struggle for survival, we will fail the way they fail. The knowledge and the practice of the truth make you a sweatless winner... Not all winners sweat to win. Sweating is a curse. It symbolises struggle... It is the blessings of God that make rich without adding any sorrow. They are released through obedience. Your expertise will not make rich.' (81–2) By the time he gets to *Prophetic Wings* (2000) there is no place at all for work; all success is due to the gifts of the man of God.

Accra and many cities and towns in Ghana there is a growing phenomenon of churches taking over factories and warehouses and converting
them into places of worship rather than places of production of goods and
services to create jobs for the teeming unemployed youth, many of whom
are in the very churches... [It is] strange that in this era of globalisation
and international competition some Ghanaians in the name of worship
would spend precious productive hours of weekdays sitting at church
houses and praying instead of working, yet when the same people go
back home, they eat and use other services that other people worked to
produce when they were worshipping. When people have to rest in the
evenings, sleep well to regain their energies for the next day's work, they
spend all those hours in 'all night' sessions, just to go back to the office
the next day to doze off when they have to work and expect miracles to
raise their standard of living... The *Guide* would want to draw the attention of our compatriots to the simple fact that there is no nation that
develops through miracles. There is no alternative to development, apart
from hardwork, Amen.'[40]

The Chairman of the National Commission on Civil Education has
called the attitude of Ghanaians to religion 'unproductive and unfavour-
able to national development'. Commenting on the proliferation of
churches in the country, he continued: 'Some places of worship operate
all day long and productive hours are spent every day on worshipping and
praying, to the neglect of work.' He referred to a garment factory which
had ceased production 'just because the managing director has turned
born-again and his pastor wants the factory premises to be used as a place
of worship.' He further deplored the situation on university campuses and
other tertiary institutions 'which are virtually being turned into seminaries by certain groups of students who organise prayer sessions during class
hours'. This was not conducive to academic success: 'If you spend all
your time praying on campus without studying, you will definitely fail
your examinations.'[41] He said his Commission's focus for 2002 was to
bring leaders of religious bodies to address this matter of religion and productivity. In August 2002 he returned to this theme, arguing that Ghana's
recurring revivals and conventions were contributing 'to poverty in the

[40] *Daily Guide*, 7–13 Feb. 01, 5. The same point is made in an editorial in *Love and Life* (1–7
Oct. 00, 4): a new phenomenon has appeared—'the holding of church services on working days... On these days, instead of being at work contributing to the productivity of
their companies and the development of the country, church members take permission
from their employers and spend vital hours in the church at the expense of productivity.'
[41] *Graphic*, 16 Jan. 02, 1. The Graphic's editorial that day (entitled 'Prayer and Productive
Work') shared his alarm, calling for 'a balance between prayer and work to increase our
fortunes for the prosperity of all'.

country because church members are left with very little time to pursue economic activities that would help alleviate the poverty in their lives.'[42]

At the same time the government minister responsible for the Brong Ahafo Region rebuked churches that teach their members to pray for prosperity without engaging in any economic ventures. 'All they do is embark on daily prayers, all-night sessions and expect manna to fall from heaven. Such deceitful teachings do not emanate from God.' He claimed that 'such attitudes of laziness and apathy' are 'not helping the country's development'.[43] A week later, at a clergy meeting in Kumasi, a bishop repeated this charge—that pastors getting their congregation 'to pray all day long without releasing them to go and work will not help society'.[44] Osofo Ameve, the head of Afrikania, obviously incensed by the accusation from a deputy government minister that pouring libations at state functions retards national progress (because, as we see in the next chapter, such idolatry incurs God's wrath), retorted: 'It can be stated with certainty that all-nights and all-day prayer camps and churches that divert the mind of our people from their work are directly responsible for the stagnation of our progress.'[45]

A London-based Ghanaian economist published a lengthy analysis of Ghana's economy after one year of Kufuor. After dealing with strictly economic factors like privatisation, inflation, unemployment and falling commodity prices, he concluded: 'Our attitudes to work must change. To quote Karl Marx: "Labour creates man"... Ghana has been praying for economic success... Now we have to work to be productive. Let us try and work conscientiously at least for five days and rest on the seventh. If we believe that we will succeed, we have to back it with action. Week-long church going is not productive and will not help our efforts in building a fast-growing economy.'[46]

Some discern important differences within the charismatic sector, and note their significance. The *Chronicle* columnist 'Steve Biko' wrote two pieces in praise of Otabil for being different precisely on this point: in insisting that development comes from hard work and not from miracles. The columnist laments: '[The messages of most pastors] are nothing but poison disseminated to ruin the lives of the uncritical, the gullible. [When I heard Otabil preaching about work], I was convinced I was right in the impression I had formed that he was a different man of God. These days most of the so-called men of God do not counsel their flock to work hard

---

[42] *Graphic*, 31 Aug. 02, 2.
[43] Ibid.
[44] *Guide*, 4 Sept. 02, 7.
[45] *Graphic*, 12 Sept. 02, 19.
[46] *Daily Mail*, 15 Feb. 02, 1.

and order/plan their lives properly. No, all their messages centre round the word MIRACLE. In Je-e-e-sus' name.'[47] Thus many Ghanaians complain that the preachers speak only of miracles, and do so on weekdays when their listeners should be working. Thus it is a widely held perception that many new churches—probably most of them—do little to encourage a work ethic. Ghanaian observers are facing an issue that Western professional scholars of religion only infrequently advert to.

Of three other factors Weber thought important—investment, internal asceticism and deferral of gratification—this writer never encountered the second and third, and as regards investment also this Christianity pushes in another direction altogether. Invariably, the wealth of the Christian is for evangelisation, not for investment. In the words of Adamson Aromaegbe at WMCI, 'The purpose of the anointing is to get wealth; the purpose of the wealth is to establish the covenant, and the purpose [of that] is that all the nations of the earth can hear his word.' (27 Oct. 00) Sam Korankye Ankrah is equally explicit: 'God prospers us for the sake of his work so that we may save souls through evangelism.'[48] This is standard faith gospel teaching. (Because saving souls is precisely the business of the preacher, we find again that this theology is particularly adaptive.) In as much as all wealth is thus sacralised by being devoted to evangelisation, this arguably represents a step back beyond the Industrial Revolution. One of the developments that made the Industrial Revolution possible was that as a result of the Reformation wealth tended no longer to be consumed in chantries and masses for the dead, and thus was freed for investment. Here perhaps is another example of something seemingly so Protestant being catholicised.[49]

Garner has argued that in the new South Africa Pentecostal churches are creating 'the kind of social change "from below" that will assist in the creation of a broadly-based market economy'.[50] It would be premature and too sweeping to make such a blanket claim for Ghana's new churches. A few explicitly set out to contribute to the building of a modern economy, and others may do so indirectly; although it is not part of their

---

[47] *Chronicle*, 8 June 01, 2.
[48] *Pentecostal Voice*, 1 (Apr.–June 2000), 16.
[49] In a perspective like Berger's, modern Ghanaian Pentecostalism, with its 'mystery, miracle and magic', is of course the functional equivalent of medieval Catholicism (Peter L. Berger, *The Sacred Canopy: Elements of a Sociological Theory of Religion*, New York: Anchor Books, 1969, 111).
[50] Robert C. Garner, 'Religion as a Source of Social change in the New South Africa', *JRA* 30(2000), 314.

conscious agenda and at first sight even conflicts with their theology, they may strengthen work habits, but this is a case that has not been proved. Indeed most Ghanaian observers of the scene are sceptical.

Of course, even if these churches did encourage hard work, this would still not give Ghana a modern economy. Irrespective of the number of Christians who might be working hard, there would be little change in the obstructive political system, which leads us to the subject of the next chapter.

7

POLITICAL ROLE

As we have noted, Ghana's mainline churches are characterised by their involvement in education and development. Development activity is now also found in some Pentecostal denominations—witness the Assemblies of God Relief and Development Services. Moreover, the mainline have been characterised by an element of direct political involvement, which has led them to pronounce on issues of human rights and even to train election monitors.

Spiritualising politics

The newer churches that are our focus here relate to politics very differently. They tend in particular to think in terms of spiritual causality—in two ways which, though closely linked, are clearly distinguishable. The first we can call an 'enchanted' approach. Demons are responsible for the political situation, and their spiritual power must be broken. Robert Ampiah-Kwofi's *Breaking Generational Curses* offers an example. 'National curses always have a nature of affecting the entire population for evil. They often result in civil wars and great poverty in nations.'[1] These curses can often be thought of as having their origins in African traditions. This is the view of Ampiah-Kwofi: 'Our immediate ancestry and culture were steeped in idolatry and heathenism.' These curses are causing Ghana's evils and must be broken.[2]

Thus Duncan-Williams talks in terms of territorial spirits: 'That's why poverty in this area, prosperity in other area. You are dealing with different

---

[1] Robert Ampiah-Kwofi *Breaking Generational Curses*, Accra: the author, 2000, 17. Ampiah-Kwofi's *The Restored Anointing*, 1998, has a very different slant; in this second book, problems arise not from spirits but from complexes, childhood traumas and repression. The two approaches seem incompatible, and indeed, given the origins of many pastors' books in Ghana, it is not impossible that it was ghosted by another.

[2] Frank Hutchful also talks in terms of curses affecting whole groups, even nations, *Pulling Down the Altars*, Accra: the author, 2000.

territorial spirits.' (*21 Oct. 00*) Heward-Mills too can state: 'Africa is dominated by territorial spirits of poverty, superstition and war. That is why the continent, although blessed with human and natural resources, is plagued with backwardness and under-development. [By contrast] Europe is dominated by territorial spirits of atheism, homosexuality and immorality.'[3] Hughes talks of a spirit dominating Africa, manifesting itself in eight social phenomena. 'They are idolatry, ancestral worship, polygamy, famine, drought, civil wars, poverty and pull-him-down syndrome.'[4] So too Marcus Hester at Duncan-Williams's ACI convention (28 Nov. 00): 'We are here to break the spirit of poverty in Ghana... God spoke to me: in five to seven years there's going to be great prosperity in Ghana.' This will not be through political or economic reform, but (as might be expected) through Christians giving more to their churches. Three days later the same speaker, in a follow-up sermon dealing with the procedure to adopt when giving does *not* in fact bring the promised prosperity, moved to the explanation of a 'national curse' arising from the 'sins of the forefathers'. (He said that Benin too suffered from such a curse, as the cradle of voodoo; and even Chicago was only now coming out of a curse arising from the career of Al Capone.)

In this way spirits can be thought to cause a nation's problems. But there is a second understanding, less 'demonic', which can be called 'biblical', for its basic idea is that found in the Books of Kings (in fact in the whole deuteronomistic history from Joshua to Kings), and in the Chronicler's history (namely Chronicles, Ezra and Nehemiah). The key text is II Chronicles 7.14: 'If my people who are called by my name humble themselves, and pray and seek my face, and turn from their wicked ways, then I will hear from heaven, and will forgive their sin and heal their land.' According to this thinking, the national plight is caused by apostasy, particularly failure to worship God properly on the part of the leader. This approach is given regular expression in Ghana's Evangelical newspaper *The Watchman*, edited by an original and independent-minded charismatic, Divine Kumah. It is given classical form in his book *Is Ghana under a Curse?* in which he argues that Ghana was made a Christian country by the British colonisers (another illustration of the lack of anti-colonial animus that contrasts so starkly with Caribbean or African American forms of charismatic Christianity). All Ghana's leaders have deviated from this, in just the same way as Israel's kings forsook the Lord. There have been degrees of apostasy, of course, and for a while Acheampong acknowledged the need for God (hence the abundance of

---

[3] Heward-Mills, *Lay People*, 117.
[4] Hughes, *God's Hands*, 39 (see all 38–44).

food between 1972 and 1976).[5] Under Rawlings, however, the apostasy was almost total, and this is the reason for the divine punishment evident in national collapse. The answer, prescribed in Chronicles, is simple; if the leader will turn back to him, God will heal Ghana.

It should be explained that rumours always circulated about Rawlings resorting to juju both to acquire and to maintain power. One famous practitioner of secret arts from the Volta Region, Torgbi Akakpo Ahiaku or Yeye Boy, was widely thought to have ensured the success of Rawlings's second coming; he met a particularly frightful death soon after, which was sometimes alleged to have been engineered by the PNDC for the reason that only he could provide the magic for others to overcome Rawlings.[6] Moreover, when Rawlings and the Vice-President of his first term (1992–6) fell out, Vice-President Arkaah revealed in a BBC interview that he had been asked by Rawlings to accompany him to a local shrine to solve the nation's problems, but he had declined.[7] It was this suspicion of juju that caused a furore when at the launching of the NDC election manifesto in August 2000 Rawlings pricked his finger and signed the first copy with his blood, which was then auctioned for 160 million cedis. Many Christians, often referring to the saving blood of Jesus, found this act diabolic, and some linked it with the ritual murder of many women around Accra.[8] Even an opposition party found Rawlings's act indicative of an 'infernal ulterior motive'.[9]

This Chronicles text (II Chron 7.14) is pervasive in this Christianity, used both explicitly and implicitly. To get an idea of its range of application, consider the following almost random examples. Apostle Ntumy used the text at an all-night prayer session organised by the Ghana Pentecostal Council at Kaneshie Sports Complex to pray for peace in the approaching elections.[10] Steve Wengam of New Life Outreach in Tema, using 'Righteousness exalts a nation' (Prov 30.34), specifically notes: 'The Bible does not say good governance exalts a nation, [or] that good policies

---

[5] Kumah, *Is Ghana?* 55.

[6] *Chronicle*, 1 March 02, 8.

[7] *Voice*, 22–23 May 95, 1; and 29–30 May 95, 1 (containing an account of an attempt—by Rawlings?—to kill Arkaah by juju).

[8] Over twenty women had been murdered around Accra over the preceding few years. These 'serial killings' were popularly called 'ritual murders'; some reports claimed that at least some had been drained of all blood, which would add credence to that theory (*Graphic*, 21 Dec. 00, 9).

[9] *Chronicle*, 22–29 Aug. 00, 12; Apostle Ahinful in *Mirror*, 19 Aug. 00, 16 (but rejoinder *Mirror*, 9 Sept. 00, 2). Ahinful's column (25 Nov. 00, 16) discusses three sources of 'spiritual backing': juju, the occult, and 'charismaticism'. He implies that all are (equally?) effective, although a Christian should restrict himself to the latter.

[10] *Pentecostal Voice*, Oct.-Dec. 2000, 5; this text is also cited in the editorial on the previous page.

exalt a nation… Any time God visits a nation the economy of that nation changes. [Like the dry bones of Ezekiel 37] Ghana will rise again! There is hope for the economy… If our leaders will turn back to God… God blesses Ghana and our economy [flourishes].' (*8 April 01*) Similarly R. Jones Jr of Philadelphia preaching at an ACI convention (26 Nov. 00) said: 'Ghana in the 1950s was liberated from [the British]. But Ghana has not learned to say: "Lord, save us"… If we are going to be economically empowered it is not the things we learnt in school [that will do this], it is "My people see my face and turn from their wicked ways and I will see their face and heal their land."' This text was even quoted to explain that national apostasy was responsible for a fuel shortage in early 2001: 'All the happenings in the world today are controlled from the spirit realm… Ghana is suffering her share of the devil's bite on our fuel, because we have broken our [pledge] of intimacy with the owner of our nation.'[11]

This 'biblical' view might be seen as very political, but it is political in a very special sense, because political issues as recognised in a modern political science department or discussed in World Bank reports can hardly arise. This thinking might well lead one to vote against Rawlings, because he like King Ahab is bringing God's punishment upon the nation (and Kumah in *The Watchman* was sometimes savage in his denunciation of Rawlings). Yet this understanding would not normally or naturally lead to pressure for an independent judiciary, accountable systems at the Bank of Ghana, transparent tendering at the Divestiture Commission, or procedures rather than personal whims in approving rice production schemes.

Consider the case of Enoch Agbozo, an important figure in the rise of Ghana's charismatic Christianity, although he is often passed over since he remained in fellowships rather than founding a church of his own.[12] Agbozo had no time for Rawlings's NDC regime. Just after the 2000

---

[11] *Christian Eye*, 8–22 April 01, 1. This text seems in the blood. It is quoted far beyond church circles; see Lt.-Gen. Joshua M. Hamidu (former Chief of Staff and later to become Kufuor's National Security Chief) in his press statement on the state of Ghana on his return from twenty years of exile. (*Dispatch*, 18–24 Aug. 00, 5–8) It is also quoted by the Governor of the Bank of Ghana expounding his spiritual economics urging trust in God 'to lift Ghana's economy'. Citing Moses, Daniel, Elijah, David and Solomon, he is reported to have said: 'The US dollar is always stable because it has its trust in God Almighty—"In God we Trust"… Really if we trust God and obey his commands He'll not disappoint us.' (*Christian Messenger*, 13, 4 [2000], 12) In Ghana's business weekly Ashimolowo has an article explaining Africa's plight—after 'God gave the African the first opportunity to rule the world'—in terms of idolatry. (*Business and Financial Times*, 18–24 Nov. 2002, 13) It is of interest to note how central this text was for US fundamentalism during its fallow years (1925–50); see Joel A. Carpenter, *Revive Us Again: the Reawakening of American Fundamentalism*, New York: Oxford University Press, 1997, 116–19.

[12] For Agbozo's importance, see Asamoah-Gyadu, *Renewal*, 155–7. He is 'the *de facto* father of charismatism in Ghana'. (Hughes, *God's Hands*, 48)

election which ended NDC rule, he proclaimed: 'Now has come an opportunity for Ghana to abandon the old order of Satanism, idolatry and bloodshed, evil, wickedness, violence and death, unrighteousness, injustice, exploitation and oppression, bribery, corruption, robbery, lawlessness and disorderly conduct as the basis of governance.' For Agbozo it was clear that Kufuor's election 'is a blessed seal to the redemption act of God towards our country... God Almighty has done a great, marvellous and wonderful thing for us. His name be praised forever.' What then is now required of Ghanaians? 'All that God Almighty requires from Ghana now is the worship of him alone, abandoning Satan and idolatry. He will bless Ghana with abundance if we do so.'[13]

Here this biblical viewpoint is expressed with stark simplicity. Not only is it God who will bring about the desired order, but nothing else is required of Ghanaians but worship of the true God. Here an elected leader is not regarded as a functionary, to be judged on criteria of effectiveness and productivity; the leader's role is still sacral, hence Ahinful's urging of Kufuor 'not to taint or soil the divine sacredness of his presidential incumbency' by pouring libations to ancestors. 'Such Satanism... will destroy what he has got through popular fasting and prayers to the Supreme God...and will incur God's anger to the detriment of the Ghanaian populace.'[14]

It is this tendency to spiritualise that characterises the politics of so many of Ghana's new churches. This spiritualising is done in various ways which we have already touched on, and we need only summarise them here. First, the faith gospel teaches that circumstances are simply not relevant in comparison with what the Word of God says must be the case. A variation is simply to bypass normal political considerations. In the words of Heward-Mills: 'If you live in Africa, you will find yourself surrounded (with) many unsolvable problems. There are many hopeless situations in this great continent. Today, I am offering you an answer which is not found through governments or politicians. The master key to your blessing is to name it, claim it and take it!'[15] There the faith gospel ('name

---

[13] *Free Press*, 10–16 Jan. 01, 6. David Yonggi Cho seemingly made the same point when on his visit to Ghana he took the opportunity to tell President Kufuor: 'Ghana, with the present leadership, would be a great country just like Korea if she is God-fearing.' (*Graphic*, 30 Aug. 01, 16)

[14] *Mirror*, 6 Jan. 01, 16. In September 2002 a government minister attributed Ghana's economic plight to this pouring of libations to ancestral spirits at state functions. His remarks were supported by many Pentecostal pastors, including Apostle Ahinful. (*Mirror*, 21 Sept. 02, 28, and 28 Sept. 02, 16)

[15] Dag Heward-Mills, *Name it! Claim it! Take it!*, Accra: Lighthouse Chapel Publications, 1999, 40. He made the same claim in a sermon: 'In Africa many of the problems have no solutions... today, God is bringing solutions.' (*10 Aug. 00*)

it and claim it') is unqualified. This idea that words achieve what they say is quite common. This thinking lay behind the charismatic objection to the Kufuor government's opting for 'Highly Indebted Poor Country' (HIPC) status in 2001; if one says that Ghana is poor and heavily indebted, it will be poor and indebted. Thus Ashimolowo preached against 'going HIPC' at the 'Winning Ways' convention. He lamented: 'How can they give such a designation to a nation and they accepted it? They gave a nation prophetic word; they said you are a Highly Indebted Poor Country, and you said "Yes, Lord"'. Ashimolowo claimed that 'God sent him to Ghana this season to reject the HIPC proposition for Ghana.'[16]

Also, in many of its forms, the faith gospel leads Christians to ignore the wider body politic. It is only believers that receive God's blessing, but that is as it should be. In Heward-Mills's boast, 'National curses of poverty and continental curses of poverty and backwardness have no effect on me!'—which implies that national poverty and backwardness are not issues calling for Christian concern,[17] a view commonly heard at Winners'. 'Stop grumbling about Rawlings. You are a child of God and not a child of Rawlings. Halleluiah! Stop grumbling about the economy. Only ensure that the commanded blessing is manifested upon your life. Full stop.' (11 June 00) Also: 'No matter the degree of hardship on the earth, the covenant will exempt you from them all. Your financial greatness is hitched on [flows from?] a working covenant... Covenant has no respect for the economy of any country. It has no bearing on whatever is happening on the political setting of any country. It unlocks heaven's wealth and makes it available to (all) within the covenant fold.' (23 June 00)

Another way of spiritualising politics, pervasive in Ghana, is given classic expression in these words of Joyce Wereko Brobby, addressing an Anglican diocesan conference: 'Only the Word of God can change human society for the better, and not governments.'[18] Joyce Wereko Brobby is a

---

[16] *Christian Eye*, 8–22 April 01, 1 and 20 May, 2 June 01, 1. HIPC status gives a country certain debt relief, but with conditionalities imposed by donor countries. There are political arguments against 'going HIPC'—e.g. Japan will give only grants, not loans, to HIPC countries; 'Going HIPC' would entail what might be considered an unacceptable restriction of sovereignty—but Ashimolowo's argument is on another plane altogether.

[17] Also Heward-Mills: 'Even if there is a shortage, for you you will eat and never lack' (*26 Sept. 00*); James Saah of ACI: 'Now the economy is difficult in Ghana, I am blessed more than when things were better. Not a (inaudible) goes by when he blesses me with foreign currency.' (13 Dec. 00)

[18] *Graphic*, 6 Oct. 99, 11. Again she writes (*Chronicle*, 16–18 Mar. 01, 6): 'Our society will change as men, women and children, youth and adults come to the saving knowledge of Jesus Christ.' Joyce Wereko Brobby was not only the wife of one of the seven presidential candidates in 2000. She attended Achimota where she was a friend of Rawlings. She was the PNDC Secretary for Information (1983–4), Education (1984–6), Local Government and Rural Development (1987), and later worked at the Castle, even as Special Assistant

significant figure in Ghana: a leading PNDC official and prominent charismatic Christian, as well as a school friend of Rawlings. Her statement
fits well with Ghana's almost national symbol, the *Gye Name*, proclaiming 'God alone'. The sentiment is widely encountered. Thus Lawrence
Tetteh: 'No political strategy will bring peace; no economic strategy will
bring peace; no sociological strategies will bring peace; the only way to
peace is God's way.' (12 Dec. 00) Or Heward-Mills: 'Africa needs not
political changes but Jesus Christ.' (4 Nov. 00)

However, to the statement that 'Only the Word of God can change
human society for the better, and not governments', one can surely reply
that there are any number of ways in which government can improve
society—by ensuring an efficient and equitable judiciary, a functioning
education system, a competent police force, protection of private property, and functioning systems of electricity and water distribution. But
many of Ghana's charismatics do not see government as geared to such
mundane practicalities. Their sights are set on higher goals altogether. In
a newspaper article on reconstructing the nation of Ghana (as Nehemiah
rebuilt the city of Jerusalem), Enoch Agbozo writes: 'Turning and establishing Ghana into God's kingdom glory state, a Beulah land and crown
of glory to God as a blessed end-time Christian nation and star of Africa
(Isaiah 62) is a great and high vision and mission agenda for the church
body in Ghana as a whole.'[19] But while Christians articulate this admittedly noble vision, schools lack textbooks and classrooms roofs, and the
police lack not only vehicles but typewriters and paper. Any administration that could remedy these deficiencies would make a significant contribution. Nobody denies that Ghana would change if all citizens became
paragons of love, truth, justice and every other Christian virtue. But Ghanaian society would also change if it had an Auditor General, Controller
and Accountant General, Serious Fraud Office, Electoral Commission,
Commission on Human Rights and Administrative Justice that worked
efficiently and were truly independent, and a Public Accounts Committee of Parliament which exercised its oversight (it has not done so since
constitutional rule was introduced in 1992).

---

to the Chairman of the National Commission on Democracy (1988–91). She is also an
important Christian figure, having worked for the Haggai Institute and Campus Crusade,
founding her own 'Salt and Light Ministries', becoming a member of the Executive
Council of the Bible Society of Ghana and the Christian Council, and one of the board of
regents at CUC. In June 2001 she became chief executive of the Ghana Chamber of
Mines. (*Graphic*, 22 May 01, 23; *Mirror*, 28 Oct. 00, 12) She is a recognisably public figure, to such an extent that in mid-2001 she was used to advertise hair relaxant on TV.
[19] *Times*, 16 Sept. 00, 14.

A related way of diverting attention from practical effectiveness is to set up all debates in terms of morality. This is widespread in Ghana.[20] What might elsewhere be considered administrative or institutional issues are here far more likely to be framed as moral ones—paradoxically because, as we have seen, there are whole areas of charismatic life where morality does not greatly intrude. An outsider cannot but be struck by the lack of emphasis in Ghana on institution-building, and the corresponding emphasis on moral reform.[21] It is a continuing lament in the media that moral standards have collapsed. It is the reason often cited why the churches should retake control of their schools—proponents forgetting that most of Ghana's élite have been produced by these church schools which are supposed to inculcate such moral probity; Nkrumah had degrees from an American seminary. A good example is Kudadjie's *Moral Renewal in Ghana*.[22] Admittedly he is a moral philosopher, and his focus (evident from his title) is morality, and as an educationalist he is concerned with developing moral awareness. But he has expectations of government that would be considered excessive in the industrialised world, where the state is seen less and less as tasked with making people moral. Its task is not producing the Greek ideal of moral excellence (*arête*), or raising up a nation of the redeemed or replicating Calvin's Geneva, but effectively delivering the necessary infrastructure and institutions for its citizens to function. Thus a state has come to be judged on far narrower criteria—the impartiality and effectiveness of administrative and legal structures, which are much easier to monitor than morality in individuals. It is sometimes suggested that the 'moralising of politics' is a contribution that new churches can make in the third world, but envisaging these matters in moral terms sometimes leads if not to a dead end, at least to a great deal of empty and obfuscating rhetoric (of which Ghana's leaders, Rawlings included, have provided their share).

In a similar way Kwame Gyekye, in his philosophical treatment of corruption, tends to downplay the institutional and focus on the moral issue. Like Kudadjie he sees the solution in moral education.[23] The much less ambitious objective of establishing systems and structures is more

---

[20] Kweku G. Folson, Professor of Political Science at Legon: 'Most Ghanaians… believe that the basic national problem is that of morality.… and since there is no other way of changing this than preaching, we have all become preachers.' (Foreword to Mike Oquaye, *Politics in Ghana 1972–1979*, Accra: Tornado Publications, 1980, xvi)

[21] The Busia Foundation symposium on 'Social Values in Ghana' (13 March 01) illustrated this preoccupation with morality, as did the forum at the Institute of Economic Affairs in July 2001. (*Dispatch*, 11–17 July 01, 5)

[22] Joshua N. Kudadjie, *Moral Renewal in Ghana: Ideals, Realities and Possibilities*, Accra: Asempa, 1995.

[23] Gyekye, *Corruption*, 46.

deliverable. The churches are frequently heard lamenting the collapse of moral standards, often implying that this is the cause of Ghana's ills. But industrialised countries do not have a higher GDP because of their leaders' morals. There may be little to distinguish Rawlings, Tony Blair and George W. Bush in terms of morality; each probably enjoys power and would prefer as few restrictions on it as possible. The difference (and it is a significant difference) is that structures and institutions prevent leaders of industrialised countries from transgressing certain limits—not perfectly of course, but significantly. An attempt to develop such structures and institutions in Ghana would bring considerable benefits, but any possible drive to that end is often short-circuited through transposing the debate on to the purportedly higher plane of morality.

There is one variant of charismatic political theology which is less frequently heard in Ghana, although visiting Nigerians occasionally introduce it. Elkanah Hanson, preaching at ACI ('My teaching and prophesying changed the political history of Nigeria' because 'Today the President is a born-again Christian'), preached essentially that a nation is in trouble when the Holy Spirit is not in charge. Only Christians should rule; the heathen must be removed.[24] Similarly Chigbundu at Alive Chapel prayed just before Ghana's elections that God would not allow the 'Sons of Ishmael [Muslims] to rule in the land'. This is not the threat to Christians in Ghana that it is to Nigerian Christians. In Ghana, for historical reasons, the ruling élite will be Christian for the foreseeable future. Hanson and Chigbundu provide examples of a particularly Nigerian variant of spiritual politics, with only the most limited application in Ghana.

Thus in all sorts of ways many charismatic churches, though concerned with national issues, contributed little to debate on modern government. They tended to spiritualise or moralise issues out of the mundane plane on which political issues have been most fruitfully addressed.

'Implicit politics'

Some observers have indeed argued that spiritualising the issues may yet be a contribution to the modern political debate; it may not be the way political debate is conducted in the West, but identifying spiritual causes can still change the physical situation through 'implicit politics'. Consider Birgit Meyer's discussion of deliverance, using Eni's *Delivered from the Powers of Darkness* as her starting-point: 'Anthropologists have realised the inadequacy of conceptualising imaginations of evil as expressions of

---

[24] Elkanah Hanson, *Understanding the Holy Spirit in Politics*, Port Harcourt: El Shaddai Ministries, 1999.

"false consciousness" in favour of viewing them as peoples' attempts to understand their situation and grapple with changing conditions.' Precisely. However, she immediately goes on: 'Imaginations of evil are not mere reflections of ill-understood social, political and economic conditions. Rather, they are fields within which people produce meanings enabling them to analyse critically and thereby shape their life conditions.'[25] We should consider especially these last phrases: 'analyse critically' and 'shape their life conditions'. Nowhere in her article does she show how this conception of evil leads to *critical* analysis, or even what this might entail; nor does she show, concretely, how the 'life conditions' of Africans are thereby affected, and how one might establish that this spiritual worldview was actually shaping, by a process of cause and effect, and for good, the situation in Africa. In the same article she writes: 'One should understand ideas about the Devil and demons not as a distortion of reality but as powerful images people draw on to make sense of their reality in a critical way.'[26] Undoubtedly they use these images to make sense of their reality, but what exactly is meant by that qualifier 'in a critical way'?

An even more striking example is furnished by Ellis and ter Haar, in an important article relating demonology to African politics, and utilising not Eni but a very similar book by Kaniaki and Mukendi.[27] The article well shows how African understandings of power invariably involve the spiritual realm; that demonic interpretations have political implications; and that the recent proliferation of religious groups with such ideas is probably related to the collapse of African states. However, even here the authors appear to make the same unexplained jump as Birgit Meyer; they show only that these conceptions are formulated to make sense of Africa's political situation, but not that they have a positive effect on the political situation. They well accomplish the first: 'Distinguishing between good and evil and understanding the nature of evil are major preoccupations of the popular religious tracts' which they discuss.[28] They rightly show (citing the former Archbishop of Lusaka as an exponent of such demonology) that 'Milingo's success, and his downfall, were his ability to articulate people's problems in terms which they understood exactly.'[29] These and

---

[25] Birgit Meyer, '"Delivered from the Powers of Darkness": Confessions of Satanic Riches in Christian Ghana', *Africa* 65, 1995, 237.

[26] Ibid., 252, note 28.

[27] Stephen Ellis and Gerrie ter Haar, 'Politics and Religion in Sub-Saharan Africa', *Journal of Modern African Studies* 36,2 (1998), 175–201. Kaniaki and Mukendi, *Snatched from Satan's Claws: an Amazing Deliverance by Christ*, Nairobi: Enkei Media Services, 1991.

[28] Ellis and ter Haar, 'Politics', 196.

[29] Ibid., 199.

similar statements can be accepted, but the authors conclude by implying that something more is happening than an attempt to *understand* reality: 'Religious movements in the long term may offer not just a new basis for legitimising power, but even a means of restructuring some sort of apparatus which will fulfil the functions of government.'[30] That is formally unexceptionable (they may indeed), but the impression is created that a slightly stronger sense is intended (they not only may, but do). Indeed, their main point seems to be that some restructuring of government systems is actually taking place—some pages earlier they stated that 'many peoples in what used to be called the Third World are reordering the systems by which power is acquired and distributed in their societies.'[31] However, Ellis and ter Haar have not proved that politics in Africa is being reordered in any way by the demonology in question, nor shown what might count as evidence for this claim and how we might assess it.[32]

As a third example, consider Ruth Marshall's treatment of the charismatic sector in Nigeria (admittedly she is not dealing directly with the theological dimension of these churches, much less focusing exclusively on the demonic elaborations, as in the previous examples). However, she too manifests the same slippage we have just noted. Her concluding remarks mention the 'self conscious movement which sees itself as changing society and making history'. No one could argue with this, since the charismatic sector does indeed see itself as transforming society. However, in the following paragraph Ruth Marshall seems to go much further, claiming that the churches in question indeed 'amount to a conceptual and practical challenge to the "power monopolies"' of Nigeria.[33] The word 'practical' takes the argument to another level; she has already claimed that 'what is being created is…an expressive and pragmatic act of individual and collective reconstruction.'[34] The innovations are said to be at both 'the conceptual and practical levels'.[35] Her argument is perhaps best summarised in this statement: '"The power in the name of Jesus", the spiritual power called upon by born-agains in their prayers, the authority behind the exorcism of evil spirits, and the protection each born-again

[30] Ibid., 201.
[31] Ibid., 195.
[32] Their example of Mozambique's Napramas does not prove to me the effectiveness of 'addressing what we might regard as political or economic or even military problems by religious discourse and action', any more than the 'religious movements whose object is to make rain fall' which is the example immediately following (ibid., 199).
[33] Ruth Marshall, '"Power in the Name of Jesus": Social Transformation and Pentecostalism in Western Nigeria "Revisited"' in T. Ranger and O. Vaughan (eds), *Legitimacy and the State in Twentieth Century Africa* (London: Macmillan, 1993), 242.
[34] Ibid., 223.
[35] Ibid., 234.

has against misfortune, is also temporal power, the power to impose categories of perception on to the world of real things, to realise the symbolic
realm of the spiritual by transforming the world of practice.'[36] This stress
on words like 'practical', 'practice' and 'pragmatic' appears to denote
some idea of external, observable consequences for Nigeria's political
structures. Yet in what way have the charismatics transformed the public
sphere in Nigeria? Is the country less corrupt, more transparent, more
governed by law? No evidence is given of such transformation, nor is it
indicated what might count as evidence, and how we might assess it.
When it is argued that these charismatic Christians manage to 'vanquish
on the spiritual plane [the] destructive forces' of the Nigerian political
system,[37] we want to know whether this vanquishing *remains* on the
'spiritual plane' or whether it has any observable practical effect on public life. According to Transparency International, Nigeria is still, even
with its born-again President, the second most corrupt country in the
world, and its position on the UN Human Development Index is pitifully
low for a country of such wealth. How many years must we wait until the
transformation effected by the flourishing born-again churches and deliverance ministries cause it to rise up the scale?

All these are serious observers with profound insights into Africa's
charismatic explosion, but they seem on this point to have shown only,
first, that Africans use this demonic cosmology to make sense of the evils
that befall them, and, second, that many African Christians claim to be
transforming the societies around them. These authors have not shown
that Africa has thereby been transformed in any way.

The 2000 transition

Several of the churches we are considering addressed themselves specifically to political issues as Ghana's 2000 elections approached. Their different positions are revealing.

Agyin Asare, as one would expect from his general emphasis on miracle
cures, expects much from God's miraculous intervention. From Ezekiel's
dry bones he preaches: 'The economy is beyond repair by human standards, but God [will intervene]... If we are going to discover mineral
resources, God will do it. It will not be by knowledge [the standard reference to Zech 4.6]; it is the spirit of the Lord, so all will say—this is the
doing of the Lord. Glory to him.' (*16 Sept. 00*) 'It is God who sets people
in positions of authority... God uses rulers as instruments of mercy or

[36] Ibid.
[37] Ibid., 238.

chastisement, determined by whether people of God pray or not... If we will pray God will give us the kind of ruler we need [and] he has prepared for us.' So 'the kind of government we get as a nation is dependent on the prayers of the saints. If we pray, God will intervene to influence those in authority so blessings and favour will be in our land.' (*21 Oct. 00*) Again, 'If God gets hold of leadership, the nation prospers. If the devil gets hold of the leadership, there is a lot of problems.' He explained how the Devil got hold of David to number all Israel (I Chron 21.1) with resulting disaster. The church can hold back the judgements of God as Abraham did for Sodom and Gomorrah. 'As Elijah was able to change the land by his intercession, we are able to change the land by our intercession... Some of the nations prospered because of God's intervention. Botswana used to be among the poorest countries in the world, but is now one of the richest because diamonds were discovered. Equatorial Guinea [had nothing] but now oil has been discovered.' So 'We need the hand of God. We need the intervention of God.' With the ensuing prosperity, 'We will take the world for Jesus... that's the reason we need good government.' (*28 Oct. 00*; very similar 5 Nov. 00) From his sermons it is clear that he was profoundly influenced by the civil wars in West Africa, and also by the 1994 ethnic 'war' around Tamale in the north which forced him to move to Accra.

Sam Korankye Ankrah preached a series on 'Election 2000—Ghana in Search of a Leader', based on Israel's search for a king (I Sam 8.4–7 and 19), which clearly illustrates what we have called above the 'biblical' approach: 'If the leader is accursed we are all accursed. If [he is] chosen by God, we are a blessed people.' (*4 Nov. 00*) 'Using the Word of God as a standard', he said that 'the wrong person can cause God's anger to destroy the land... So vote for a godly man, according to the Word of God, so that this land will be saved.' He recounted his vision (to great applause): 'I see a man of God ruling this land. I see righteousness, our shops filled with goods, hospitals, beautiful cars, good roads, a nation moving forward, a nation taken from glory to glory!' There was much good sense against tribalism ('I bind the spirit of tribalism'), much lamenting of the general lack of tolerance and the 'winner take all' attitude in African politics, and much of value in defining a 'godly man'— one who 'treats people with dignity'. The general thrust was the deuteronomistic one ('Because you honour me, I will also honour you'), but this was confused somewhat by stating that the immoral Clinton ('Look at the women he has slept with!') would easily win again, were he able to stand, 'because [in the United States] people don't care about his morality; they care about his performance.' Korankye Ankrah, paradoxically, seemed to endorse this American attitude by stating that although Ghana's constitution limits the President to a maximum of two terms, 'I would be the first to advocate three, four or five terms if we had a man who cancels our situation' (i.e. one able to bring Ghana prosperity). As we have already had cause to note, one of the problems with preaching from just a few notes, or even none, is that it can sometimes lead to imprecision, inconsistency or worse; with Korankye Ankrah this danger is considerable.

Duncan-Williams did not deliver a series of sermons, but on 2 December 2000, just before the election, he spoke out, mainly to reassure people that all would be well and chaos would not ensue: 'The Lord has assured me that he will save Ghana.' 'In the next five to seven years the economy of Ghana will flourish. I have assurance from God. This city [*sic*] is coming out of a coma.'[38] At the Sunday service the following day, with many media people covering his remarks, he spoke in the same vein: 'I do not expect any violence… the same God who delivered us in 1992 will deliver us in 2000.' Using Philippians 4.6–8 ('Have no anxiety about anything, but in everything by prayer… let your requests be made known to God') he stated: 'There are some pastors in this country [for whom] prayer is a taboo, who think philosophy, logic and reasoning answers everything.'[39] Then in a common charismatic rhetorical device, he repeated the text several times, replacing 'by prayer' with other expressions—'by debate', 'by reasoning', 'by argument', 'by logical speculation', 'by intellectual explanation', with the congregation shouting after each misreading: 'No!' He stated that God is not logic; God is bigger than reasoning. 'I am confident that come December 7 Ghana will still be intact.'[40]

---

[38] This service was remarkable in that for a period of about forty minutes forty or fifty pastors gathered around Duncan-Williams, some holding his arms up in the way Moses was supported (Ex 17.12), because it had been announced that, like Moses, 'his destiny affects millions'. Four microphones were in action, and the noise was deafening. This is testimony to the primacy accorded to Duncan-Williams within Ghana's charismatic sector.

[39] Given the acknowledged tensions within the charismatic sector, this might legitimately be interpreted as a reference to Otabil.

[40] For Duncan-Williams's calls for peace, see *Graphic*, 3 Jan. 01, 14; *Times*, 4 Jan. 01, 10. Duncan-Williams's approach to politics is revealed in a sermon delivered at Salifu's Alive Chapel, 'The Mystery of the Oil' [1998]. 'The church must pray that the decrees and decisions of eternity shall be executed. Listen to me; you cannot leave the destiny of this nation to be determined by political powers. They don't know how to govern. When we talk about governance, it is the church…it must be people from within the church.' And later: 'I was talking to a former head of state friend of mine in one of these African nations [Matthieu Kerekou of Benin?]. He was here and we had dinner and we were talking and I perceived that he would become the next president of his nation, and when he was going back to his nation, I told him there is a man of God in his city he must see. He said, "No, I have my own bishop that prays with me", and I said "You don't understand. I know your bishop, he does not have the calling and anointing to deal with the political devils." I said he can cast out devils, he can cause cripples to walk, but he does not have

Otabil did not preach a special series, but a few weeks before the elections he delivered a sermon entitled 'Thy Kingdom Come' based on Matthew 6.9–13 (the Lord's Prayer) and, to the knowledge of this writer, was the only church leader to reveal any awareness that there is no simple correlation between biblical Israel and modern Ghana. Whereas Agyin Asare and Korankye Ankrah were effectively operating with some form of representative sacral kingship (if a leader honours God, God will bless the nation), Otabil distinguished various types of government in history (feudalism, monarchy or chieftaincy, and republicanism) thus giving humanly-determined and culturally-conditioned institutions a significance not suggested elsewhere. In a republic, said Otabil, 'power resides with the people', so a president does not have the same power as a chief. 'A president is a servant of the people who elected him. If we don't understand this, we allow people who become leaders to assume a monarchical position of sovereignty, and when they do that they take the power from the people, invest it in themselves, and use it for their own pleasure.' Ultimately God is sovereign, but he has always 'ruled through human institutions'. He continued: 'Many of us think sovereignty rests with the person we are electing. No, it rests with us the people. It is us the people who release our sovereignty to him to exercise it on our behalf and not on his own behalf.' Thus 'voting is dependent on identifying a person to whom you can delegate your sovereignty.' So check the candidates' assets and liabilities—all have plenty of both—and vote for the person whose assets in your opinion most outweigh his liabilities, 'and remember, after four years, you are not bound to give that same person your sovereignty [again]. One of my greatest desires is for me to see a day when we can rotate people with our thumbs [ballots]. That day will be when we can say we belong to the Republic of Ghana, the day when we can dispatch people and say "Go", "Come", "Go", "Come". When that day comes politicians will not joke with us again, or take us for granted. They will respect you because they know that power is in your hands.' Otabil was the only charismatic pastor heard by this writer to raise issues of power and authority in a way that could be handled in a social science course, understanding political systems as man-made, and the president as a political functionary rather than God's vicegerent.[41]

---

the unctions and the insight and the skills to manoeuvre in political arenas. So I said maintain him as your bishop, but the man you need to contact is that guy there because he has the assignment and the authority to deal with political devils.'

[41] Concluding this sermon, Otabil delivered this prayer: 'Father, today we come into agreement with your word and with your spirit and with the name of Jesus, and by faith we push back every spirit of evil, of uncertainty, of injustice, instability, corruption. We push back every spirit of destruction, fighting, of warfare. We push it back in the name of

Salifu at Alive Chapel not only spiritualised things, but introduced a note of self-interest. On 3 September 2000 the congregation were told: 'Real leaders of the nation are the spiritual leaders. When these people are positioned well in the nation, the nation will prosper.' Just before the election run-off, Salifu proclaimed: 'We need a president that fears God.' (24 Dec. 00) He said he did not want a Minister of Defence who was capable merely in the natural sphere: 'I need a president who puts a man who fears God as the Minister of Defence.' Using the stock examples of Elisha and Joseph, he went on: 'We need people who when tough times come can enter into their bedroom and pray. We need a president who seeks God, we do not need a president who drinks blood [serves false gods].' The need was for people who believe in the Bible, who will read the Bible for themselves, who 'will appoint Christians to become ministers of state', who will appoint people 'who prophesy and it shall come to pass'. The service ended that day with the visiting Chigbundu beseeching God for 'a man after your own heart who would [honour] prophets in this land'.

With such importance given to the spiritual and moral, many charismatic—and mainline—churches are fair game for politicians who can employ the appropriate rhetoric. They are easily co-opted. Politicians vie to speak at religious functions—for example, Mrs Rawlings addresses the

---

Jesus. By faith we do warfare in the realm of the spirit against spiritual wickedness in high places. We pull down the strongholds of evil, we capture every thought, plan, idea that is against your will and against the welfare of this nation, in the name of Jesus. We bind every effort of evil, of Satan, against this nation in Jesus' name. We declare that Ghana is covered under the blood of Jesus and we declare that the light of God destroys every darkness from our land in the name of Jesus. We declare, let there be light in Ghana. Let there be peace, justice, that Christ be king over Ghana, in Jesus' name. Amen. Praise God. Alleluia.' Such a prayer paradoxically would be more characteristic of many of the other pastors we are considering.

The nearest to Otabil is Gordon Kisseih, whose services are televised as weekly programmes entitled 'Treasures of Wisdom'. In 2001 he presented a whole series on 'Strategies to Transform a Nation', built around Ezekiel's dry bones vision (Ez 37). Kisseih talks of structures, and adding value to exports like timber and cocoa and gold, but in the last resort reverts to the idea of blessing (Prov 28.20) and insists: 'God will take away unemployment from this land.' He concludes: 'I am convinced in my spirit that this is my time, this is the time for my nation.' (*8 April 01*) Another strategy he recommends is to have a national day of thanksgiving to God: 'Any nation that acknowledges God, God raises it up.' (*6 June 01*) This last point is encountered frequently in Ghana's charismatic sector. As one letter to the editor expressed it, 'America is the only continent in the world which among all their holidays observe one day set aside every year as thanksgiving day of the Lord, for their crop yield throughout. By this, no wonder, America, despite the increase in crime there, they are one of the richest nations in the world.' (*Chronicle*, 28 Feb–1 March 01, 2)

Pentecostal Council or opens a Women's Aglow conference.[42] Rawlings himself addressed an international convention of the African Faith Tabernacle church a few days before the first round elections, and unashamedly used the occasion to promote his NDC.[43] Christianity was well co-opted in a massive 'Thanksgiving Service' for Rawlings organised by the charismatic sector in the National Theatre on 12 November and attended by, among many others, Agyin Asare and Apostle Ntumy of the Church of Pentecost.[44] Rawlings received a plaque citing how 'the President has transformed the country from the point of moral and economic collapse to a proud, hopeful, stable and democratic nation.'[45] The Rev. S. Asore, Head of the Assemblies of God and a member of Rawlings's (advisory) Council of State, declared: 'This is a man God has given to us.'[46] Mrs Rawlings took the opportunity to instil virtue: 'Most significantly we appear only once, which calls for the utilisation of the opportunity for the upliftment of mankind otherwise that person has not lived in the image of God.'[47]

This obfuscating Christian rhetoric is plentiful in Ghana. One sycophantic columnist in the state-owned *Graphic* could even end an article previewing the election: 'Brothers and sisters, can you wage war against God and his anointed? No! Therefore, do not blaspheme any more. Be contented.'[48] An NDC official went so far as to describe Rawlings's intended successor Mills, as Joshua to Rawlings's Moses and, even further, to call Mills 'the comforter sent by President Rawlings to console Ghanaians after his retirement, just as Jesus Christ sent the Holy Spirit to comfort mankind after his ascension.'[49]

If, like *the Watchman*, one refused to have any truck with Rawlings because he was an idolater and thereby bringing God's wrath upon Ghana, one could still rally to his intended successor Mills because he was totally

---

[42] *West Africa*, 16–22 May 94, 866. *Graphic*, 22 Aug. 00, 13. Mrs Rawlings readily uses born-again diction. For example, in denying media accounts of her daughter Ezanetor's former boyfriend's ordeal at the hands of the security forces, she claimed her daughter was born-again and it was this which had led to the break-up with him. (*Guide*, 29 Aug.-4 Sept. 00, 1)

[43] *Graphic*, 6 Dec. 00, 17.

[44] *Graphic*, 13 Nov. 00.

[45] *Guide*, 16–22 Nov. 00, 1.

[46] *Chronicle*, 14 Nov. 00, 1.

[47] *Guide*, 16–22 Nov. 00, 1.

[48] *Graphic*, 17 June 00, 7.

[49] *Chronicle*, 7–8 Aug. 00, 6. The NPP could use this language just as effectively; their preelection conference in Ho more resembled a crusade (*Chronicle*, 11–12 Sept. 00, 1 and 12). Kufuor's final front-page advertisement before the first round election read simply: 'I strongly believe that God (Allah) will use me to deliver his people on December 7.' (*Graphic*, 5 Dec. 00, 1)

born-again (as he may indeed be). As the elections neared, Mills could play on Christianity in a way denied to Rawlings. This, the report of a press conference, offers some not untypical Mills rhetoric: 'He said that he has come to realise, after being the Vice-President for four years, that there are many problems that they cannot solve as human beings, and that it is only God who can assist us to solve all the problems. "Our prayer has always been that God will lead us in all our endeavours and set us on the right path. We are therefore convinced that with the help of God we shall succeed in all we are determined to do for the nation."' When asked whether he would reopen the unsatisfactory inquiry into the 1982 murder of the judges, he hedged: 'I will however take consolation in the Bible. "Vengeance is mine, says the Lord", and also if you look at Philippians 3.13 Paul says, "I forget the past which is behind me. What I do is to strive for what is ahead of me."'[50]

Shortly before the run-off election, Mills used Christianity for all it was worth, at a reception for the Accra football team Hearts of Oak which had just beaten Espérance of Tunisia to become the champion club of Africa.[51] Four days before the election run-off GTV screened highlights of a reception Mills gave for the victorious team at State House. Flanked at the top table by numerous clergy—mainline, Pentecostal and Charismatic—Mills began his speech: 'Dear Brothers and Sisters in Christ'. He used Proverbs 21.21, 'Victory belongs to the Lord', to show that there is a spiritual dimension to all success, even in football. He linked this with the presidential run-off in a few days, referring to his surprise selection by Rawlings to succeed him: 'I believe I am on a mission from God. One moment I am an ordinary government functionary, the next I am the second most powerful person in the land, in an office that others fought for for years. If this is not a miracle I don't know what is... It has become apparent to me that God has not finished with me yet... I need your prayers. Nothing I do will succeed unless I have the support of God.' After his speech, there was a presentation of Bibles and daily prayer guides to all the Hearts team by Agyin Asare. This was a clear manipulation of Christianity. While the NDC were plotting to win the election by every means at their disposal, Mills took the opportunity to present himself nationally as the anointed and God-fearing leader the deuteronomic history requires. Many churches fell for it totally.[52]

[50] *Guide*, 11 Oct. 00, 1, under headline 'Osofo [i.e. Reverend] Mills speaks out'. This cutting was posted on the official notice-board of Duncan-Williams's ACI.

[51] Mills had been president of the club and it was associated with the NDC, just as Asante Kotoko, of which Kufuor had been chairman, was associated with the NPP. On 9 May 2001, the game between these two clubs, that some media had hyped as a re-run of the elections, led to disturbances in which 126 died.

[52] On the morning of the first round elections, the *Chronicle* broke the story that the

It should be noted that Agyin Asare, after the defeat of his champion Mills, immediately regrouped, and at Kufuor's post-election Thanksgiving Service on 4 March 2001 read the prayer. Building on Daniel 4.17 ('The Most High is sovereign over kingdoms of men, and gives them to anyone he wishes'), someone who had prayed every week over the NDC candidate Mills had no difficulty endorsing Kufuor, praying to God: 'We asked you to give us your own man, and you have given us [your man]. We have gathered to say "Glory to you". When you set a man in place [you give him what is necessary]. We thank you for what you are going to do.'[53]

It is interesting that Agyin Asare could be similarly involved in neighbouring Ivory Coast. In early December 2000, just at the time of Ghana's first round elections, Ivory Coast had been plunged into chaos, with President Laurent Gbagbo, who had taken power in an uprising against military rule, banning his main rival, former Prime Minister and northern Muslim Alassane Ouattara, from presidential and parliamentary elections. As a result, the UN withdrew its support for elections. Clashes took place in which scores of dead were reported, and it was also said that police had incited the burning of a mosque. The United States, the EU and France all condemned Gbagbo's manipulation of the elections, but immediately afterwards Agyin Asare preached at a thanksgiving service for Gbagbo held in a stadium in Abidjan. His message (based on II Sam 23.2–4) was what he has preached in Ghana: all leaders are put in authority by God (Rom 13.1, and Ps 75.6), as the result of the prayers or lack of prayers of the people. But God who raises up people can also cast them down (as in Ghana, he used the example of Nebuchadnezzar) unless they rule in the fear of the Lord. When God influences leaders, there is peace and blessing ('Blessed is the nation whose God is the Lord'), but when the Devil influences leaders, there is confusion, disorder, chaos (as with David and his census, II Sam 24, I Chron 21). What is significant here is not the wealth of sound advice that Agyin Asare gave to Gbagbo, but the role he played in offering legitimacy to a very dubiously elected president. His opening text, 'All authority is from God' (Rom 13,1), must have been music in Gbagbo's ears, for by every other standard his legitimacy was very slight. It was ominous that Agyin Asare seemed to see little danger in thus legitimising Gbagbo[54] and in being willing to involve

---

supposedly childless Mills had an illegitimate son being brought up by his sister in Cape Coast. One 'Concerned Reverend Minister' took out a full-page advertisement in the *Graphic* (22 Dec. 00, 15) to defend him: 'Even Abraham, the man who is described in the Bible as the father of the Christian faith, did it.'

[53] It is worthy of note that Otabil, who had spent the previous decade earning a reputation for opposing the NDC, did not attend this apotheosis of the NPP.

[54] TV coverage of Agyin Asare meeting Gbagbo also showed Agyin Asare's American mentor Morris Cerullo in attendance. Agyin Asare was invited by Gbagbo for an

himself in what seen from one angle was a struggle between Christians and Muslims.

Thus there is no single attitude to politics or political role within this charismatic sector. Many charismatic leaders could denounce the regime, because of its supposed idolatry, and therefore favour change.[55] Duncan-Williams actively supported the NDC, claiming that the New Testament gives no mandate for criticising the government and its officials, even if they are doing bad things.[56] He was also closely associated with the annual thanksgiving services that Rawlings orchestrated through the 1990s. The *Free Press* noted that 'the national Day of Thanksgiving was meant to serve Rawlings not God', and another newspaper was not far from the mark with its headline labelling the 1995 service 'NDC Rally on Church Platform'.[57] Agyin Asare, despite the spiritual nature of his theology, was known to be very close to NDC candidate Mills. Heward-Mills had every reason to have negative opinions about the NDC, his church headquarters having been the object of political thuggery, but generally his energies went into the one thing necessary, evangelism and church planting.[58] Otabil joined considerable pragmatism to radical re-thinking—vote for whoever you think would serve you best, but unless the whole political culture is changed, Ghana has no future. Winners' scarcely touched explicitly on politics, partly perhaps because, as Nigerians, the leaders were reluctant to be seen to interfere,[59] but at a deeper level it stemmed from

---

'official' visit in March 2001 (*Graphic*, 26 Mar. 01, 3, where there is a photo of Agyin Asare praying with the President's family).

[55] In very different ways. Matthew Addae-Mensah of Gospel Light International could see God's hand in the Kufuor victory: 'The number 8 was Mr Kufuor's divine appointment. He would have won first round if the election had taken place on December 8, which was his birthday. Divinely, Mr Kufuor's victory was interrupted when the election was changed to December 7. God had to reschedule Mr Kufuor's victory. [Addae Mensah] disclosed that when you take the number 2 from 28, you still have the number 8, the number of Mr Kufuor's divine appointment with God. If you add 6 and 2, which is Mr Kufuor's age, you still have the number 8. The number 2 stands for the second round.' (*Chronicle*, 8–9 Jan. 01, 5) But Enoch Agbozo denounces this as an 'occultist-spiritist explanation', and a 'numerical and astrological arrangement which takes from God's redemption of Ghana from Satan... Let us not give glory to stars, numbers, Satan and man. This is an abomination.' (*Chronicle*, 20–21 Feb. 01, 7)

[56] *Chronicle*, 16–17 Feb. 00, 4; & 17–20 March 00, 4.

[57] *Free Press*, 25 Feb. 3 March 1994, 4; *Voice*, 23 March 2 April 1995, 1; see Gifford *AC*, 86–7.

[58] After the transition, he could be critical of the NDC in allusions to their misuse of law (25 Dec. 00), and the need to have personal contacts before anything could be achieved (21 Jan. 01: 'We pray that it won't be like that again') and in print even before the change of regimes: see *Solomonic Success*, 4–7; *Principles of Success*, 14, 41.

[59] Togo deported the Winners' pastor in Lomé 'before he does more harm in the cordial relations existing between Togo and Nigeria'. This Nigerian pastor had denounced the

their theology: politics does not really matter because a Christian prospers quite independently of the context. Salifu wanted spiritual men, even prophets like himself, to have political authority. Thus the diversity was wide.

Reform of culture

We remarked of Otabil above that he goes far beyond economic or political structures and confronts the issue of culture as a factor in development. He consciously addresses Ghanaian culture, aspects of which he sees as ill-adapted to the modern world.

However, there is another more subtle way in which culture can be considered. David Martin has long argued that although most Pentecostals do not directly confront political issues—indeed, most are so powerless that to expect it would be unreasonable—they nevertheless may function very politically by slowly and subtly transforming cultural values in areas like power and gender relations. He puts his argument succinctly: 'In societies where politics is carried on by corrupt clienteles, a reform of culture through religion may well be the best option the populace has.'[60]

Before considering some of the issues involved here, we should make two provisos. First, some Western observers often suggest that members of charismatic churches manifest a conviction and commitment of an altogether superior order to that of mainline Christians, whose adherence is largely nominal. This may have been true of Latin America in the 1980s, but it is not true of Ghana today. No Ghanaians function with this understanding; all accept that nominal adherents are as plentiful in charismatic churches as in the mainline ones—and conversely that committed Christians are as evident in mainline as in charismatic churches. In 2001 Heward-Mills's LCI completed the computerisation of their records; only about one-third are categorised as committed in any deep sense. One of the reasons why Otabil has no choir or officials on the platform when he preaches is that he is not prepared to have the impact of his message diluted by association with people whose morals he cannot vouch for. It has been said that in places like Botswana with its AIDS pandemic the majority of women teachers are unmarried—deliberately so, because to marry is effectively to sign one's own death warrant. In such circumstances 'sects'—in the hard sense like the SDAs and Jehovah's Witnesses, where fidelity is more assured—can play a significant social role. But in Ghana

---

Togolese people as 'the very embodiment of laziness' as a result of their voodoo shrines (*Crusading Guide*, 5–11 Sept. 00, 12).
[60] David Martin, *TLS*, 18 Dec. 92, 22.

the new charismatic churches are not seen as intensely counter-cultural, world-renouncing or ascetic in that sense; hence the word 'sect' is quite inappropriate to describe them. (This is why one should be hesitant about describing Ghana's new Christians as 'Evangelical', if conversion in some hard sense is to be considered one of their defining characteristics.)

Also, Ghana was never like Guatemala, where Christian groups were forced to be apolitical at the risk of their lives; and in Ghana the United States was never fighting communism and its presumed fellow-travellers with any methods that came to hand. On the contrary, northern agencies have for many years now been fostering civil society and encouraging pluralism. Since northern donors were contributing half of Ghana's budget, public involvement and advocacy could hardly be proscribed. Certainly many Ghanaians were harassed and some opted for exile, but the repression was of a totally different order from that in some Latin American countries, as outspoken criticism in newspapers like the *Chronicle* and then on radio talk-backs increasingly revealed.

Let us briefly consider some of the areas where churches might have on impact on culture. The first is 'peaceability', by which Martin means that these churches encourage a climate of peace, a prerequisite for development. In Ghana all the churches, in what almost became a crusade, put enormous emphasis on campaigning for peace before and during elections.[61] On one level, as a few pointed out, this was effectively playing into the hands of the NDC. The Reform Party protested about the chorus for peace sung by the traditional and religious leaders. 'These people are basically irresponsible… It is irresponsible if someone is consistently poking his finger into my eyes and you are not cautioning the person but preaching to me to exercise restraint. You cannot have peace without justice. You cannot have justice if there is no fairness.' The party decried 'the silence of traditional and religious leaders in cases of infractions by President Rawlings'.[62] The NPP likewise objected to playing up issues of bloodshed to scare Ghanaians away from voting for others. Rawlings continually insisted 'There will be peace only under the NDC', and one of the advertisements on the ubiquitous NDC billboards urged, rather unsubtly, 'Vote NDC for Peace'. The NPP feared that all this talk was meant to provide 'an excuse to introduce unconstitutional measures under the pretext

[61] We can cite just a few examples. For Duncan-Williams, see *Evening News*, 27 Nov. 00, 1; for CAC, see *Times*, 29 Aug. 00, 3; for CCG, see *Graphic*, 20 June 00, 11; for Methodists, see *Graphic*, 29 April 00, 11; for Deeper Life, see *Graphic*, 19 Dec. 00; for International Pentecostal Holiness Church, see *Spectator*, 18 Nov. 00, 14; for Apostolic Faith Ministry International, see *Graphic*, 5 Sept. 00, 11; for Church of Pentecost, see *Mirror*, 23 Dec. 00, 22.

[62] *Chronicle*, 15 Nov. 00, 1.

of some imaginary threat to security.' One political analyst decried this as part of a whole 'campaign to moralise politics': 'The NDC has delegated the job of attacking the opposition to its underlings... and is running on the ostensibly benign and apolitical theme "Praying for Peace".... While there is certainly a place in politics for the public show of piety, it is no substitute for a vigorous debate on the issues.'[63] The churches were also preaching that the loser should accept the verdict of the polls, which again—given that the NDC were attempting to manipulate the outcome— was effectively a sign that the churches were playing into the hands of the NDC. Ghana was indeed fortunate that the NPP victory was so obvious and undeniable that the NDC was forced to accept it.

However, on a more important level Martin is surely correct. The threat of civil war in Ghana was real—and, before the elections, concerned bodies repeatedly broadcast a song beginning 'Liberia, Sierra Leone, Angola, Burundi' listing the African countries destroyed by civil war. In Africa anything is better than a civil war, as is clear from a glance at Ghana's neighbours Liberia and Sierra Leone, both of which have been totally brutalised and set back generations. It is only the peace prevailing in Ghana that enabled important advances to take place almost by stealth, in some cases becoming evident only in the election itself and its aftermath.[64]

Second, we should consider issues of gender. Obviously these churches provide opportunities—not many, but a few—for women to assume leadership roles. But even if top leadership positions are still difficult to attain, women are often involved as ushers, choristers, prayer warriors and evangelists. These churches also give enormous importance to marriage. As we have mentioned, it is accepted that the young women who join choirs are seeking husbands, and these marriages are modern and monogamous. Fidelity is the ideal even if not often spoken of, and marriage is a partnership even if the husband is definitely the head.[65]

---

[63] Daniel A. Smith, in "Election 2000: Debating the Issues?" CDD briefing paper, Sept. 00, writes: 'The NDC is not the only public party making a calculated effort to play upon the public's underlying fear that the elections may not be peaceful. Other parties have also side-stepped important issues facing Ghanaians, choosing instead to pray to a higher authority for the country's salvation.'

[64] Otabil made this point at the launching of the Agyin Asare Gospel Crusade. Responding to the criticism of the charismatic churches, he said: 'Can you imagine what Ghana would be like without these churches? (The youth) would have gone on the streets and cut off each other's heads out of frustration... Ghana would not have survived without the new churches, because they have the majority of the youth. [We are] a stopgap between our poverty and total destruction.' (31 Mar. 01)

[65] David Martin, who has written that Pentecostalism 'is a woman's movement' uses the nice phrase of Pentecostal marriage: 'patriarchalism in theory and consensuality in practice'. (David Martin, *Pentecostalism: the World their Parish*, Oxford: Blackwell, 2002,

The overall importance of this for women is undeniable. If all Ghanaians have incurred hardship over the last decades, the greater share has fallen on women. Their lives have become particularly hard, ekeing out a living, finding husbands, rearing children (often alone), or coping with barrenness and the intolerable pressure it brings from in-laws. One woman interviewed on why women in particular would join these new churches responded: 'I might have gone crazy by now if I had not resorted to seeking divine intervention in solving my problems.'[66] The way women's needs are met has been well researched—by Tetteh for women frequenting prayer camps and by Quame for those in charismatic churches. The latter study shows the numerous structures set up to address the needs of women at ACI: the 'Fruit of the Womb' prayer and deliverance session for childless women, the solidarity 'Day-Born Meetings' (meetings of those born on a particular day of the week), the Singles Department, the 'Pre-Marital Department', the 'Post-Marital Department', the 'Pastors' Wives Association', and the women's wing of the church called 'Women in Action'. All churches provide forums for women; thus in August 2001 Heward-Mills and his pastor wife conducted a 'Daughter, you can make it' convention, with 'lady pastors ministering… on women's issues, the challenges women face, relationships etc.' Christie Doe-Tetteh's Solid Rock Chapel in September 2001 hosted a women's convention entitled 'The Excellent Woman'. These women's sessions are mainly targeted gatherings for inculcating self-esteem, providing encouragement and overcoming blockages, in much the same way as is characteristic of meetings of these churches generally.[67] The general message of winning is often directed at women specifically. We have seen Otabil insisting that women must raise their sights. They must not be content to be just 'hairdresser, seamstress, secretary, teacher, nurse': 'Take those [professions] away and most of you will have nothing to do.' (*8 Aug. 02*) Otabil again: 'Most of you women have great potential but you will die pathetic creatures… A woman's lot is not to depend on a man. Have your own house, car… I'm looking for purpose-driven, achievement-orientated women.' (*29 Aug. 02*)

If women run the risk of witchcraft accusation, some of these new churches—such as Otabil's—are gently undermining the mindset that permits such denunciations, while others like Salifu's function because of

---

169 and 98 respectively) This picture is disputed by Rekopantswe Mate, 'Wombs as God's Laboratories: Pentecostal Discourses of Femininity in Zimbabwe', *Africa*, 72, 4 (2002), 549–68.

[66] Golda Armah, 'Do Women seek "Miracles" to solve Problems?', *Graphic*, 31 Aug. 00, 8.

[67] Tetteh, *Dynamics*: Quame, *Christian*, esp. 54–69.

this very mindset. The mothers, aunts and grandmothers readily named as witches and responsible for all manner of ills suffer, although it might be argued that deliverance from a witchcraft spirit in church is far preferable to banishment to a witches' camp.[68]

Third, consider the understanding of success. In general, traditional culture has vested much in keeping communities united by preventing individuals from prospering much more conspicuously than their fellows. Witchcraft accusations have often functioned in this way. Obviously, this new Christianity, by constantly glorifying success, is well calculated to change such attitudes and legitimise wealth creation by individuals, because it presents success as a blessing, a person's right, and almost godly. Moreover, pastors with their Mercedes cars, luxurious houses and expensive clothes must be doing much to undermine this attitude. However, there is another side to this. 'Big Man' syndrome is the curse of Africa. The pastors themselves do not greatly advert to the fact that their cars and houses (acquired through a particularly adaptive theology of tithing and seed faith) are purchased at the expense of the people they are theoretically serving, in just the same way as Rawlings and his entourage thrived from their 'revolution.' In the same month as the President of Nigeria's senate was impeached for, among other things, 'bringing his total of official vehicles to 32',[69] *Winners' World* carried an article about their founder's acquisition of a private jet. One might argue that the church leader and his jet, far from illustrating God's faithfulness to his chosen, is just the Nigerian Big Man syndrome transposed on to a Christian plane.

Fourth, where the inculcation of democratic virtues is concerned, one must bear in mind that many of these churches are not really communities or fellowships at all. Some are, and many others began in that way, but just as many are now composed of clients of a particular 'Man of God'. Certainly the famed 'cell groups' often taken as almost characteristic of these churches have become far less significant in the last decade.[70]

---

[68] Recently a Presbyterian organisation has been exorcising witches at the Gambaga witches' camp, thus enabling many women to return home; numbers at the camp were 87 in mid 2002, down from 140 three years before. (*Graphic*, 8 Aug. 02, 19)

[69] *Graphic*, 10 Aug. 00, 5; *Economist*, 12 Aug. 00, 39.

[70] In the late 1980s most of Ghana's major charismatic churches started to establish local branches in residential suburbs, because transport to the central church was both difficult and expensive, and because they were all beginning to lose members to new churches arising in the suburbs. With this proliferation of branch churches, the rationale for cell-groups was less convincing, even though all pastors I spoke to insisted on the crucial role they still played. Even Winners', which of set policy has no branches, has only '109 fellowships of between seven and 15 members each' (interview assistant pastor, 7 May 01), which at the most generous calculation comes to a grand total of 1,635 members involved; this is only about 15% of its weekly attendance.

More significantly, it is widely admitted that there has been a move away from egalitarian tendencies to a more authoritarian ethos. What may have begun as fellowships in the early 1980s became churches and even denominations, and leaders, originally called simply 'Brother' (or more rarely 'Sister'), became 'General Overseer' and then perhaps 'Bishop' or 'Archbishop'—a noticeboard at LCI has proclaimed Heward-Mills as 'the Megabishop'. Many church leaders have acquired honorary doctorates—a title is as important in this sector as in society at large—and many too move around with bodyguards, a great status symbol in Ghana.

The prophetic phenomenon has brought this trajectory to its culmination. Prophets are persons of a totally different order from their congregations, with special gifts—and even here we have seen the rise of 'Major Prophet' and 'Mega Prophet'. Oyedepo, founder of Winners', provides a glimpse of a prophet's standing. He recounts spending a four-day meeting with all his pastors deciding on a mission policy. Immediately afterwards, however, God spoke to him to reverse the policy agreed: 'That settled it.'[71] Because of his status he is totally unchallengeable: 'The moment you doubt prophetic utterances, you are damned.'[72] Again, 'When you go against the prophet, it is actually God you are rising up against.'[73] He gives an example of a man speaking against a prophet, and dying while the meeting was still in progress.[74] 'Prophets are the carriers of God's power, and this power is like a river. One characteristic of rivers is that they flow downhill, not uphill. ... If you must partake of what the prophets carry, you must accept them as being placed above you.'[75]

The leaders of these churches have thus become increasingly important figures, and their otherness can be trumpeted quite unashamedly.[76] A church whose founder is alive and in office may convoke all the meetings required by its constitution (where one exists), but it is widely admitted that such churches do not function in such a way as the exponents of civil society might hope as nurseries of democratic virtues. Subordinates

---

[71] Oyedepo, *Prophetic Wings*, 18.

[72] Ibid., 47.

[73] Ibid., 111.

[74] Ibid., 163. He continues: 'You become a victim of whatever you criticise in the prophet. If you pick on his prosperity, you die in poverty. If you pick on his success, you become a public and established failure.'

[75] Ibid., 120. Not surprisingly, receiving from a prophet is linked with giving to him beforehand: 'Friend, you need prophetic encounters that will last you all the days of your life. And you can obtain them by giving to the prophet.' (ibid., 133; see all 129–47)

[76] See Heward-Mills: 'A church needs a strong leader to move it forward. Democracy and numerous committees are not helpful when you need strong leadership.' (*Solomonic Success*, 16) 'A committee does not run a church. A church needs a strong leader supported by wise and loyal assistants.' (*Secrets of Success*, 21)

are often not prepared to speak up, and often when they do they may come to regret it (there are many stories of consequent redeployment). Even Otabil's ICGC, although it has board meetings, does not have as many as are required by its constitution; indeed, according to many of his own pastors, Otabil has used his increased stature to make himself totally unaccountable. Some pastors have brought their wives into leadership positions, probably to entrench their personal control. The older, 'classical' Pentecostal churches score much more highly in this area; because their founders are dead, some of the authority exercised is institutional rather than personal, and committees can function properly as committees. Even here, however, anomalies persist. When the CACI was bidding farewell to its chairman, the church's president presented him with some benefits including an 'unspecified sum of money as a gratuity, and other allowances'.[77] It was ironical that exactly at this time some media were revealing the undisclosed sums that Rawlings's NDC (with some collusion from the incoming NPP élite) had voted themselves as 'end of service' benefits. In these cases both the church and political élites were looking after their own in a way that was best kept from the masses. Where general financial accountability is concerned, these churches are not obvious models of transparency; I know of none that publishes yearly accounts or the salaries of its pastors, and subordinate pastors appear to be dealt with on a basis of patronage.

Fifth, over the issue of social capital, or the element of trust infusing society, we have noted that far from the born-again sector being distinguished by unity and harmony, pastors tend to be wary of one another. After all, they are in many way rivals for a substantial but not unlimited catchment (one of the agendas behind the 'Breaking Barriers' convention of the 'Winning Ways' superstars was to break the barriers between the charismatic leaders and effect a more obvious harmony). At a much deeper level, however, we have observed at several points that enormous explanatory value is given to 'enemies' (again, we have argued that this stems from a traditional religious understanding). We have cited numerous examples of explanations through personal forces of evil, very often within families.

It is also revealing to see how these churches understand themselves. Heward-Mills makes a constant theme of loyalty and disloyalty, and in his *Loyalty and Disloyalty* they are seen as places of enormous conflict, each a veritable bear-pit.[78] The church is *his*: 'I encourage people to walk

---

[77] *Graphic*, 27 Feb. 01, 9.
[78] Heward-Mills, *Loyalty and Disloyalty*, Accra: DgTP, 1998. See also *Secrets of Success*, 26; *Principles of Success*, 7–8; 14–16; 19, 29; 35–6.

out of my church if their hearts are not with me.'[79] His position is unassailable: 'I am here because God has put me here. There may be people who are even better pastors than I am, but God put me here instead of them.'[80] He describes recalcitrant members as traitors, villains, anarchists, mutineers, rebels, betrayers. He refers often to potential enemies: 'The friend of my enemy is also my enemy' and 'Any new person is a potential traitor until proved otherwise.'[81] 'To have a culture of loyalty you must constantly prune out disloyal elements that find their way into our midst.'[82] Signs of disloyalty are manifested by one who 'thinks too much money is being spent on the head',[83] who 'does not contribute to a joint effort which is intended to bless and appreciate their pastor',[84] and who tells the pastor 'You are not always right.'[85] 'A subversive associate constantly listens to tapes from external ministers and learns from them. But he never listens to his own head pastor's tapes.'[86] By contrast, a loyal assistant genuinely admires his pastor and praises him,[87] 'makes complimentary remarks about everything that he has preached',[88] spontaneously celebrates his birthday and presents him with gifts.[89] Both the advice and the illustrations indicate that harmony is not a given. In one sense, there is nothing remarkable in this preoccupation with internal cohesion under authority. Established churches have set orders and procedures—Catholics and Anglicans have canon law—to structure and regularise, to resolve disputes, to discipline and to promote. Many of these new churches have absolutely nothing except the pastor's vision, and in order merely to survive they have to institutionalise and routinise. Even so, the picture emerging in some cases provides little comfort to those who would like to see charismatic churches as democracies in microcosm, or places where disputes can be procedurally resolved. Some churches are moving to structure themselves along the lines of the unchallengeable Big Man rather than accountable leadership and popular participation.[90]

---

[79] Heward-Mills, *Loyalty*, 6
[80] Ibid., 90.
[81] Ibid., 70 and 99.
[82] Ibid., 48.
[83] Ibid., 111.
[84] Ibid., 114.
[85] Ibid., 120.
[86] Ibid., 142.
[87] Ibid., 127.
[88] Ibid.
[89] Ibid., 134.
[90] And Heward-Mills suggests that inter-church sniping is just as serious: 'I have discovered to my surprise that pastors are best at slandering other pastors and helping to destroy other ministries.' (*Anomaa Nsem*, 19–25 Dec. 00, 4)

Finally, there are the related issues of time and work habits. According to Landes, no country can hope to modernise until it has interiorised the importance of time.[91] In Ghana all sorts of activities are notoriously late in starting. In many cases this seems deliberate; one of the ways by which the leader shows that he is a Big Man is by keeping the little boys waiting. The immeasurable waste of time that results must be one of the reasons why productivity in Ghana is so low. These churches are doing little to improve this, since few of their services and conventions begin on time. The internal structure of gatherings is not geared to help this interiorisation, because the first sixty to ninety minutes invariably consist of praise and worship, or feature choirs and groups. The crowds build up during this time, and even choir members and musicians saunter in during this period. Murdock in 'Winning Ways' insisted on the importance of interiorising time if one wants to be successful in any area of life. Of Ghanaian pastors this writer has heard only Otabil gently chide his members for not being there at the time a service was scheduled to start.

The political role of these churches does not lend itself to easy summary. At one end of the spectrum there is a form of Christianity that challenges the entire political culture—as at Otabil's ICGC. Yet this is only one possibility, and by no means the most characteristic. Others bring an exclusively spiritual or moral focus to issues that are just as much matters of efficiency, competence and professionalism. Obviously this does not automatically or invariably keep one bound in the realm of the supernatural. The poultry magnate Kwabena Darko, one of Ghana's most successful businessmen, is himself a Pentecostal pastor. Kofi Coomson, owner of Accra's *Chronicle* and contender for the prize (if one were awarded) for the greatest conspiracy-theorist in Ghana throughout the 1990s, seeing the NDC as responsible for every ill, is a member of Agyin Asare's WMCI. So too is Kabral Blay-Amihere, the politically sophisticated former head of the West Africa Journalists' Association and ambassador for the Kufuor government.[92] These are instances where a form of Christianity that stresses spiritual causality did not prevent attention being given to mundane causes as well. Nevertheless, there are a great number of Ghanaian charismatics for whom the stress seems to fall exclusively on the spiritual. We outlined here a debate of some importance: that involving the conceptualisation of evil as caused by demons. This might be an

[91] David Landes, *Revolution in Time: Clocks and the Making of the Modern World*, Cambridge, MA: Harvard University Press, 1983.
[92] Kabral Blay-Amihere, *Fighting for Freedom*, Accra: Trans Afrika News (2001).

implicit way of challenging malfunctioning political systems. Proponents have shown that Ghanaians may conceptualise evil through these
means and thereby make their lives liveable, but it has not been shown
that political systems are thereby reformed in any meaningful sense.

Many Ghanaians are sceptical here too. They would argue that the
modern world—which Ghana tried to join through the ERP and all the
IMF and World Bank activity throughout the 1980s and '90s—is marked
by the pursuit of technically efficient means of securing this-worldly
ends. In the process of modernisation, technical rationality has gradually
displaced supernatural influence and moral considerations in ever-wider
areas of public life, replacing them by considerations of objective performance and practical expediency. This system functions on the basis of a
particular kind of rationality. It may be asked whether a form of religion
so manifestly different in its explanatory processes can contribute greatly
to the rationality that the modern world introduced and seemingly requires. David Martin has written: 'Pentecostalism in Africa is a collective
raft pointed with determination towards modernity.'[93] Akrong, writing
equally sweepingly about the same Christianity, strongly disagrees, seeing charismatic Christianity as 'nothing but the repackaging of traditional witchcraft mentality in Christian categories'. He concludes: 'By
far the most serious challenge this [charismatic] mentality poses to our
society is the enthronement of a magical world-view with its dualistic
subtleties that lures us to passivity, dependence, surrender of the power to
make choices and accept responsibilities. Painfully, these are the very
ingredients that destroy identity and personal initiative in a highly com-
petitive world where we have to make important choices every day.
Tragically, the magical world-view which this mentality reinforces is
hardly the kind of mentality that will help us as a society to participate
fully in the modern world where the operating paradigm is rationality and
scientific thinking—the basic requirements for proper functioning in the
global village.'[94]

---

[93] Martin, *Pentecostalism: the World*, 152.
[94] Abraham Akrong, 'A Neo-Witchcraft Mentality in Popular Christianity', *Research
Review*, New Series, 16, 1 (2000), 11. See also Quame: 'Because of its charismatic out-
look, [Duncan-Williams's church] has employed the African medium to interpret life and
its concerns... Here the African interpretative scheme is never challenged. It is rather
endorsed and enforced all the time.' (*Christian*, 152)

8

CONCLUSION

One fact can be agreed on: Ghanaians themselves view their new Christianity with some unease, and many have profound misgivings about it, sensing that it is socially dysfunctional. 'Stop these Disgusting Preachers', blazons one newspaper headline. 'Ruining Lives in Je-e-esus' Name' is another.[1] Editorials frequently urge caution: 'Beware of the Charlatans' (the *Spectator*) and 'Beware of False Prophets' (the *Graphic*).[2] One editorial says that all these new churches should have been 'one of the best things to have happened to Ghana, but unfortunately the reverse is the case.'[3] The disquiet arises on several scores. There are frequent reports of sexual lapses by these new pastors: (e.g. 'Pastor Traps Girl, 16, and impregnates her'[4]) and about theft and fraud, particularly over visas ('Miracle Pastor Dupes Woman'[5] and 'Playboy Pastor, Girlfriend, Convicted'[6]). Such stories provide staple fare for reports in the tabloids (even the *Mirror*) and in their correspondence columns.

There are misgivings also about the effects of their teaching. Their understanding of witchcraft is often faulted. One writer deplores the injustice done by 'pastors and priests who have turned into witchhunters. Indeed, they have, by their false doctrines, destroyed many homes after declaring either a mother, wife or an in-law a witch.'[7] Many think the

---

[1] *Spectator*, 11 Aug. 01, 2, *Graphic*, 8 June 01, 2.

[2] *Spectator*, 30 Sept. 00, 3 and *Graphic*, 22 Aug. 00, 7; see also *Graphic*, 17 Oct. 00, 7; 6 Nov. 00, 7; 27 March 01, 7; and 6 Oct. 00, 7; also specifically on the Great Light Worship Centre in Kumasi, (*Guide*, 7–13 Feb. 01, 5; *Gospel News*, Jan. 01, 8).

[3] *Love and Life*, 1–7 Oct. 00, 4.

[4] *Spectator*, 26 Aug.–1 Sept. 00, 1.

[5] *Spectator*, 20 July 02.

[6] *Daily Guide*, 7 Aug. 01, 3.

[7] Tina Aforo-Yeboah, 'Murder in the Name of Witchcraft', *Spectator*, 28 April 01, 13. In a much-publicised case a woman who protested during a service at the price the pastor was charging for a small bottle of olive oil was taken outside and tied to a tree as a witch; the woman later died, and the pastor was charged with murder, although the case was dismissed since the inquest showed that the woman died from natural causes (*Daily Guide*, 4 June 01, 1, and 4 July 01, 1; *Crusading Guide*, 10–16 July 01, 5).

faith gospel's prosperity emphasis is self-serving: 'The establishment of a "Christian" church has become the shortest route to raise oneself above the poverty line.'[8] Others fear that the insistence on miraculous divine provision militates against development. In the words of one politician, 'Promising people to reap where they have not sown not only encourages them to be corrupt but also lazy. Until the various religious bodies redefine their doctrines on miracles and urge the people to work diligently, the government's quest to increase productivity in the country [will] never materialise.'[9] A *Graphic* editorial laments the increasing tendency to explain everything in terms of spiritual forces: 'It seems our society is gradually being swallowed by superstition. The numerous churches that dot the various residential areas daily attribute all the afflictions of the individual to the devil and his or her prosperity to the divine. Once a society is built on such a mystical foundation, hard work and perseverance fail to take hold...'[10] There have been yet more misgivings since pastors began to trumpet their ability to cure AIDS. These churches are generally considered to be of little help in combating the threat of an AIDS epidemic: 'Preachers of the gospel are now preachers of prosperity and instant miracles with little or no reference to morality in their messages.'[11]

Mainline churches have repeatedly voiced misgivings. The 71st Synod of the Presbyterian Church of Ghana was 'deeply concerned' about 'the use of the name of God to cheat and rob innocent people'.[12] The National Congress on Evangelisation (NACOE 2001) expressed serious concern about 'a growing absence of God's word from the pulpits and in our Radio and TV Christian programmes';[13] in an interview the General Secretary of the CCG called on this NACOE conference to 'flush out false pastors, prophets'.[14] Such reservations come not only from the mainline churches, which might feel under threat through loss of numbers; the

---

[8] Kwame Gyasi in *Spectator*, 31 March 01, 3. Also, 'This country produces more priests now than doctors because the priestly profession is now an avenue to quick money. This is what our Christian society has become today.' (*Chronicle*, 5 Sept. 02, 3)

[9] *Graphic*, 6 July 01, 11.

[10] *Graphic*, 16 Sept. 02, 7.

[11] Eunice Menka, 'Condoms, the Church and HIV/AIDS', *Times*, 28 June 00, 6. Churches making such claims include the Synagogue Church of all Nations (*Mirror*, 28 April 01, 1); the Ebenezer Worship Centre International (*Newsmaker*, 16–22 Oct. 00, 3; *Guide*, 5–11 Oct. 00, 9; 24–30 July 01, 5); the Apostolic Faith Mission International (*Daily Guide*, 28 Aug. 01, 4); Winners' (claimed at service, 1 Sept. 02); even Kwamena Ahinful, *Mirror* 4 Aug. 01, 16; Lawrence Tetteh, *Do Miracles still Happen?* London: World Miracle Outreach, 1999 (a story he tells often, e.g. at his crusade 15 Sept. 00). For an editorial protesting, 'Pastors and AIDS claims', see *Daily Guide*, 19 June 01, 5.

[12] *Christian Messenger*, 13, 7 (2000), 3.

[13] *Christian Messenger*, July–Aug. 01, 3.

[14] *Graphic*, 4 June 01, 3.

Chairman of the Church of Pentecost has said: 'The greatest threat to Christianity and society these days is the preaching of false doctrines.'[15]

In mid-2002 the Accra Metropolitan Assembly raised the monthly rent for churches hiring classrooms from 50,000 cedis ($7) to 600,000 ($85), and introduced a deposit of 2.4 million cedis, probably not only to tax what are widely seen as commercial ventures, but also to attempt to damp down the charismatic explosion.[16] At the same time a *Graphic* editorial was calling for oversight: 'It is time Ghanaians extended the critical scrutiny [brought to bear on] politicians and other public office holders to religious leaders.'[17]

With the widespread disquiet goes recognition of the variety within this Christianity. This, along with its ability to change over time, has constituted a serious difficulty for this study: if charismatic Christianity is so protean, how helpful is it to write about it as one reality? Ghana's Charismatic Christianity is considered here as a broad spectrum rather than as two or more separate things. In the view of some Ghanaian charismatics a prophet like Salifu is not representative, and it is not valid to use him (or Bempa or Vagalas or Apraku) to build up a picture of Ghanaian charismatic Christianity, but that response must be rejected. Salifu is certainly not representative of Ghana's charismatic movement, but he none the less represents a significant and growing strain within it, and to leave him out of the discussion for whatever reason would be intellectually dishonest. Nor is Otabil representative. He and Salifu stand at opposite ends of the spectrum, and between them there is tension amounting to incompatibility. It is virtually unthinkable that Otabil would be invited to speak at Salifu's

[15] *Graphic*, 30 March 00, 11. In the same article one Pentecostal church actually suggests forming an umbrella body to 'send a draft proposal to Parliament on what it considers as a true Christian doctrine, which could promote the national good, for adoption'. Other charismatic pastors calling for some regulation include the Church of Bethesda (*Chronicle*, 13 July 01, 4), the prophet Owusu Bempa (*Spectator*, 12 April 01, 4), the Apostolic Church of Ghana (*Graphic*, 16 Aug. 00, 14), and Deeper Life (*Chronicle*, 4 Jan. 01, 5 and 20–22 April 01, 4).

[16] *Chronicle*, 6 June 02, 8; Apostle Ahinful, *Mirror*, 15 June 02, 16. Since the pastors of the new churches are often viewed as businessmen, the question of tax has raised its head, for in the eyes of many these should not receive the tax exemption hitherto accorded the mainline churches with their massive involvement in development. Churches are exempt, except for monies earned in trade or business. Since these newer churches are almost by definition involved in selling books and tapes—sometimes they are veritable media empires—they are subject to tax on any gift over 50,000 cedis. Again, the newer churches are considered to be avoiding tax by filing few returns. See *Graphic* 20 April 00, 1, and 19 May 00, 32; *Spectator*, 3 March 00, 1. The revenue services ran a seminar on 18 May 2000 for 'bishops, presiding pastors, overseers, apostles, prophets of the Christian faith' to educate on tax law.

[17] *Graphic*, 22 July 02, 7.

Alive Chapel. For one thing, Salifu's congregation would not understand
Otabil's 'big English', and the issues he addressed would leave them
cold—why does he not speak of visas, husbands, children, the reversing
of curses, the detection of witches and the routing of demons? Conversely,
Salifu's concerns would doubtless embarrass Otabil. Yet when one moves
from a direct comparison of extremes, a different picture emerges.

Consider Duncan-Williams, who is best understood as a preacher of
the faith gospel. Yet he ordained Salifu (along with Owusu Bempa).
Although Duncan-Williams at his ACI does not place stress on witches
and demons with Salifu's persistence, he has preached at Salifu's Alive
Chapel, and fits in with little adjustment. In a sermon on 'Family Curses'
he intimates that every evil is to be understood as a curse: 'God visits the
iniquities of the father unto the fourth generation of those who serve
idols. Now everyone of you seated here, some way somehow there is
some kind of idol in your background.' (2 Oct. 98) In another sermon at
Salifu's entitled 'The Mystery of the Oil', he is as magical as Salifu,
enforcing 'divine curses on the spirit of armed robbery', and reversing
curses on businessmen reluctant to pay debts to a church member: 'I said
[to this church member], "Anoint yourself with oil and go back to them
and tell them that they either sign for you to get your money or they are
located [removed?]." They laughed. You know some of these intellectual
guys think they can play down the supernatural. One of them went to
Kumasi, and on his way coming [back] he had an accident and he died.
Another had an attack of a stroke and got paralysed and he died.' On the
fortieth anniversary of Ghana's independence, Duncan-Williams in a sermon explained recent earthquakes in terms of demonic dislocation.[18] His
world-view is essentially the same as Salifu's. For example, discussing
'Spiritual Hosts of Wickedness' he can argue: 'Also in this category are
marine and water spirits—Satan's Navy. The witches and territorial spirits are Satan's Air Force and demons form his ground troops.'[19]

Likewise, Eastwood Anaba can write a preface to one of Salifu's books.
Korankye Ankrah delivers the graduation address at Owusu Bempa's

---

[18] He had asked for an explanation. 'God's reply apparently was that he had heard our
prayers on behalf of the nation and that these prayers had caused a shake in the spiritual
realm. The shaking supposedly caused some powerful demons to fall on our land, resulting in the tremors. Then he said God asked him to pray that the demons will be sent away
to their abode.' (*Watchman*, April 97, 1)

[19] *Binding*, 19. A new Christian magazine has articles on Duncan-Williams, Korankye
Ankrah, Owusu Tabiri and Christie Doe-Tetteh, and also an article entitled 'Nude Sub-
marine Women invade Churches' which states: 'It has been revealed that over 30 million
mermaid girls have been released by the Queen of the Coast from their oceanic residence
into the world and specially assigned to churches to lure pastors, weaken committed
believers and corrupt choristers.' (*Church Watch*, vol 1 no. 1, 11)

Bible Institute.[20] And although this writer never heard Lawrence Tetteh subsume everything under witchcraft as starkly Chigbundu, he runs crusades in Chigbundu's church in Benin City, and Chigbundu speaks in Tetteh's church in London. Chigbundu also preaches at Duncan-Williams' ACI. In this writer's experience Myles Munroe, Mike Murdock and Matthew Ashimolowo have never indulged in the magical rituals of Winners', but all preach at Winners' Lagos headquarters, and Oyedepo speaks at Ashimolowo's annual London 'Gathering of Champions' (as does Otabil).[21] Besides, Agyin Asare was ordained by Oyedepo. Thus between most of them there is at least no perceived incompatibility. They themselves recognise the unity within their diversity.[22] Despite this unity, we have avoided writing of an essence of Ghana's new Christianity, preferring to suggest characteristic emphases. All charismatic churches highlight success, victory and wealth. The stress on victory is constitutive and indispensable, and provides the real appeal of this Christianity. These Christians are generally those whom the world has marginalized, and as globalisation gathers pace they risk being marginalized further. This contextualised Christianity claims that it has the answer to the marginalisation of Ghanaians, and can remedy the lack, the poverty, the desperation; it will change you from a nobody into a somebody.

We have touched on other important reasons for charismatic growth, and can recapitulate some here. The worship is participative and exhilarating. Testimonies enable non-professionals and the voiceless generally to express themselves and be heard. Where cell groups exist, they can provide a sense of solidarity. Charismatic churches give opportunities to play a role—as usher, deacon, security officer. Those with real leadership skills can exercise them. These churches provide employment in a country where employment is scarce—one academic has estimated a wastage of up to 75% of 'skilled human resources in Ghana due to lack of employment opportunities'.[23] There are similarly restricted opportunities for higher education. Only 31% of the nearly 17,000 students qualifying for entry to the University of Ghana could actually be admitted in 2000–1;[24] some have their entry deferred for some years. Not a few of them go into evangelisation where, as we have seen, an adaptive faith gospel can

---

[20] *Free Press*, 31 Jan.–6 Feb. 01, 5.

[21] In the period covered by this research Munroe and Murdock are, after Oyedepo himself, the preachers most featured in Winners' monthly *Winners' World* (see e.g. Dec. 2001, 8 and 16; Feb. 2002, 14).

[22] Compare Nigeria, where the splits are public. See also the attacks by other pastors on Prophet T. B. Joshua (*Excel*, 27 Jan.–3 Feb. 3000) and on various faith gospel preachers.

[23] *Graphic*, 12 July 00, 13.

[24] *Graphic*, 30 Oct. 00, 14.

ensure a livelihood. For others and for those just missing the university entry qualifications, the mushrooming Bible Schools provide a chance to take studies further; Ghana's society is one where white-collar jobs confer status. The number of proposed church universities can be expected to take this tendency further, for most of them will emerge from upgraded Bible schools or seminaries, and will produce even more ministerial graduates needing employment.[25]

All such factors are significant, and none should be downplayed. To quote Landes on another issue, 'We are dealing here with the most complex kind of [issue], one that involves numerous factors of variable weights working in changing combinations.'[26] Yet these churches have proliferated primarily because they profess to have the answers to Ghana's real problems, expressed in an idiom to which many Ghanaians naturally respond. The ills that beset Ghanaians are often explained in terms of spiritual forces, and many of these religious leaders claim the powers to control these forces.

A secondary aim of this book has been to relate these churches to Ghana's attempts to join the world economic system—an equally complex issue. There is no simple link between a religion and its public effects. The present author's position is well expressed by Steve Bruce: 'I do not want to insist that ideas or belief systems "cause" behaviour in the sense that the same ideas always produce the same outcomes irrespective of circumstances. But, equally well, I see no reason to suppose religious ideas are without consequences.'[27] Religions are about 'world construction' and 'world maintenance'. They provide ideas and values that order lives. They determine (not exclusively nor immutably, of course, but nevertheless powerfully) what attitudes and actions are considered legitimate, or prescribed, or irrelevant, or forbidden. They help establish which situations are experienced as unchangeable, which acceptable and which subject to improvement. My study of the religious situation in Ghana has not convinced me that much of Ghana's new Christianity leads naturally to many of the benefits sometimes suggested, benefits like a new work ethic. However these churches often instil motivation or self-belief—one meets scores of people who attest to ambitions fostered and goals attempted, some even who attest to the discipline and order brought into

---

[25] See van de Walle's observation, about capacity building in Africa: 'Pretty quickly… Africa was generating the wrong mix of graduates, given its most pressing needs.' (*African Economies*, 130)

[26] Landes, *Unbound Prometheus*, 8.

[27] Steve Bruce, *Fundamentalism*, Cambridge: Polity, 2000, 109; also, 'It would be bizarre if something that took up so much of so many people's wealth and time… did not matter.' (ibid., 103)

their lives (although I myself would not consider these representative). This is important, yet if Ghana is to join the modern world economy the greatest need is the development of transparent and accountable structures, systems, procedures and institutions to regulate all aspects of society. The Rawlings years did not contribute greatly in this regard, and it is still too early to know if the Kufuor regime marks any great advance. Already some are disappointed. Kufuor's declaration of zero tolerance for corruption remains largely a declaration. There has been little effort to empower those institutions that might regulate procedures.[28] As for fostering structural reform, the role of these churches since the 1980s has been mixed. We addressed these issues in the last two chapters, and will merely repeat here that while some of these churches focus attention on structures, others not only do not, but actively divert attention from them. The claim that charismatic churches of themselves or as such must be fostering socio-political reform has not been proved. Nearly all operate on neo-patrimonial or patronage rather than accountable bureaucratic lines, encouraging the emergence of the 'Big Man' rather than empowering the ranks. Van de Walle has noted that in Africa since the 1980s increasing government austerity and rapidly growing aid resources have displaced patrimonial dynamics to the aid sector—to such a degree that the aid regime has actually slowed down reform and helped sustain patrimonialism.[29] There is more than a suspicion that this displacement is also evident in Christianity, the other booming sector of Ghana's economy.

Yet change is inevitable. Ghana is changing rapidly as it is caught up in the wider world, albeit as part of the periphery forced to enter globalisation on terms set by others. The churches too are changing in many ways. One trajectory may be towards a greater social awareness. Otabil is the one charismatic figure who emerged from the Rawlings years with his status enhanced, and his success inevitably attracts imitators. And he is the one who has made this structural focus his concern (connecting, as already remarked, with a widely shared perception among the class he attracts). The questions he raises, the solutions he suggests, the areas he declares to be a Christian's concern, are all likely to assume greater

---

[28] Sobering analyses are found in E. Gyimah-Boadi, *Confronting Corruption in Ghana and Africa*, CDD Briefing Paper, May 2002; Lord Cephas M-Yevugah, 'Building a Corruption-Free Society', *Business and Financial Times*, 26 Aug–1 Sept. 02, 18–19. President Kufuor, at a Presbyterian dedication ceremony made a '"presidential" donation of 10 million cedis ($1,500) as his contribution to the project'. (*Chronicle*, 1 Sept. 02, 12) The cheering congregation were obviously delighted, but the way public accounting functions in Ghana means that it is almost impossible to know where that money came from.

[29] Van de Walle, *African Economies*, esp ch 5.

prominence. There may be some evidence of this shift already. For example, at Duncan-Williams' Sunday service on 7 April 2002 there were many familiar motifs: give and you will prosper; achievement is 'sweatless'; Duncan-Williams through his anointing will break the yoke of poverty and cast out the demons holding back finances; a Christian should be distinguishable from others, distinguishable on the score of prosperity, and God will bring this about. Then, however, Eastwood Anaba spoke on Joshua 5.10–12, a text telling how the Israelites' ceased to be provided with manna and instead had to grow corn for themselves. He insisted: 'You don't have to think to get manna; for corn you have to think.' Fending for themselves brought responsibilities, but also advantages—manna lasts only a day while corn is enduring, and manna is only for personal use while corn supports a nation. Taking corn as an acronym, he expounded how C stood for creative powers, O for order and organisation, R for risk, and N for networking (or cooperation with others). Anaba was aware of the novelty here; he described the text as 'traumatising'. An academic and a pastor of the church who were both present told me that this development was new, and both claimed, unprompted by me, that it reflected the current unavoidability of motifs introduced by Otabil. Another observer used the phrase the 'Otabilisation' of Ghana's charismatic Christianity to describe this suggested shift. And things continue to evolve.

Two final issues need to be mentioned. The tension between the local and the international in this Christianity should be borne in mind. We have seen that so many themes like motivation to success, prosperity, 'sowing and reaping', the demonic and, most recently, the prophetic role are to be found in charismatic Christianity around the world. In Ghana certain practices, expressions, even mannerisms can be traced to their origins outside the country. Authorities like Hagin, Copeland, Price, Wagner and Benny Hinn are drawn on often, openly and explicitly. Even key words—'doorways', 'legal rights', 'curses', 'blood covenants', all the words that would be found in certain American authors—betray particular origins. If most external influences are recognisably North American, the Nigerian influence of the likes of Idahosa and Chigbundu is also tangible.

There are some motifs that have no particular resonance in Ghana. Although media is crucial to all charismatic Christianity, owning Evangelical radio stations seems a Latin American preoccupation. The precise issues of inner city deprivation associated with the likes of Dallas-based T. D. Jakes do not really resonate in Ghana. Also, the anti-slavery and anti-colonialism strand of African American and Caribbean Christianity are not significant—the insistence on being victims and oppressed is not strong in Ghana. Key concerns of American fundamentalism—even the inerrancy of the Bible, especially of the prophecies establishing the identity of Jesus—are not prominent; probably few Ghanaian charismatics have ever heard the Bible's inerrancy questioned. Duncan-Williams in one place implies that Catholicism is a Satanic spirit blocking God's work, and Ashimolowo's broadcasts, originating from London, sometimes declare the mainline churches in Britain godless. However, attacking deficient 'liberal' churches is not a major issue in Ghana,[30] and the Nigerian staple of denouncing Islam is heard only infrequently.

However, even when the message is formally the same, there are obvious differences in reception. Many visiting evangelists or TV preachers mention witchcraft, by which they often mean the occult; yet witchcraft is a different reality in Ghana, a natural and immediate category for experiencing and explaining reality. Even if Rebecca Brown or Derek Prince might be found speaking of water spirits and snake spirits, these two are totally counter-cultural in the West. However, in Ghana, where water and snake spirits are everyday realities, stories of possession and witchcraft are not counter-cultural. Nor is the stress on curses exclusively African, but the linking of curses to ancestral religious practices is. So while nearly all Ghanaian charismatics may find a visiting preacher like Munroe or Yonggi Cho totally compatible with everything encountered in their local Ghanaian church, much of the visitor's preaching could well be received in a sense somewhat different from that intended by him.

Lastly, it is often said, and meant as praise, that the charismatic churches, or the Pentecostal generally, meet the needs of Africans. It is also frequently heard, and meant as a criticism, that the mainline churches were unable to meet those needs. However, could the mainline churches meet some of those needs? Williamson admitted it bluntly: 'The [mainline] church has not provided a creative answer to the Akan's problems. It may well be that, at least by the church as historically implanted, no such answer was possible.'[31] It is notable that the official Catholic Church seems to have opted not to meet those needs that Salifu addresses so directly, or at least not in his way. Even though one of the thrusts of the Second Vatican Council (1962–5) was to make the Catholic church more open to other cultures, it is best understood as the Catholic Church's coming to terms with the modern world which (in matters ranging from democracy to historical scholarship) it had rejected for so long. Coming into line with modernity in fact largely set it against much non-Western religion.[32] In statements since, it has been increasingly rejecting the

---

[30] Duncan-Williams, *Binding*, 25.

[31] Williamson, *Akan Religion*, 156–7.

[32] Christopher Comoro and John Sivalon write: 'The worldview and cosmology of pre-Vatican II Roman Catholicism were in fact an inculturated understanding based on a

understanding of evil so common is charismatic circles. This process reached a climax in September 2000 when the Vatican issued an instruction regularising healing services in the Catholic Church. This instruction was widely seen as prompted by the activities of the Zambian Archbishop Emmanuel Milingo, who would be quite at home in Salifu's strain of Ghana's charismatic Christianity. Thus for all the Catholic insistence on inculturation, a most pervasive and persistent element of Ghanaian traditional religion is increasingly not desired. Of course, in Ghana the Catholic Church is very sensitive to the religious imagination of many of its members, but the official Catholic explanation of evil is of another order altogether.[33] The mainline Christian churches, though perhaps numerically now centred in the developing world, keep their official theology firmly centred in the West.[34]

---

culture and consciousness very similar to traditional African culture. Vatican II, while marking an opening up to the world was in fact opening up to a world, worldview and culture of modernity that are quite different from African culture. As the church accommodated itself to scientific and secularised culture, it moved dramatically away from the cultures of indigenous people around the world.' ('Tanzania: Marian Faith Healing Ministry' in Thomas Bamat and F. Wiest (eds), *Popular Catholicism*, Maryknoll, NY: Orbis, 1998, 170)

[33] Congregation for Divine Worship, *Les formes multiples de la superstition*, dated 26 June 1975; Congregation for Divine Worship, *New Rite for Exorcism*, formally released 26 Jan. 1999; Congregation for the Doctrine of the Faith, *Instruction on Prayer for Healing*, dated 14 Sept. 2000. No less a figure than Mary Douglas argues that the Catholic Church could learn much from the understanding of evil of the Lele in the Congo; it appears that this is precisely what the Catholic Church declines to learn; Mary Douglas, 'Sorcery Accusations Unleashed: the Lele Revisited 1987', *Africa*, 69 (1999), 177–93, esp. 189–90.

[34] I would disagree with Jenkins, *Next Christendom*, 198, 202, who argues that the Catholic Church, for demographic reasons, must espouse the 'Southern' viewpoint.

BIBLIOGRAPHY

Aboagye-Asamoah, Samuel, *A Plea from Hell*, Accra: SonLife, 2000.
Achampong-Baifie, Kwaku, *Commanding Power in Offensive Warfare*, Accra: the author, 1996.
———, *The Sacrifices of God: the Pouring of Libation*, Accra: the author, 1992.
Acquah, Rita, 'The Church of Pentecost Prayer Camps: a Study of the Macedonia, Paradise and Salvation Prayer Camps', Legon, BA Hons thesis, 1997.
Adatura, Rockeybell, *Allah, Yahweh, and God of the Traditions*, Accra: the author, 1999.
Addae-Mensah, Matthew, *Walking in the Power of God*, Belleville, Ontario: Guardian Books, 2000.
Addo, Ebenezer Obiri, *Kwame Nkrumah: a Case Study of Religion and Politics in Ghana*, Lanham, MD: University Press of America, 1997.
Adu-Boahen, Stephen, *Deliverance from Demons*, Kumasi: the author, 1999.
———, *How to Obtain God's Free Salvation and Maintain it*, Kumasi: the author, 1999.
———, *The Great Tribulation and the Antichrist who is to come*, Kumasi, the author, 1999.
Agyin Asare, Charles, *Miracles, Healings, Signs and Wonders*, Tamale(?): Power Publications, 1992.
———, *It is Miracle Time 1 & 2*, Accra: the author, 1997.
———, *New Testament Ministers' Manual*, Accra: the author, 1998.
———, *Rooted and Built up in Him*, Accra: Miracle Publications, 2nd edn 1999.
Akrong, A., 'Neo-Witchcraft Mentality in Popular Christianity', *Research Review*, New Series, 16, 1 (2000), 1–12.
Akrong, Abraham, 'The Historic Mission of the African Independent Churches', *Research Review (NS)*, 14 (1998), 58–68.
Allen, A.A, *The Riches of the Gentiles are yours*, Benin City: Calvary Publications, orig edn, 1965.
Ameve, Kofi, *The Divine Acts: Holy Scriptures for Sankofa Faith*, Accra: Afrikania, n.d.
———, *The Origin of the Bible: the Old and New Testament*, Accra: Afrikania, 3rd edn, 1991.
Amoako, Elisha Salifu, *From Ignorance to Knowledge*, Accra: the author, 1997.
———, *Your Angel will come*, Accra: Alive Publications, 1999.
———, *Vision and Provision*, Accra: the author, 2000.
———, *Power to Make Wealth I*, Accra: Alive Publications, 2001.

Amorin, Kokuga, *Holy Bible our Key to true Success and Lasting Happiness*, Accra: Amorin Publishing, 1999.

Ampiah-Kwofi, Robert, *The Restored Anointing*, Accra: the author, 1998.

———, *Breaking Generational Curses*, Accra: the author, 2000.

Anaba Eastwood, *The Key of Discipline: your Open Door to Success*, Accra: the author, 1998.

———, *The Restored Anointing*, Accra: the author, 1998.

———, *Elevated Beyond Human Law through the Fruit of the Spirit*, Bolgatanga: the author, 1995.

———, *Breaking Illegal Possession: Dislodge the Enemy and possess the Land*, Bolgatanga, the author, 1996.

———, *The Oil of Influence*, Bolgatanga: Desert Leaf Publications, 2000.

———, *Birthrights, Blessings and Crumbs: Attitude determines the Portion*, Bolgatanga, Desert Leaf Publications, 2001.

Anderson, Allan H. and Walter Hollenweger (eds), *Pentecostals after a Century: Global Perspectives on a Movement in Transition*, Sheffield Academic Press, 1999.

Ansah, H. Akrofi, *Revelation Made Simple I*, Accra: the author, 1999.

Appiah, Joseph, *Joe Appiah: the Autobiography of an African Patriot*, Accra: Asempa, 1996.

Aryeetey, Ernest, Jane Harrigan and Machiko Nissanke, *Economic Reforms in Ghana: the Miracle and the Mirage*, Oxford: James Currey, 2000.

Asamoa, Ansa, *Socio-Economic Development Strategies of Independent African Countries: the Ghanaian Experience*, Accra: Ghana Universities Press, 1996.

Asamoah-Gyadu, Johnson, 'Renewal within African Christianity: a Study of some Current Historical and Theological Developments within Independent Indigenous Pentecostalism in Ghana', PhD thesis, University of Birmingham, 2000.

Ashimolowo, Matthew, *It's Not Over till it's Over*, London: Mattyson Media, 1996.

———, *Breaking Barriers*, London: Mattyson Media, 2000.

Assimeng, Max, *Saints and Social Structures*, Tema: Ghana Publishing Corporation, 1986.

———, *An Anatomy of Modern Ghana*, Accra: Ghana Academy of Arts and Sciences, 1996.

———, *Foundations of African Social Thought: a Contribution to the Sociology of Knowledge*, Accra: Ghana Universities Press, 1997.

———, *Social Structure of Ghana: a Study in Persistence and Change*, Tema: Ghana Publishing Corporation, 2nd edn 1999.

Atiemo, Abamfo O., *The Rise of the Charismatic Movement in the Mainline Churches of Ghana*, Accra: Asempa, 1993.

Atiemo, Abamfo Ofori, 'Mmusuyi and Deliverance; a Study of Conflict and Consensus in the Encounter between African Traditional Religion and Christianity', MPhil thesis, University of Ghana, 1995.

Ayee, Joseph R.A., *Saints, Wizards, Demons and Systems: Explaining the Success or Failure of Public Policies and Programmes*, Accra: Ghana Universities Press, 2000.

Ayittey, George B.N., *Africa in Chaos*, London: Macmillan, 1999.

Ayitey, Wisdom K., *Broken Chains: Deliverance from Curses and Demons*, Accra: the author, 2001.

Bankole, Yemi, *Four Hour Interviews in Hell*, Lagos: Christian Charter Books, 1999.

Banning, Sampson Joseph, *Pan African Renaissance and the Hidden Prophecy*, Accra: the author, 2001.

Bediako, Kwame, *Jesus in African Culture: a Ghanaian Perspective*, Accra: Asempa, 1990.

———, *Christianity in Africa: the Renewal of a Non-Western Religion*, Edinburgh University Press, 1995.

——— ——, *Jesus in Africa: the Christian Gospel in African History and Experience*, Akropong-Akuapem: Regnum Africa, 2000.

Berger, Peter L., *The Sacred Canopy: Elements of a Sociological Theory of Religion*, New York: Anchor Books, 1969.

Blay-Amihere, Kabral, *Fighting for Freedom*, Accra: Trans Afrika News [2001].

Boahen, Adu, *Ghana: Evolution and Change in the Nineteenth and Twentieth Centuries*, Accra: Sankofa, rev. edn 2000.

Boison, Charles Dadzie, *Spiritual Militants: an Insight into Spiritual Discipline and Warfare in Christianity*, Accra: Ahenpa Publishers, 1996.

Bruce, Steve, *Fundamentalism*, Cambridge: Polity, 2000.

———, *Politics and Religion*, Cambridge: Polity, 2003.

Carpenter, Joel A., *Revive Us Again: the Reawakening of American Fundamentalism*, New York: Oxford University Press, 1997.

CDD, *Democracy Watch* (quarterly newsletter) Accra: CDD.

———, *Popular Attitudes to Democracy and Markets in Ghana*, Accra: CDD, 1999.

———, *Elite Attitudes to Democracy and Markets in Ghana*, Accra: CDD, 2000.

———, Media Coverage of the 2000 Elections, Accra: CDD, 2001.

Chabal, Patrick, and Jean-Pascal Daloz, *Africa Works: Disorder as Political Instrument*, Oxford: James Currey, 1999.

Challenge Enterprises, *Spiritual Warfare* (compiled for National Prayer Conferences 1999), Accra: Challenge Enterprises, 1999.

Chigbundu, Abraham, *I believe in Deliverance: Deliverance made Easy*, Benin City: Voice of Freedom, 1995.

Clapham, Christopher, *Third World Politics: an Introduction*, London: Routledge, 1985.

———, 'Democratisation in Africa: Obstacles and Prospects', *Third World Quarterly*, 14 (1993), 423–38.

———, 'Governmentality and Economic Policy in Sub-Saharan Africa', *Third World Quarterly*, 17 (1996), 809–24.

Cleary, Edward L., and Hannah W. Stewart-Gambino, *Power, Politics and Pentecostals in Latin America*, Boulder, CO: Westview Press, 1997.

Coleman, Simon, *The Globalisation of Charismatic Christianity: Spreading the Gospel of Prosperity*, Cambridge University Press, 2000.

Comoro, Christopher, and John Sivalon, 'Tanzania: Marian Faith Healing Ministry' in Thomas Bamat and F. Wiest (eds), *Popular Catholicism*, Maryknoll, NY: Orbis, 1998, 157–82.

Cox, Harvey, *Fire from Heaven: The Rise of Pentecostal Spirituality and the Reshaping of Religion in the Twenty-First Century*, London: Cassell, 1996.

Damuah, Okomfo, *Miracle at the Shrine: Religious and Revolutionary Miracle in Ghana*, n.d.

Danso-Boafo, Kwaku, *The Political Biography of Dr Kofi Abrefa Busia*, Accra: Ghana Universities Press, 1996.

Dempster, Murray W., Byron D. Klaus and Douglas Petersen (eds), *The Globalisation of Pentecostalism: a Religion made to Travel*, Oxford: Regnum, 1999.

Diamond, Larry, 'Rethinking Civil Society: Toward Democratic Consolidation', *Journal of Democracy*, 3 (1994), 4–17.

Dickason, C. Fred, *Demon Possession and the Christian*, Eastbourne: Crossway Books, 1987.

Dickson, Kwesi A., *Theology in Africa*, London: Darton, Longman and Todd, 1984.

Douglas, Mary, 'Sorcery Accusations Unleashed: the Lele Revisited 1987', *Africa*, 69 (1999), 177–93.

Dovlo, Elom, 'The Role of Religious Bodies in Ghana's Political Development Process', *Legon Journal of the Humanities*, 8 (1995), 1–12.

Duah, Grace B.F., *Deliverance: Fact or Fantasy?*, Accra: the author, 1997.

Duah, J.K., *The Day of the Lord is Near*, Accra: FBN Publications, 1999.

Duncan, Spencer, *Releasing your Miracles: Understanding how to operate God's Principles in order to receive your Miracles*, Accra: the author, 2001.

Duncan-Williams, Francisca, *Reflections: the Untold Story*, Accra: Action Faith Publications, 2002.

Duncan-Williams, N., *You are Destined to Succeed!*, Accra: Action Faith Publications, 1990.

Duncan-Williams, Nicholas, *Destined to make an Impact*, Accra: Action Faith Publications, 2002.

———, *Binding the Strong Man*, Accra: the author, 1998.

———, *Birthing the Promises of God in Travail*, South Bend, IN: Bishop House, 1999.

———, *The Price of Greatness*, Accra: the author, 1999.

Ellis, Stephen, and Gerrie ter Haar, 'Religion and Politics in sub-Saharan Africa', *Journal of Modern African Studies*, 36 (1998), 175–201.

Eni, Emmanuel, *Delivered from the Powers of Darkness*, Ibadan: Scripture Union, 1987.

Essel, Michael, *The Treasure Within You: Using your Inner Resources*, Accra: Essel Library Publications, 2000.

Essilfie, Joseph, *Don't Kill your Future*, Accra: Ephphatha Publications, n.d.

———, *Hope for the Hopeless*, Accra: Ephphatha Publications, n.d.

Etounga-Manguelle, Daniel, 'Does Africa Need a Cultural Adjustment Program?' in Lawrence E. Harrison and Samuel P. Huntington (eds), *Culture Matters: How Values Shape Human Progress*, New York: Basic Books, 2000, 65–77.

Ferguson-Laing, George, *Building your Life according to God's Pattern*, Takoradi: the author, 1997.

————, *Worship and the Blessing of God*, Takoradi: the author, 1997.

Foli, Richard, *Towards Church Growth in Ghana*, Accra: Trust Publishers, 1996.

Fomum, Zacharias Tanee, *Deliverance from Demons*, Yaounde: the author, 3rd edn 1993.

————, *The Way of Spiritual Warfare*, Yaounde: Christian Publishing House, 2nd edn 1996.

Frempong, Henry, *Christianity: a Religion of Power, Dignity and Privileges*, n.d.

Freston, Paul, 'Charismatic Evangelicals in Latin America: Mission and Politics on the Frontiers of Protestant Growth' in S. Hunt, M. Hamilton, T. Walter (eds), *Charismatic Christianity: Sociological Perspectives*, Basingstoke: Macmillan, 1997, 184–204.

————, 'Evangelicals and Politics: a Comparison between Africa and Latin America', *Journal of Contemporary Religion*, 13 (1998), 37–49.

————, *Evangelicals and Politics in Asia, Africa and Latin America*, Cambridge University Press, 2001.

Friedman, Thomas L., *The Lexus and the Olive Tree: Understanding Globalisation*, New York: Anchor Books, rev. edn 2000.

Garlock, Ruthanne, *Benson Idahosa: Fire in his Bones*, Tulsa, OK: Harrison House, 1981.

Garner, Robert C., 'Religion as a Source of Social Change in the New South Africa', *JRA*, 30 (2000), 310–43.

————, 'Safe Sects? Dynamic Religion and AIDS in South Africa', *JMAS*, 38 (2000), 41–69.

Gellner, Ernest, *Cause and Meaning in the Social Sciences*, London: Routledge and Kegan Paul, 1973.

Ghana Catholic Bishops' Conference, *Pastoral Guidelines for the National Pastoral Congress*, Accra: GCBC, 1997.

Ghartey, John B., *Understanding the Names of God I*, Accra: Living Word Publishers, 1996.

————, *God's Programme for Time and Eternity: a Concise Study of Biblical Dispensations*, Accra: Living Word Foundation, 2000.

Gifford, Paul, 'Prosperity: a New and Foreign Element in African Christianity', *Religion*, 20 (1990), 373–88.

————, *Christianity and Politics in Doe's Liberia*, Cambridge University Press, 1993.

————, 'Ghana's Charismatic Churches', *JRA*, 24 (1994), 241–65.

————, *African Christianity: its Public Role*, London: Hurst, 1998.

Goodhew, David, 'Growth and Decline in South Africa's Churches 1960–91', *JRA*, 30 (2000), 344–69.

Gyekye, Kwame, *Political Corruption: a Philosophical Inquiry into a Moral Problem*, Accra: Sankofa, 1997.

Gyimah-Boadi, E., *Governance, Institutions and Values in National Development*, Accra: ISSER, 2001.

Hansen, Nancy, *Deliverance*, Accra: n.d.

Hanson, Elkanah, *Understanding the Holy Spirit in Politics*, Port Harcourt: El Shaddai Ministries, 1999.

Hanson, Susan, *A Nation touched by the Fire of Heaven*, Accra: the author, 2000.

Hayes, Thomas F.K., *Satan on the Run: You can pursue and surely take back what Satan has stolen*, Accra: the author, 1999.

Heward-Mills, Dag, *Frugality*, Accra: Lighthouse Chapel Publications, 1997.

————, *The Beast of Prodigality*, Accra: DgTP, 1997.

————, *Loyalty and Disloyalty*, Accra: DgTP, 1998.

————, *Lay People and the Ministry*, Accra: Lighthouse Chapel Publications, 1999.

————, *Name it! Claim it! Take it!* Accra: Lighthouse Chapel Publications, 1999.

————, *Principles of Success*, Accra: Lighthouse Chapel Publications, 2000.

————, *Secrets of Success*, Accra: Lighthouse Chapel Publications, 2000.

————, *Solomonic Success*, Accra: DgTP, 1999.

————, *Supernatural Power*, Accra: Lighthouse Chapel Publications, 2000.

Hughes, Joshua Swain, *God's Hands over Africa*, Accra: Horizon Publications, 1999.

Hunt, Stephen (ed.), *Christian Millenarianism: from the Early Church to Waco*, London: Hurst, 2001.

Hutchful, Frank, *Pulling down the Altars*, Accra: Design Solutions, 2000.

Jeffries, Richard, 'The Ghanaian Elections of 1996: Towards the Consolidation of Democracy?', *African Affairs*, 97 (1998), 189–208.

Jenkins, Philip, *The Next Christendom: the Coming of Global Christianity*, New York: Oxford University Press, 2002.

Joyner, Rick, *The Harvest: the Prophetic Word of the Nineties and Beyond*, New Kensington, PA: Whitaker House, 1993.

————, *The Prophetic Ministry*, Charlotte, NC: Morning Star Publications, 1997.

Kisseih, Gordon, *The Benefits of Fear of the Lord*, Tema: Gordon Kissieh Publications, 1999.

Konrad Adenauer Foundation, *Promoting a Sustainable Democracy and the Social Teachings of the Catholic Church: Preparation for the Year 2000 Election Observation*, Accra: KAF, 1999.

Koomson, A. Bonnar (ed.), *Prospects for Private Broadcasting in Ghana*, Legon: School of Communication Studies, 1995.

Korankye Ankrah, Sam, *God's Favour operating through Covenants*, Accra: the author, 1998.

————, *Is this Prophecy from God?*, Accra: the author, 1998.

Kudadjie, Joshua N., *Moral Renewal in Ghana: Ideals, Realities, and Possibilities*, Accra: Asempa, 1995.

Kumah, Divine P., *Is Ghana under a Curse?* Accra: SonLife, 2000.

Kwami, S.Y., *Deliverance: a Scriptural Approach*, Accra: the author, 1998.

————, *Holy Spirit Baptism and Speaking in Tongues?*, Accra: the author, 1998.

Kwarteng, K.A., *Pastor Livingston*, Accra: the author, 2001.

Landes, David S., *The Unbound Prometheus: Technological Change and Industrial Development in Western Europe from 1750 to the Present*, Cambridge University Press, 1969.

Landes, David, *The Wealth and Poverty of Nations: Why some are so rich and some so poor*, London: Little, Brown, 1998.

Larbi, E. Kingsley, *Pentecostalism: the Eddies of Ghanaian Christianity*, Accra: CPCS, 2001.

———, *God and the Poor*, Accra: CPCS, 2001.

Laryea, Ebenezer Anang, *The Origin of the Black and White Race: Great Revelation*, Accra: E. A. Laryea Publications, 2001.

Lauer, Helen, 'Two Dogmas of Modernity: Potential Impediments to Enlightened Development Planning in Ghana', *Legon Journal of the Humanities*, 8 (1995), 37–53.

Lehem, *God with Us*, Accra: Zetaheal Church, 2000.

Longman, Timothy P., 'Empowering the Weak and Protecting the Powerful: the Contradictory Nature of Churches in Central Africa', *African Studies Review*, 41 (1998), 49–72.

Marsden, George M., *Fundamentalism and American Culture: the Shaping of Twentieth Century Evangelicalism 1870–1925*, Oxford University Press, 1980.

Marshall, Ruth, '"Power in the Name of Jesus": Social Transformation and Pentecostalism in Western Nigeria "Revisited" ' in T. Ranger and O. Vaughan (eds), *Legitimacy and the State in Twentieth Century Africa*, London: Macmillan, 1993, 213–46.

Marshall-Fratani, Ruth, 'Mediating the Global and Local in Nigerian Pentecostalism', *JRA*, 28 (1998), 278–315.

Martey, Emmanuel, 'Deliverance Ministry in the Church: a Theological Assessment', *Trinity Journal of Church and Theology*, 9 (1999), 18–25.

——— and Mary Gerald Nwagwu, *The Gospel, Poverty and the Displaced in Africa: the Case of the West African Sub-Region*, Accra: WAATI, 2000.

Martey, Samuel, *Africa Kills her Children*, Tema: Resurrection Faith Ministry, 1998.

———, *Understanding the Mystery of the Anointing Oil*, Tema: Resurrection Publishers, 1999.

Martin, David, *Tongues of Fire: the Explosion of Protestantism in Latin America*, Oxford: Blackwell, 1990.

———, *Pentecostalism: the World their Parish*, Oxford: Blackwell, 2002.

Matthew, B., *How to Become Rich: Conquer Poverty for Yourself*, Accra: the author, 1999.

Meyer, Birgit, '"If you are a Devil, you are a Witch, and if you are a Witch, you are a Devil": The Integration of "Pagan" Ideas into the Conceptual Universe of Ewe Christians in Southeastern Ghana', *JRA*, 22 (1992), 98–132.

———, '"Delivered from the Powers of Darkness": Confessions of Satanic Riches in Christian Ghana', *Africa*, 65 (1995), 236–55.

———, '"Make a Complete Break with the Past": Memory and Post-Colonial Modernity in Ghanaian Pentecostalist Discourse', *JRA*, 28 (1998), 316–49.

———, 'Commodities and the Power of Prayer: Pentecostalist Attitudes towards Consumption in Contemporary Ghana', *Development and Change*, 29 (1998), 751–76.

————, 'The Power of Money: Politics, Occult Forces, and Pentecostalism in Ghana', *African Studies Review*, 41 (1998), 15–37.

————, *Translating the Devil: Religion and Modernity among the Ewe in Ghana*, Edinburgh University Press, 1999.

Munroe, Myles, *Maximising your Potential: the Keys to Dying Empty*, Shippensburg, PA: Destiny Image, 1996.

Murdock, Mike, *The Covenant of Fifty-Eight Blessings*, Denton TX: Wisdom International, 1994.

————, *31 Reaon People do not receive their Financial Harve$t*, Dallas, TX: Wisdom International, 1997.

————, *Secrets of the Journey: Leadership Secrets for Excellence and Increase*, Dallas: Wisdom International, 1997.

————, *Secrets of the Richest Man Who Ever Lived: 31 Master Secrets from the Life of King Solomon*, Dallas: Wisdom International, 1998.

————, *31 Secrets for Career Success*, Dallas: Wisdom International, 1998.

Ntumy, Michael K., *Financial Breakthrough: Discovering God's Secrets to Prosperity*, n.d.

Nugent, Paul, *Big Men, Small Boys, and Politics in Ghana*, London: Pinter, 1995.

————, 'Winners, Losers and Also-Rans: Money, Moral Authority and Voting Patterns in the Ghana 2000 Election', *African Affairs*, 100 (2001), 405–28.

Oduro, Emmanuel, *Dry Bones Can Live: Turning your Hopeless Situations Around*, Kumasi: Oduro Jesus Life Publication, 1994.

————, *How to touch God for your Miracle*, Kumasi: the author, 1998.

————, *Powerful Quotations to overcome Witches, Wizards, and Bad Spirits*, Kumasi: the author, n.d.

Okaigbe, Godwin O., *Dreams, Interpretations and Prayers, I, II, III*, Lagos: the author, 1998–2000.

Olukoya, D.K., *Deliverance from Spirit Husband and Spirit Wife (Incubi and Succubi): Release from Evil Spiritual Marriage*, Lagos: Battle Cry Ministries, 1999.

————, *Overpowering Witchcraft*, Lagos: Mountain of Fire and Miracles Ministries, 1999.

————, *Power against Marine Spirits*, Lagos: Battle Cry Ministries, 1999.

————, *Your Foundation and your Destiny*, Lagos: Battle Cry Ministries, 2001.

Omari, T. Peter, *Kwame Nkrumah: the Anatomy of an African Dictatorship*, London: Hurst, 1970/new edn Accra: Sankofa, 2000.

Opoku-Akyeampong, Daniel Kofi, *The Road to Prosperity*, Accra: Waterville Publishing House, 1997.

Oquaye, Mike, *Politics in Ghana 1972–1979*, Accra: Tornado Publications, 1980.

————, 'Law, Justice and the Revolution' in E. Gyimah-Boadi (ed.), *Ghana under PNDC Rule*, Dakar: Codesria, 1993, 154–75.

Osabutey, Ralph, *How to Receive Bountifully from God*, Accra: the author, 2001.

Osei, Victor, *Breaking through Barriers and Limitations II*, Kumasi: the author, 2000.

Otabil, Mensa, *Beyond the Rivers of Ethiopia: a Biblical Revelation on God's Purpose for the Black Race*, Accra: Altar International, 1992.

————, *Enjoying the Blessings of Abraham*, Accra: Altar International, 1992.
————, *Four Laws of Productivity: God's Foundation for Living*, Accra: Altar International, 1992.
————, *Buy the Future: Learning to Negotiate for a Future Better than your Present*, Lanham, MD: Pneumalife, 2002.
Owiredu, Charles, 'The Concept of Prosperity in the Old Testament and its Contemporary Relevance in the International Central Gospel Church (Ghana)', MPhil thesis, CUC, 2000.
Owusu Ansah, Kwame and Bea, *Bribery and Corruption and How to overcome it*, Kumasi: Great Line Publications, 1998.
————, *Genuine or Counterfeit Pastor-Prophet?*, Kumasi: the authors, 1999.
Oyedepo, David O., *The Law of Faith*, Lagos: Dominion Publishing House, 1985.
————, *The Miracle Seed*, Lagos: Dominion Publishing House, 1985.
————, *Covenant Wealth*, Lagos: Dominion Publishing House, 1992.
————, *Releasing the Supernatural: an Adventure into the Spirit World*, Lagos: Dominion Publishing House, 1993.
————, *The Hidden Covenants of Blessings*, Lagos: Dominion Publishing House, 1995.
————, *Breaking Financial Hardship*, Lagos: Dominion Publishing House, 1995.
————, *Riding on Prophetic Wings*, Lagos: Dominion Publishing House, 2000.
Peale, Norman Vincent, *The Power of Positive Thinking*, Lagos: Blessed Family Publishing, n.d.
Pemberton, Carrie, *Circle Thinking: African Women Theologians in Dialogue with the West*, Leiden: E. J. Brill, 2003.
Pepra, Regina, *The Second Coming of Christ I: the Opening of the Seals*, Kumasi: God Cares Publications, 1996.
Percy, Martin, *Words, Wonders and Power: Understanding Contemporary Christian Fundamentalism and Revivalism*, London: SPCK, 1996.
Pobee, John S., *Religion and Politics in Ghana*, Accra: Asempa, 1991.
————, *Religion and Politics in Ghana: a Case Study of the Acheampong Era*, Accra: Ghana Universities Press, 1992.
Quame, Valencia, 'Christian Faith Communities and their Approach towards the Concerns of Women: a Comparative Study between the Christian Action Faith Ministries and the Presbyterian Church of Ghana', MPhil thesis, University of Ghana, 1999.
Rathbone, Richard, *Nkrumah and the Chiefs: the Politics of Chieftaincy in Ghana 1951–60*, Oxford: James Currey, 2000.
Saah, James Kweku, *The Road to the Double Portion: Achieving God's Purposes God's Way*, London: Design Solutions, 1994.
————, *The Finger of God*, Accra: the author, 1999.
Sackey, Brigid M., 'Aspects of Continuity in the Religious Roles of Women in "Spiritual Churches" of Ghana', *Research Review NS*, 5 (1989), 18–33.
————, 'Spiritual Churches in Kumasi 1920–86: Some Observations', *Africana Marburgensia*, 24 (1991), 32–49.
————, 'Evangelisation of Ghana: Historical and Contemporary Roles of Women', *Research Review NS*, 15 (1999), 39–59.

———, 'Religious Beliefs and Practices as Paradigms for Development', paper delivered at seminar on African Traditional Religions and Development at TICCS, 1–3 Nov. 1999.

———, 'Charismatics, Independents and Missions: Church Proliferation in Ghana', *Culture and Religion*, 2 (2001), 41–59.

Sampong, Kwasi Addo, 'The Growth of Prayer Centres in Ghanaian Christianity: the Quest for Health and Wholeness', MTheol thesis, Regents Theological College, 2000.

Sandbrook, Richard, and Jay Oelbaum, *Reforming the Political Kingdom: Governance and Development in Ghana's Fourth Republic*, Accra: CDD, 1999.

Sarpong, Clement Owusu, *The Converted Pastor*, Accra: the author, 1996.

Shorter, Aylward, and Edwin Onyancha, *Secularism in Africa: a Case Study: Nairobi City*, Nairobi: Paulines, 1997.

Shorter, Aylward, and Joseph N. Njiru, *New Religious Movements in Africa*, Nairobi: Paulines, 2001.

Smith, Daniel A., *The Structural Underpinnings of Ghana's December 2000 Elections*, CDD, 2001.

———, 'Consolidating Democracy? The Structural Underpinnings of Ghana's 2000 Elections', *JMAS*, 40, 4 (2002), 621–50.

Smith, Daniel A., 'Consolidating Democracy? The Structural Underpinnings of Ghana's 2000 Elections', *JMAS*, 40, 4 (2002), 621–50.

———, and J. Temin, 'The Media and Ghana's 2000 Elections' in Joseph R. A. Ayee (ed.), *Deepening Democracy in Ghana: Politics of the 2000 Elections*, Accra: Freedom Publications, 2001, 160–78.

Soku, Leonard, *From the Coven of Witchcraft to Christ I*, Tema: the author, rev ed 2000.

Subritzky, Bill, *Demons Defeated*, Chichester: Sovereign World, 1982.

———, *How to Cast out Demons and Break Curses*, Lagos: Frontline Publishing House, 1992.

Tackie-Yarboi, N.A., *Dreams of the Night: How to Reverse Negative Dreams*, Accra: Hallel Productions, 1998.

———, *The Believer's Mind*, Accra: the author, 1998.

———, *Victory over Depression*, n.d.

Tetteh, J.N., 'The Dynamics of Prayer Camps and the Management of Women's Problems: a Case Study of Three Camps in the Eastern Region of Ghana', MPhil thesis, University of Ghana, 1999.

Tetteh, Lawrence, *Do Miracles Still Happen?* London: World Miracle Outreach, 1999.

Tilton, Robert, *How to Kick the Devil out of your Life*, Dallas, TX: Robert Tilton Ministries, 1988.

Van de Walle, Nicolas, *African Economies and the Politics of Permanent Crisis, 1979–1999*, Cambridge University Press, 2001.

Van Dijk, Rijk A., *Christian Fundamentalism in Sub-Saharan Africa: the Case of Pentecostalism*, Copenhagen: Centre of African Studies, 2000.

Wagner, C. Peter, *Apostles and Prophets: the Foundation of the Church*, Ventura, CA: Regal Books, 2000.

Walley, Pauline, *Receive and Maintain your Deliverance on Legal Grounds*, London: PWCC, 1997.

Westwood, John, *The Amazing Dictator and His Men*, Accra: Nestreco (n.d., actually 2001).

Williamson, Sidney George, *Akan Religion and the Christian Faith: a Comparative Study of the Impact of Two Religions* (ed. Kwesi A. Dickson), Accra: Ghana Universities Press, 1965.

Wilson, Bryan R. (ed.), *Rationality*, Oxford: Blackwell, 1974.

INDEX